Penguin Books
The Rain Forest

Olivia Manning was born in Portsmouth, Hampshire, spent much of her youth in Ireland and, as she put it, had 'the usual Anglo-Irish sense of belonging nowhere'. She married just before the war and went abroad with her husband, R. D. Smith, a British Council lecturer in Bucharest. Her experiences there formed the basis of the work which makes up *The Balkan Trilogy*. As the Germans approached Athens, she and her husband evacuated to Egypt and ended up in Jerusalem, where her husband was put in charge of the Palestine Broadcasting Station. They returned to London in 1946 and lived there until her death in 1980.

Olivia Manning's publications include the novels *Artist Among the Missing* (1949); *School for Love* (1951); *A Different Face* (1953); *The Doves of Venus* (1955); *The Balkan Trilogy* (1960–65), which consists of *The Great Fortune* (1960), *The Spoilt City* (1962) and *Friends and Heroes* (1965); *The Play Room* (1969); *The Rain Forest* (1974); and *The Levant Trilogy* (1977–80), which consists of *The Danger Tree* (1977, *Yorkshire Post* Book of the Year award), *The Battle Lost and Won* (1978) and *The Sum of Things* (1980). She also wrote two volumes of short stories, *Growing Up* (1948) and *A Romantic Hero* (1967). She spent a year on the film script of *The Play Room* and contributed to many periodicals, including the *Spectator*, *Punch*, *Vogue* and the *Sunday Times*. Olivia Manning was awarded the CBE in 1976.

The Balkan Trilogy and *The Levant Trilogy* form a single narrative entitled *Fortunes of War* which Anthony Burgess described in the *Sunday Times* as 'the finest fictional record of the war produced by a British writer. Her gallery of personages is huge, her scene painting superb, her pathos controlled, her humour quiet and civilized. Guy Pringle certainly is one of the major characters in modern fiction.'

Olivia Manning

The Rain Forest

Penguin Books

PENGUIN BOOKS

Published by the Penguin Group
27 Wrights Lane, London W8 5TZ, England
Viking Penguin Inc., 40 West 23rd Street, New York, New York 10010, USA
Penguin Books Australia Ltd, Ringwood, Victoria, Australia
Penguin Books Canada Ltd, 2801 John Street, Markham, Ontario, Canada L3R 1B4
Penguin Books (NZ) Ltd, 182–190 Wairau Road, Auckland 10, New Zealand

Penguin Books Ltd, Registered Offices: Harmondsworth, Middlesex, England

First published by William Heinemann Ltd 1974
Published in Penguin Books 1977
Reprinted 1983, 1984, 1986, 1988

Printed and bound in Great Britain by
Cox & Wyman Ltd, Reading
Set in Monotype Times Roman

To Isobel English, Neville Braybrooke, Francis King
with love

PART ONE

The Bat

1

The Fosters, Hugh and Kristy, both at the mid-seasonal age of thirty-five, journeyed to Al-Bustan on the Thursday boat. The other Englishman on board exchanged a glance with Hugh then turned his back on him. Hugh, newly appointed to the Al-Bustan government service, decided that this man was also an official. Seeing in his classical, bearded face a romantic father image, Hugh was attracted to him but too nervous to approach him. The voyage had lasted five hours and during that time the two men had remained apart.

Kristy, who had perched herself on the cover of the companion-way, was in no state to approach anyone. She was untidy and felt exhausted. They had flown, via Paris, from London to Nairobi, then risen at dawn to catch the early plane to Réunion, that being the only one that connected with the boat. Of course, the whole journey could have been done in a more leisurely fashion. They could have spent a few days in Nairobi. At Réunion, had they waited, they might have been picked up by the inter-island heli-copter: but the helicopter was unreliable and Hugh would not risk it. Harassed by the need to know the worst about his new job, he had resented even their five hours of sleep in the Nairobi airport hotel.

For ten years Hugh had been a writer of film-scripts, working when he chose to work, which was every day and all day, and seeing himself a free man. Like other script-writers known to him, he could not say exactly what had happened, but, at a time when a whole new generation of effective, ambitious young men was making itself noticed, he found his work disappearing from under him. He could not, as he usually did, expect to pay this year's income-tax out of next year's earnings because it seemed there

7

would be no earnings. So here he was, obliged to attend an office at fixed hours and be answerable to other men.

Every stop on the route suggested to him that he seize the chance to fly back home again so, to counter his panic, he insisted on haste. Away from his friends, he began to feel isolated in misfortune; the more isolated because Kristy did not depend on his success. She had her own career as a writer and, if need be, could keep herself. While it seemed to him that the ten years of their marriage had gone down in nothingness, she could account for their every minute. She had preserved them in her novels.

Looking up at her where she sat with her black hair limp from the heat, her face white in the glowing pallor of the light, he could see she was tired out: but, for all that, he could imagine her mind still working away like an eccentric wheel.

Hugh knew he should have been glad that Kristy had chosen to come with him, but he was not glad. He never knew what she would do or say next. Her outspokenness had gone down well enough among their London friends but would it go down on Al-Bustan? He would have preferred to face this new life without the worry of her. And she, if she had to spend her time writing, could do it as well at home. He looked away from her, knowing that their marriage, begun in love, was breaking up in rivalry and discontent.

The island should have been in sight by now but a sea mist blanketed the boat. They were making their way through it at about two knots with the siren braying and other sirens answering. There was nothing to be seen, only the fog enclosing them like a dirty pearl. The decks were littered with baggage and people sprawling on it, asleep from boredom. Families had grouped themselves to pass round saucers of beans or chapattis with curry. The boat reeked of curry but now another smell was beginning to seep through: a sweet, heavy flower smell. The name of Al-Bustan meant The Garden and this was the garden's scent.

Kristy, bemused by heat and the monotonous drift through opaque haze had forgotten they were going anywhere. She was cogitating a story that did not belong to her: it was Hugh's story, though he was never likely to write it. It concerned his mother who, at the age Hugh and Kristy had now reached, had com-

8

mitted suicide. Her husband had fallen in love with another woman and the wife could not face life without him. Or, perhaps, she had wanted to spite him; or merely to frighten him. She may have expected him to come back and find her in a coma. But he did not come back: he stayed out all night. It was Hugh who found her, but too late. He had risen at 8 a.m. and, thinking she was asleep, had got his own breakfast and gone to school. When he came back in the late afternoon, she was still asleep. Only she was not asleep: she was dead.

Kristy had kept that story at the back of her mind since first hearing it, not from Hugh – nothing would induce him to speak of it – but from a man who had been his friend at school. She had never gone close to it, thinking it a claustrophobic, incestuous sort of story, not her own. Now, as though the move from its setting had released her inhibition about it, she had begun to consider it. Hugh had been ten when his mother had died in that way. What sort of woman could, for the sake of a faithless husband, abandon a dependent child? And, what was worse, leave him with an ever-present sense of guilt? – for had he tried to waken her when he rose at eight o'clock, he might have been in time to save her.

The guilt she had surmised from a look that came on his face, a furtively defensive look, when someone unwittingly spoke of suicide. What he felt, she imagined, was a peculiar sinking of the heart: and that was something he must suffer for the rest of his life.

Other emotions, too. Chagrin? A sense of unjust deprivation? Grievance, of course. What else? Never quite certain of him, she looked for him among the people on the deck and saw him moving towards the bows. He was a youthful-looking man, not as tall as he would wish to be but with a blunt, kindly face that won people to him. He was, with his fair hair, distinctive among the crowd of dark-haired Arabs and Indians. His hair was his most striking feature. It was of so clear a gold that it looked metallic and, even in this light, flashed as he turned his head. She could see he was making his way, diffidently, but with a purposeful diffidence, towards the Englishman who stood in the fore of the ship. The man, facing out to sea, was unaware of this advance and Hugh, moving in on him, went with the caution of a hunter. Feeling his expectancy, Kristy felt an old irritation: and yet she was sorry for him. She knew she added to his insecurity. Without her, he could adapt to any situation: with her, he was anxious and on edge. In London, they had almost reached the point of separating yet, when she had the choice, she had chosen to accompany him. She did not want to live alone. They were, she thought, both lost children, though neither was ever likely to admit this to the other.

The shape of the island had appeared like a shadow on the fog, and the passengers were stirring and putting their bundles together. Hugh, who had ceased to watch for it, was astonished to see it there. Its size surprised him: it looked more like some dangerous obstacle, a rock or a giant iceberg, than an objective. Having reached the bearded Englishman, he was sufficiently roused to speak: 'So we've got here at last.'

'We're an hour late, but fog's not unusual at this time of the year.'

Encouraged, Hugh introduced himself then realized that the other man had not meant to encourage him. He stared at Hugh with critical and insolent directness, obviously deciding whether or not to waste time on him, and when he spoke at last, he gave his name grudgingly: 'I'm Simon Hobhouse.' He looked Hugh up and down then added, in the tone of an examining magistrate: 'May I ask what you are doing here?'

Hugh did not take offence. Having exalted the man, who was less than ten years his senior, to the paternalistic order, he was able to answer with genial mildness: 'I'm taking up a temporary job with the government. I'm to monitor the Indian satellite and bring out a news-sheet. The idea is to interest the ministers in world politics; to widen their outlook. At the moment, apparently, they're all stuck in local affairs.'

Hugh, having done bigger things, could speak lightly of his new job but he did not expect Hobhouse to see it as ludicrous. He was startled when the man threw back his head and shouted: 'So you're bringing world politics to Al-Bustan! Oh, my God!'

'You're not in the OCS?'

'I most certainly am not.' Hobhouse turned, dismissing Hugh,

10

then, on second thoughts, swung round again: 'Why did you have to come four thousand miles to take a job like that?'

Hugh was about to explain when Hobhouse said: 'Don't bother to tell me.' He pointed to the island: 'Watch.'

The boat was sliding into the harbour. The sun, that had been out of sight all day, was now appearing; a fireball sinking in a welter of red. The island was taking on colour, first showing as a watery blur of green and gold, then, as though shifted into focus, appearing so immediate and defined that Hugh had the illusion of seeing it through a magnifying glass. Its façade rose almost sheer from the water-front and seemed to overhang the boat. It was covered in greenery. At the water's edge, there were coconut palms while above, from the harbour right up to the Arab city, vegetation was so crowded that trees and bushes jutted from ledges with roots clinging like fingers. The trees were all burdened with flowers or fruit or nut clusters held in webby bags like the young of spiders. The fruit was so profuse it not only grew on branches but out of tree trunks.

A road wound uphill. Villas stood among gardens and at the top of the island was the Medina, a small unit of pinks and cream, spined with minarets like a hedgehog. Above the city, divided from it by a stretch of grass, was the rock ridge that ran across the island from east to west. Suddenly, as though they had materialized when he was looking elsewhere, Hugh saw that two vast peaks rose from the ridge, forming the apex of a mountain range greater than the Himalayas; a drowned range of which nothing could be seen but this one mountain-top, Al-Bustan.

The sinking sun lit everything with a syrup light, as richly pink as the heart of a pumpkin. Under this light the greens deepened and took on lustre. For a moment the island seemed a mosaic of incandescent stones, olivine, jade and malachite inset with coral, then, in an instant, night came down. Lights appeared. The scene was gone.

Hugh, turning to his companion, found that he, too, had gone. As the boat bumped the quay, a clamour rose among the passengers struggling to be first ashore: but Hobhouse was off before any of them. Hugh could see him making a brisk, independent departure down the gangway, a bag in each hand, a rucksack on

11

his back. There were only two taxis on the quay. He threw his luggage into one of them, sprang in after it and was driven away. Meanwhile the passengers, massed together, were fighting their way down the gangway as porters and safragis fought their way up.

A Nubian in a silk kaftan was the first on deck. He shouted at Hugh: 'You for Praslin?'

'No, Daisy Pension.'

The Nubian made a scoffing sound and pushed into the crowd, demanding of any likely person: 'You for Praslin?'

Hugh could see Kristy still up aloft, gazing down as though too weary to attempt a descent. He called to her and collecting as much of their baggage as he could carry, set out to emulate Simon Hobhouse. He was surrounded at once by jeering porters who snatched the bags from his hands and tossed them down to their confederates below. One bag fell and was caught, giving rise to much laughter, as it was about to slide between ship and quay.

The Praslin safragi, having collected three Kuwati Arabs for his hotel, came down the gangway at Hugh's heels. As the Fosters put foot on land, they were engulfed in porters who demanded payment, at the same time impeding the Praslin party. The Nubian sternly ordered the porters to one side and told Hugh how to deal with them: 'You give one rupee each luggage.' He watched with attentive superiority as Hugh found the money then he asked the onlookers: 'Where Daisy Pension man?'

Where, indeed! No safragi awaited Hugh and Kristy and the Praslin safragi, contemptuous and pitying, ordered the remaining taxi to take the Fosters to the pension. He then held out his hand: 'I do you service. You give three rupee.' Putting the money into the folds of his kaftan, he led his Arabs to a large American car marked: 'PRASLIN HOTEL, Pride of the Southern Seas.'

Settled into the taxi, the Fosters felt the worst was over.

Hugh said: 'Thank heaven we know where we're going' and he gazed indulgently out at the lights and crowds and hubbub of the harbour. The taxi, jolting and coughing over the pebbles, did not take wing until it reached the quiet of the upper road. Here the only lights were bulbs strung at intervals among the filmy foliage of the roadside trees. They did not reveal much but they did show Kristy a large white turreted house flying the Union Jack. The same house had been pictured on the Daisy Pension writing-paper and she said: 'We've just passed it.'

The taxi did not stop. Hugh called out: 'How far to Daisy Pension?'

The driver's face, dark, with one black eye and one white eye, jerked to his shoulder: 'Daisy Pension very long time.'

Having been told the pension was just above the harbour, Hugh dared not speak. They came to a circus cut into the cliff where a tall building shone out but offered no help. The driver shouted 'This place where sultan had great show with horses. No dirty British those times.' A long white wall ran beside the rising road. When the wall ended, the road became rough and steep and the driver accelerated to take the ascent. Skidding this way and that, the car tore through the branches of unfamiliar trees and came out at last to level ground. Here there were no street lamps and the sky, hazed with heat, gave no light. A vast darkness stretched into the distance but on the right, some half a mile away, there was a glimmer from the Arab city.

'Medina.' The driver waved towards it and switched on his headlights. As the car wavered drunkenly about the road, the lights lit a chasm on their left.

Hugh, looking to see if Kristy were aware of their danger, saw she had closed her eyes. He thought she was asleep and he alone. Alone, he could be robbed and murdered and no one would ever know.

But he was not alone and Kristy was not asleep. When he glanced again at her, she had opened her eyes and had turned towards him as he had turned towards her. Realizing she shared his fear, he caught her hand and held to it, and so they sat: feeling united and thankful, in this threatening situation, that each had the other.

The taxi, swinging right, advanced on the Medina, rocking over pot-holes and loose pebbles, and followed a wall until it reached a space where cars were parked about a petrol pump. Here, without a pause, the driver took a turn, too sharply and too fast and Kristy gave a cry and wrung Hugh's hand. They skidded but stayed upright. With a wild burst of speed, the car returned to the

13

dark road, skirting the chasm with scarcely a yard to spare. In the distance, a long way below, the Fosters could see the lights of the harbour. At last they were down again among lived-in places and their hands fell loose and they lay back, one on each side of the car, too enervated to comment on what had happened. The driver braked, flinging them forward, and they found they had stopped in front of the turreted house that flew the Union Jack.

The front door was thrown open. The figure standing within it was a Nubian, as tall, imposing and richly dressed as the Praslin safragi. His kaftan was of dark blue rep and on his head he wore a round cap crocheted in pink and white silk. As he emerged, Kristy jumped from the taxi and pointed to the driver: 'This man has taken us all round the island.'

The Nubian's large eyes seemed to jolt from his head at this accusation. He raised his brows and speaking in Arabic, questioned the driver who replied, making off-hand gestures. The Nubian shrugged and leading Kristy into the pension, said 'He say yo' want to see sights. He say yo' want see Medina.' Kristy, too tired to argue, asked for the proprietor, a Mrs Gunner.

The Nubian, who with imperious finger movements was ordering some lesser servants to bring in the Fosters' luggage, said '*Sayyidah* not yet. Here is Akbar,' he spread a large hand on his chest: 'Yo' follow Akbar now.'

Hugh appeared, looking flushed. The room they had entered was large and full of middle-aged men and women. They all stared at the Fosters and the Fosters, weary and travel-worn, saw no friendliness in their faces.

Following Akbar, Kristy paused on the stair that led up from the main room, and said 'Have we come all this way to meet these old boilers?'

'For Heaven's sake, Kristy!'

Akbar, waiting in the corridor above, threw open a door, switched on a light and said 'Very nice room. Yo' have balcony, yo' have bath here, yo' have desk, ottoman, bed, cupboards. Best room in Daisy Pension.'

'Why should they give us the best room?' Kristy asked.

'Do shut up,' said Hugh. 'You're never grateful for anything.'

Downstairs again, they found the bar had opened and they had ceased to be of interest. The bar, that had been hidden behind an ornamental grille, was now a-dazzle with fairy-lights and behind the counter there was a woman who could only be Mrs Gunner. Though less than five foot tall, thin and with the face of a mummified marmoset, she extruded authority and Akbar was her henchman. He stood beside the bar and with a movement of brow or forefinger controlled the half-dozen safragis who, their white kaftans sashed in red and each wearing a fez, carried the drinks on silver trays.

Red, it seemed, was a colour favoured by Mrs Gunner. She herself was in red. The chairs and sofas were covered in bright red haleskin, the curtains were red and at intervals, on an embossed cream paper smudged with gold, gilded cupids held out lights with red plastic shades. It was a very bright room and the brightest thing in it was Mrs Gunner. As she moved, her jerkin and trousers flashed with sequins. She was said to run the best pension in the southern seas and Hugh, observing her with respect, whispered to Kristy 'Should I introduce myself?'

'I think you should.'

Approaching her, Hugh saw that Mrs Gunner's finger-nails were as red as her hair, and her arms, bare from the shoulder, were as brown and wrinkled as cinnamon sticks. She was counting change when he came to the bar and she did not look up. After waiting some minutes, he said.

'Excuse me, Mrs Gunner, I'm Hugh Foster.'

'Oh, yes!' she kept her eyes down and her husky Cockney voice expressed no interest at all.

'We want to thank you for giving us such a nice room.'

'All the rooms are nice, dear.' She turned back to her bottles and cash register without having given him a glance and he lamely made his way back to Kristy.

Kristy, in his absence, had seated herself on a sofa between two women. The women, pointedly displeased, looked away from her and Hugh knew she felt, as he did, a sense of social failure. As he reached her, she sprang up and taking his arm, pulled him to an empty corner, breathing fiercely. 'What do you think? I tried to be friendly. You saw those women? I sat down between them and said "I'm Mrs Foster. Who are you?" and they froze. You'd think I'd insulted them.'

'They probably heard you call them "boilers".'

'Don't be absurd.'

Depressed, sweating in the humid heat, they sat at the back of the room, not knowing what was expected of them. The only positive emotion they could feel was exasperation with each other, so neither spoke. Beside them was an open doorway covered with a bead curtain. When Hugh lifted the curtain and looked into the garden, several near-by people stirred resentfully, and he let it drop again. A dinner-gong sounded and the others, rising, filed past the Fosters and went out through the curtain. Following the last of them, the Fosters found the garden air as hot and humid as the air of the room. They crossed the lawn to a large square tent which was, they discovered, the dining-room. Akbar placed them obscurely, close to the canvas wall. From where they sat, they could make cautious inspection of the other tables. On every table there was a bowl of fruit and another, smaller, bowl that contained some fragile leaves of lettuce. Mrs Gunner did not come to the tent for her meals. Akbar, presiding alone, stood by the serving-table and, when required, would pull the cork from a wine bottle. His main job, it seemed, was to keep the other safragis busy.

The light bulbs were dim. The canvas, soaked by the rains, gave off a musty smell. Kristy, turning over the tropical fruits in their bowl, said: 'This is the only encouraging sight I've seen here yet.'

Listening to the conversations near enough to be overheard, the Fosters realized that here, as everywhere, the English talked about the weather. The Fosters had been advised that the hot wet season would soon be ending and cooler weather would be on its way. It would become dry but not very dry. Owing to the slant of the island and a quirk of the trade winds, there was rain all the year round. This was thought to be an advantage though they did not know why. The people about them were knowledgeable on this subject.

'The rains were excellent this year,' one said.

'Oh, yes, and very well-spaced.'

There was turtle soup, turtle meat fried in coconut oil, sweet potatoes and yams. Those of the guests who had wine on their tables, took no more than a glass each and tightly recorked their bottles. Observing everything, Kristy asked suddenly: 'What are we doing here?'

'Do keep your voice down. I have to work with these people. You know why we're here: we've got to pay off our income-tax. And you didn't have to come.'

'This climate makes you bad-tempered.'

'I'm cross for several reasons. To begin with . . . I had to give that taxi-driver five pounds.'

'You gave him five pounds? You're mad.'

'What else could I do? We arrive in a small place where everyone gossips: can I start my career by having a row with a taxi-driver?'

Kristy started to laugh.

Apprehensively, Hugh asked: 'What now?'

She shook her head and went on laughing, making no noise but shaking helplessly while Hugh looked round to see who was watching. Only one person had noticed her and he smiled when Hugh caught his eye. He glanced away at once but the smile surprised Kristy into sobriety.

The government officers in their suits of khaki drill, the wives all much alike in flowered, sleeveless dresses of unfashionable length, seemed to keep dry by a refrigeration of the will. The newcomer – who had entered late and whose table was close to the Fosters – glistened with sweat and his clothes, too heavy for the climate, were shabby, sweat-stained and, in places, split. Bent over his food, he was still smiling as though he remembered Kristy and her laughter with pleasure. He was so different from the other inmates of the pension that Kristy whispered: 'A human being!'

He was a man in middle age, of immense size, and his face, with its broad brow and short nose, looked like the face of the sphinx, blunted by blows and attritive time. His faded auburn hair was fine in texture but his skin, coarse-grained and sallow, was like the skin of some large pachyderm. 'A white rhino,' Hugh thought, never having seen one. The man, with his broad shoulders and chest, might have been a pugilist had he not had, when the smile faded out, an expression of reflective sadness.

Hugh, having observed him, looked away but Kristy, confident of his interest in them, waited until he glanced their way, then smiled at him. He at once bent towards them, saying 'I am Ambrose Gunner: not, as people are inclined to think, the husband of Mrs Gunner; merely the son. I keep the books here. I've been expecting you.'

'I'm glad someone was expecting us,' Kristy said.

'Did you find Mrs G. abstracted? I fear she is before she's had something to sustain her. She's over eighty, you know.'

'You live here?' Hugh asked.

'Not really. I come and go. My father settled here when he retired from the navy. When he was a young man, his ship called in at Al-Bustan on the way to the China station and he was determined that one day he would come back to live here. He bought this house for a song.' Ambrose Gunner's voice was light and compelling, a beautiful voice and he was, Hugh felt, presenting it at its most subtle pitch so the Fosters might know that Ambrose Gunner's true world was not that of the Daisy Pension.

'So you're on a visit?'

'Yes. I'll be returning to London in a few weeks' time.'

Hugh sensed an arrogance about the man but Kristy, watching the slight uptilt of Ambrose's chin, the droop of his eyelids and the defensive set of his delicate mouth, thought him sensitive and vulnerable. They both regretted that he would be leaving so soon.

There was a pause then Ambrose suggested that they take their coffee together in the main room. This arrangement made, the tension of their mutual curiosity subsided, and the Fosters left Ambrose to finish his supper alone.

Out in the garden, they stopped, startled by the change in the exterior scene. The sky had cleared and they saw, for the first time, the unfamiliar stars of the southern hemisphere. The sky was indigo, of a glassy clarity; and the stars so large they seemed to be rushing towards the earth, pulsing and scintillating as they came, and casting a bluish twilight over the garden. In this uncertain light, the trees seemed monstrously tall and the fruit-bats, sweeping from tree to tree, as large as pterodactyls.

The air whined and wheezed and clicked and creaked with

night creatures. Under all the noises was the steady sibilation of the cigalas. Small grey objects sat on the lawn like a concourse of mushrooms and some of the noise came from them. Moving cautiously forward, the Fosters saw they were frogs, their moving throats glinting in the starlight and giving out a unison of croaks.

Kristy, putting her hand under Hugh's arm, said 'The isle is full of wonders' and felt, when they went indoors, that the room looked more like home. Mrs Gunner appeared through a door near the bar and moving with an unsteady swagger, clanged the grille open and shouted: 'It's m'birfday.'

A small, moustached man, pink and bristling like a shrimp, took this up flirtatiously: 'Not your birthday again, Mrs G.?'

Humorously belligerent, Mrs Gunner said: 'I suppose I can have another birfday if I want, can't I?'

The guests were quick to agree and several of the men invited her to take a drink.

The Fosters, outside the circle of jocularity, seated themselves where they had sat before and waited for Ambrose. Near them another room, entered through a glass door, ran at an angle to the main room. Though it was unlit, it sparkled for it was a glass room and the harbour lights shone through it. When Ambrose joined them, Kristy asked why there should be a conservatory on an island that was itself a conservatory.

'That,' said Ambrose, 'is the Lettuce Room – where Mrs G. grows lettuce. She'll tell you that the Daisy is "a little bit of England on the Equator" and what would England be without lettuces?'

As he sat down, Hugh was aware of an observant shuffle among their neighbours. From glances received, he could guess that, despite Ambrose's impressive bulk and air of intellectual and social superiority, he was not approved. Hugh, knowing that unpopularity was a catching condition, felt uneasy, remembering his first term at school, when, coming in late on a row between two older boys, he had been ordered to choose whose side he was on. In his innocence, he had chosen the wrong boy then obstinately refused to repudiate him. That tormented year as follower of the outcast had, Hugh felt, set a pattern for his whole future. He was perforce a nonconformist and still did not know whether nature or circumstances prevented him from conforming. But there it was! In a strange place where they knew no one, Ambrose alone had welcomed them and Hugh was again on the wrong side.

Ambrose was eager to know exactly where the Fosters had lived in London. Kristy was telling him that they had lived at Beaufort Street. They had had a large, costly, leasehold flat that had been no asset when their money ran out.

'The lease was nearly at an end and the owner said he wanted the place for himself. Not true, of course: but it meant we had nothing to sell or let, and we had to store our furniture.'

Unaware of the misfortune contained in these facts, Ambrose said longingly: 'Chelsea! My old stamping ground. My place was off the Fulham Road. Did you drink at the Birdie?'

Kristy shook her head, not caring to admit that they had drunk, much too expensively, at a Curzon Street club frequented by film people. It was too early to confide all their follies but Ambrose was so much part of their social scene, she could tell him of her encounter with the two women on the sofa. The same women were back on the same sofa and Ambrose viewed them through oblique eyes.

'How did I offend them?' Kristy asked.

'Ah! They're very important ladies. The thin, gingery, sharp-nosed one is Mrs Axelrod, leader of Daisy thought. The soft, silly-looking one is her stooge, Mrs Prince. Their husbands are 'Superscale' and you must understand that no one not Superscale can speak to a Superscale lady unless first spoken to.'

'You're joking!'

'No, I assure you.' Ambrose turned to Hugh: 'Where do you come in the service hierarchy?' Hugh did not know and Ambrose said 'You must look up your contract. It will tell you when you may speak and to whom, which parties you have a right to attend and, should you give a party yourself, whom you are obliged to invite. This and much else is implicit in your code.'

Kristy said: 'I can't believe it. How could people tolerate such restrictive snobbery?'

'Tolerate it? They live by it. They're displaced persons. Without service conventions, they wouldn't know how to behave.'

'Surely the young...?'

'But there are no young. It's a dying service. You're the youngest people here. I'm afraid you've come the wrong way on the time machine and you'll find you're back in pre-war days. If you want to be accepted, you must respect the rules.'

'I never respect rules.'

'You'll get used to them.'

'But will they get used to me?'

Ambrose laughed uncertainly, not knowing what government society would make of a young woman as rash as Kristy Foster.

Hugh said: 'But we're not limited to these people. Surely there are others around? I met a man on the boat called Hobhouse.'

'Hobhouse?' Ambrose, who had been urbane as a giver of information, frowned now, much ruffled: 'Is *that* one back?' He began to rise as though Hobhouse were a contagion and he in danger from it.

Hugh, holding to him, said: 'Don't go. Tell us about Hobhouse. Who is he? What does he do?'

'He's mad. He's a medical man without a practice. A sort of amateur scientist who despises money yet has private means. He's full of nonsense – and vicious. An impossible person.'

Disconcerted, Hugh said: 'I rather liked him.'

'I thought you did,' Kristy spoke sharply then, pretending more amusement than she felt, said teasingly: 'In fact, I rather thought you'd fallen for him.' She explained to Ambrose as though making light of the situation: 'The fact is, Hugh doesn't trust women. What he really wants is a man friend: an ideal friend. A hero.'

Ambrose was not amused and did not pretend to be. He said in a remote and lofty tone: 'I doubt whether Hobhouse would suit his book. That one doesn't want friends.'

Kristy, knowing they had upset Ambrose, felt too tired to improve matters and took herself to bed.

Ambrose, though still put out, sat on. In the same remote and lofty tone, he asked what Hugh had done before joining the service. On hearing he had once been a writer and then a scriptwriter, Ambrose relaxed and said with enthusiasm: 'We have a great deal in common. I, too, belonged to the literary scene. And I often felt the urge to write, but did not.'

'Why was that?'

'I'm so self-critical,' Ambrose sighed. He pondered his condition for several moments, then added: 'But I was in publishing. And I have reviewed novels. I had a regular column once. I think I can truthfully say I was an influence, even a power. I've a friend I'd like you to meet. Would you feel like strolling down to the harbour for a drink?'

Hugh felt more like following Kristy to bed but, relieved by Ambrose's returned spirits, said: 'If we don't stay long.'

'One drink,' Ambrose promised, 'only one drink.'

2

In the open air, Hugh was ravished by the night scents of the island. He asked: 'What scent is that?'

Ambrose sniffed vaguely: 'Probably jasmin. It's all over the place. But do tell me why you, a script-writer, wanted to come to a place like this?'

'My script-writing career collapsed. I had to get a job.'

Ambrose murmured his sympathy: 'I, too, was let down. I, too, helped the wrong people.'

'No.' Hugh did not wish to be misunderstood: 'No one let me down. The bottom fell out of the film-industry. Suddenly – or so it seemed. Chaps like me were doing all right so when the final collapse came, none of us was prepared for it.'

'You had nothing saved?'

'Not much, I'm afraid. We lived like everyone else. You had to show up at expensive clubs and restaurants or you were counted out. And we had a heavy insurance so Kristy would have something if . . . and, of course, income-tax. Our only asset was an Aston Martin and when I got this job, we sold the car to buy tropical kit.'

'But the collapse of the film-industry! How did it happen?'

'I wish I knew. I'd been asked to write the script for a big film – a "super colossal film", as they used to say – based on the "Pilgrim's Progress". I was seeing my agent to sign the contract when he rang and said there would be a few days' delay: the company saw a change coming and had decided to secure the money before going ahead. I waited. A fortnight later I was told they intended borrowing from other companies, then that they were trying to get the cash in the city, then that they were approaching private investors. A couple of months went by. My agent was optimistic: he thought a money shortage was no bad thing. He said "the industry's riddled with hangers-on, scroungers, chaps on the fiddle. This'll sort the men from the boys." Meanwhile, we were living on capital. After about three months of this, my agent stopped telephoning. When I rang him, he didn't know what to say. He told me to wait – but one can't wait forever.'

Hugh paused, unable to describe the final indignity that had brought him to Al-Bustan. He had gone to the club, the worthlessly expensive place in Curzon Street, thinking that someone must see him and offer him a job. When he entered the dining-room there were a dozen or more men known to him, all in the same position, all there with the same idea, all caught in the same despairing fantasy. They had looked up hopefully and seeing him, had looked away.

'Some of them moved to television but the work's sporadic and the rewards small. Besides, I wanted to get away. A new environment, a different part of the world. Something to revive me. I knew someone at the Foreign Office and he offered me this.'

'There are worse places.' Ambrose, nodding his understanding, lifted his large, moist face into the white light of the risen moon: 'And the film world will pick up.'

'In time, yes, but it will never be the same. Younger men were coming in and now they're working for peanuts. The good days are over.'

'I may say.' Ambrose's small voice became confidingly smaller: 'This chap we're seeing down here: he's extremely well heeled. There's no knowing! If he takes a fancy to you, he could put you back on your feet.'

Hugh laughed. He did not know how any one person could put him back where he once was, but Ambrose was convincing and Hugh, for no reason at all, began looking about him with a new excitement. He ceased to see his job as a pending prison of office routine. It was temporary. It would tide him over into better times. Meanwhile he could enjoy the equatorial sky, the shadows of the pepper trees black, like black ostrich feathers, on the white sandy road, the white distant shore where the Indian Ocean, again and again and again, rolled in with a long curling wave. Elated, he bent down and sifted the sand through his fingers.

24

'What is this?'

'Coral. Everything here is coral. They make it into blocks for building. The villas are built of coral, so are the Government Offices, the Praslin, all the new buildings. The others, like the Daisy, are adobe.' Ambrose smiled at Hugh's wonder but to him the island was a commonplace: his mind was elsewhere. 'This chap we're seeing's called Lomax. I think you'll like him. He's a bit spoilt by his money, of course. To people like us – intellectuals from the great world – ownership of cash is not, in itself, admirable. But here,' his voice dropped impressively, '*it cuts a lot of ice.*'

'Is he a native of Al-Bustan?'

'No, no. Oh, dear me, no. God knows what he's native of. He lives at the Praslin, calls it his "home from home" but I doubt if he has any other.'

Walking downhill with flat-footed dignity, Ambrose swayed under his own weight. His jacket was too tight to meet across his belly which stood out some distance in front of him. Hugh was surprised to find, when they stood together, that he and Ambrose were much of a height. Sitting, Ambrose looked enormous. On his feet, with his vast shoulders and chest, he gave the impression of a giant dwarf or dwarf giant, and Hugh was less over-awed by his bulk. Still, as he walked with head thrown back, the wind sweeping his fine hair this way and that, the street lights illuming the rubbery mounds and runnels of his face, his appearance was grandiose.

At the bottom of the hill, he was becoming breathless. He gasped: 'I have a little project in which Lomax is interested. I'll tell you later. I know you'll keep it under your hat.'

Flattered by this trust in his discretion, Hugh felt he had already made a friend.

The road opened on to the broad, cobbled area of the harbour. The shops here were brilliant and busy and young men were out walking in the night breeze. Some of the men were Indian; others were of no certain race but made up for their indefinite skin colouring with patterned shirts and western trousers, all in the most definite colours they could find. Ambrose pointed to the largest of the shops, a balconied, embellished wooden structure,

25

like a rambling lop-sided Swiss chalet, and said 'Aly's. That's where Mrs G. buys the bacon. Great shop; sells everything. There's a hairdressing establishment upstairs where the Daisy girls get their hair done.'

Through all of Aly's lighted windows, Hugh could see the movements of customers: Indians, Arabs and Mulattos, but mostly Indians. He asked if the harbour were an Indian quarter.

'More or less. The Indian shopkeepers drove the Arabs out and the blacks can't compete. Africans give credit to all their relatives then wonder why they don't make a profit. The Arabs aren't much better but they still own the cafés.'

There were three or four cafés and the chairs and tables, mingling and covering the cobbles on either side of the road, reached out to the verge of the quay. The Arab customers lolled on the chairs, whiling away the hours before empty coffee cups. The more energetic played tric-trac or ran their fingers over their amber worry beads. Hugh, following Ambrose among the tables, met here and there a sleepy stare and thought the Arabs too long defeated to care who held the island that had once been theirs. Then a voice spoke quietly behind him: 'Go home, Englishman.' Hugh turned but the faces he saw expressed nothing.

'Was that meant for us?'

'Possibly. There are, I suppose, troublemakers here but the Arabs, on the whole, are charming. Now, here we are at our little pleasure spot.'

A few doors from Aly's there was a brick building that looked like a nonconformist chapel. It had been built, Ambrose explained, by the Wesleyans but converts had been few and, in the end, the missionaries had to sell up. Now the arched entablature carried a neon sign that said: GURGUR'S GIRLS.

The manager, a sad-looking Malay, intercepted Ambrose in the hall and in an awed voice told him that Mr Lomax had telephoned to book them a banquette. He led them into the club where tables, topped with yellow plastic, stood round a dancefloor and the banquettes, scalloped round the walls, were covered with dirty yellow velvet. Lomax's booking had not been necessary: the banquettes were all unoccupied.

The lights were masked with Chinese lanterns but nothing, not even the musak, played at top pitch, could dispel the aura of Gothic vaulting and pitch-pine walls. The air was chilly and Hugh started to sneeze.

'It is a bit over-conditioned,' Ambrose apologized, 'but I like it. One can take a drink without loss of body fluids. Bit empty, isn't it. Still, early yet.' He ordered whisky to be charged to Lomax's account.

The other patrons were five young men sprawled over a table at the edge of the dance floor. As soon as they saw Hugh, they sat up and gazed at him as though his appearance confounded them. They took in the cut of his silk jacket made by a Maddox Street tailor, the line of his shoes, the set of his shirt and tie, and the length of his fair hair that curled into the nape of his neck, and then, putting their heads together, they discussed him anxiously. Hugh, disliking this attention, frowned. When they started to shout above the howl of the musak, slapping each other on the back and saying 'How are you, old bean?' and 'What'll you have, old top?' he became red and said, 'They're laughing at me.'

'*Au contraire*. They're impressed by you. They had thought themselves the height of Western elegance until they saw you. You dress with a difference. They want to be like you.'

'But that out-of-date slang!'

'Everything's out of date here. Change begins at the centre. It takes a long time to reach us.'

'What are they? Arabs?'

'Gracious me, no. No pure-bred Moslem or Hindu would be seen in this place. They're mixed breeds. Some pass for white and some for black, but they suffer the abject humility of belonging to no tribe or race.'

'I imagine they're a problem?'

'Far from it. They manage the plantations and they're the government's most loyal supporters.'

The whiskies, when they came, were the largest Hugh had ever seen. He decided that one would be enough for him. When Ambrose downed his glass and ordered another round, Hugh said he could drink no more.

'Come now! When do you most need a drink? When you've just had one. And don't worry about our host: he can afford it.'

'How did he make his money?'

'God knows. How does that sort of man make money? I wish I knew. He's a money man: he bets on certainties. But – and this one *must* admire – he will take a gamble for the good of his soul.'

The particular complacency with which Ambrose spoke made Hugh laugh: 'I take it you're referring to your project?'

'Well, yes.' Ambrose's large, sad brown eyes fixed themselves on Hugh: 'I would like to describe it to you but I'm afraid ... you will think it fantastic. You'll treat it with derision.'

'I won't, I promise you.'

Ambrose considered the project with solemn face then spoke as one launching into a life story: 'This island, I suppose you know, was uninhabited before the pirates turned up. There were only the dodos, poor trusting, wingless creatures who couldn't get away. They were at the mercy of the pirates but the pirates were at the mercy of other forces. They collected riches but if they tried to spend them, they were likely to be seized and hanged. So they were always burying the stuff. These south sea islands are full of buried treasure. There's a cache not a hundred miles from here.'

'And you know where it is?'

'I've a pretty shrewd idea. The search, however, calls for money – and faith.'

'I suppose it does.' Hugh's interest in Ambrose was dulled by this unlikely tale and Ambrose, aware of Hugh's incredulity, looked injured. His eyes, watery with emotion, shifted from him and at once their expression changed. He nodded gleefully to some object in view: 'There's Gurgur.'

A thin, sagging man was standing on the dance-floor, his head protruding from his rounded shoulders, his neck stretched, taut and wrinkled, like the neck of a rampant hen. His face, as taut as his neck, was watchful and seemed to be intently sneering at nothing.

'What does he remind you of?' Ambrose asked.

'A vulture.'

'Exactly,' Ambrose was delighted: 'And the curious thing is that his name means "vulture". When he first arrived here, the blacks called him "Gurgur" and he kept the name. I don't think he knows what it means – to him one name is as good as another; and one place is as good as another. When he appears, the cabaret begins.'

At once, as though word had gone out to the quay, the hall became full of young men. Every chair and banquette was taken and those who could not find a seat, stood behind the rest. No one spoke. The hall was in a state of avid suspense. The musak ground to a stop and Gurgur, in a voice like a computer, announced 'Miss Baba and Miss Nikki in their Bubble Dance'.

The speakers relayed 'Rustle of Spring' as the girls ran out. They were fat, elderly girls dressed in scraps of chiffon, who giggled wildly as they tossed the ball about, occasionally taking a jump and thumping down to the floor. Their limbs quivered. The young men pressed forward until there was scarcely room for the dance and Gurgur ordered them back again. When the girls kissed their hands and tripped off, the men, frantically pushing Gurgur out of the way, ran after them. Gurgur watched with a bleak grin as the first half dozen got through the curtains and the rest slunk back again.

'So that's what Gurgur is up to?' Hugh said.

Ambrose smiled. 'And he's never short of custom. The girls are imported, of course. Local girls – anyway the Indian and Arab girls – are kept on a very tight rein. They have to be virgin to make a good match.'

Two more girls came out, younger girls, plump and brown-skinned, who shook their breasts and hips till the floor groaned, the woodwork creaked and the men were in a frenzy. Ambrose, speaking beneath the uproar, said: 'Lomax.'

The tall figure in the doorway did not move until the dance ended. As the young men went pelting and crying after the girls, Lomax came slowly across the room. He observed Hugh as though displeased at finding him there. Ambrose was quick to introduce him as 'a new and desirable resident of our island. Hugh Foster, influential member of the government, and a famous writer.'

Hugh murmured: 'Please!' but it did no good. Some of the young men, frustrated in the race for the girls, were returning to the banquettes, and they gazed on Hugh in open admiration. The words 'famous writer' were breathed among them.

Their admiration, however, was not shared by Lomax. As he seated himself on a chair opposite Hugh, he flatly asked: 'What have you published, Mr Foster?'

'One novel. Some time ago.'

Lomax smiled. His smile was not so much a smile as a painful grimace as though, at long last, he had seen the point of a not very good joke. 'And you have done nothing since?'

'He's a film man,' Ambrose broke in eagerly: 'Oddly enough it was in my mind that a film should be made of our treasure hunt and, lo and behold, a film man turns up.'

Lomax, who sat with his head down, raised his thick, pale eyelids to look again at Hugh: 'You are here to make a film, Mr Foster?'

Hugh laughed to hide his embarrassment: 'I was only a script-writer. I'm here to do a temporary job for the government. I'm setting up a news-sheet.'

'Indeed!' Lomax's eyes, of a very light blue, were moving rapidly, taking in Hugh's appearance as though to assess his background: 'What are you drinking, Mr Foster?'

'I think it's my turn.' Hugh looked about for the safragi but Lomax, ignoring his attempts to buy a drink, called to the manager: 'Order me a whisky and see these gentlemen are served with what they are drinking.'

Hugh, having got through two triple whiskies, was incapable of protest. He sank against the back of the banquette and watched Lomax, as from a considerable distance. He had, at first, seen Gurgur and Lomax as similar but now, melting under the influence of his third glass of whisky, he began to think better of his host. He decided that where Gurgur was mean, Lomax had substance of a sort. He was a physically colourless man. His skin and hair reflected the biscuit tint of his tussore suit. He was perhaps fifty but his movements and manners were those of someone much older. His face, built round a long, curving, nose, should have been lean, but instead, was puffy, reminding Hugh of a picture, seen outside a police station, of a drowned man who had been a month in the water.

Ambrose was saying: 'Some cases of mine have arrived. The purser rang me and said they're pretty heavy. Think they contain books.' This information was left on the air a while then, as it gave rise to no comment, Ambrose augmented it: 'I'm expecting to find a chart in one of them.'

When Lomax said nothing, Ambrose looked expectantly at Hugh. Hugh, who had faded almost beyond the range of conversation, pulled himself together and did his best to oblige. 'What chart is that?'

Ambrose was quick to tell him: 'It's a chart which my old dad bought the first time he came here. It was his first commission. He was only a lad. One of those half-breed Portuguese – Canarians, they call them – offered it to him for five rupees. He bought it more as a memento than anything else. In those days no one could hope to raise a ship sunk in twelve fathoms of water.'

Hugh keenly inquired: 'How did it get there?'

'Ah!' said Ambrose, 'an interesting story. A pirate called Morgo was taking his gold by sea, meaning to bury it in the forest on the other side of the island. He never got there. The ship sprang a leak and went down in the bay they call Morgo's Bay.'

Hugh was beginning to believe all this: 'Where is Morgo's Bay?'

'Not far.' Turning heavily, Ambrose faced Lomax to say: 'I really think we should take a drive round to the bay. I suggest you see it before finally making up your mind to finance this venture.'

Lomax declined his head but remained silent. The lack of response did not seem to worry Ambrose whose manner became increasingly grand as he said: 'The money is nothing, of course. The initial outlay for men and equipment would be no more than 300,000 rupees. And in return, what would you get?'

Lomax smiled: 'I'd guess, nothing very much.'

Ambrose earnestly amended this: '*Au contraire.* You'd get a spiritual adventure; a search comparable with the search for the Holy Grail. *A search for gold.* Think of the interest it would rouse! If you had any business of your own on hand – any building, that is; selling of real estate; that sort of thing – think how this would draw them in. And, as I said, what a subject for a film! You've been thinking about it, haven't you?'

Lomax nodded.

Ambrose looked grieved: 'I really did hope you'd been thinking to better purpose than this.'

Lomax's lips, as full and defined as those of a stone pharaoh, lifted slightly in an expression, perverse and obstinate, that startled Hugh.

Ambrose, very hurt, shuffled to the edge of the banquette and bent towards Lomax: 'I *do* wish you'd give it serious thought.'

Lomax said evenly: 'I have done so, and will continue to do so.' His tone dismissed the matter and Ambrose, realizing he would get no better assurance, sighed and drooped like a dejected bear. Hugh thought it was time to go but Lomax, having put the treasure behind him, clearly thought the evening had just begun. Before Hugh could get to his feet, the safragi came to the table with three more glasses of whisky. Gurgur accompanied him.

Standing at one side of Lomax and bending close to his ear, Gurgur spoke rapidly in Arabic. Hugh, who had learnt a little of the language before he came out, understood that some of the words were proper names. There were African, Indian and Arab names, and, among them, the English name of Culbertson.

He asked Ambrose: 'Who are they talking about?'

'Police officers. He says it's costing him a pretty penny to keep this place open. It's the old story. He buys people, but they don't stay bought. Now, if he won't pay up, they say they'll close him down altogether.'

Hugh felt depressed because it was an old story. His mellow mood was failing and he was near sleep. Watching the sick over-hanging face of Gurgur, he asked, as Kristy had asked: 'What are we doing here?' Simon Hobhouse could not understand why he need come four thousand miles to take the job offered him, but the job had meant nothing. If you could not do what you wanted to do, did it much matter what you did? The island had offered sanctuary – but was there such a thing? He had imagined he was coming to a different place: a place still held by an ideal of inno-cence, so far from the Western world that corruption could not

32

find it. But the world had grown too small for innocence and he saw that corruption was everywhere.

He whispered urgently to Ambrose: 'Let's go.'

'In a minute.' Ambrose was sitting stiffly, waiting for Gurgur's departure. The man began to go at last and as he went, Lomax placed a hand on his arm and held to him a second or two. It was a gesture that showed Hugh the understanding between them.

Ambrose bridled slightly, preparing to say his say. When he spoke, he did so with dignified restraint: 'If you have no interest in the project, then there is nothing to keep me here. I came to see my old mother and I've stayed longer than I had intended. I have other matters in hand. I'd better not say too much at the moment but ... well, a literary friend of some importance has invited me to edit a new edition of a major poet. I am tempted. I am greatly tempted.'

To Hugh's surprise, Lomax was moved by the threat implicit in Ambrose's claim. He looked uneasy and said: 'We might take a drive to Morgo's Bay.'

This concession was not enough. Ambrose showed his contempt for it by getting himself off the banquette. He said in a lofty tone: 'You'd better think about it and give me a ring.'

Lomax, feeling a need to excuse himself, said 'After all, it's not a cheap project.'

'Do you want a cheap project? You've made your money, God knows how, and now you want a cut-price salvation.'

Lomax began to speak but Ambrose would hear no more. Calling Hugh to follow, he went with a haughty strut to the hall where he was brought up short by finding the door locked. When Hugh reached him, he was flinging his weight against it, then hammering it and bellowing in frustrated rage. The manager came running to open it and Ambrose strode out with Hugh hurrying after. At the first rise of the road, Ambrose came to a stop, breathing heavily and mopping his face.

'What a bore that man is!' he said. 'In London, I was invited everywhere. Here I waste my time with a fellow like that! What is he? A wheeler-dealer, a speculator, an extortioner, a bloody usurer. The only thing he ever reads is a balance sheet. He's disliked and he doesn't know why. He belongs nowhere. And he's

33

an insomniac. He'll sit there drinking till his chauffeur goes in and gets him.'

'Perhaps he is to be pitied?'

'I *did* pity him.' Ambrose sniffed and trudged on, grumbling to himself. A taxi, hooting up from the harbour, caused him to side-step like an irate whale and he stopped again, shouting, 'I saw his need and I pitied him. This is the thanks I get for it.' He trudged on again.

Hugh, with the road swaying about him, stood for a while, watching Ambrose who came again to a stop and then put his head against a tree. Hugh, managing to reach him, found he was striking the bark with his fists and crying: 'I want to go back to my old stamping ground.'

Hugh, his eyes wet with sleep, joined Ambrose against the tree; Ambrose's distress reminded him of his own: 'You're a free man, but I've got a wife. My wife can do what I can't do. She writes books. She never thought of it till she saw me doing it, and now she's better than I am.'

Ambrose, sobering a moment, said: 'She writes, does she? Under the name of Foster?'

'No. She's Christine Middleton.'

'Really? I've reviewed her. She's good.'

'Feminine stuff.'

'You could say that about Jane Austen.'

Finding no consolation in Ambrose, Hugh put his arms round the tree trunk, feeling the wood softening and enfolding him as he slid to the ground. Pulling him up by the arms and slinging him like a sack over his back, Ambrose trudged on, too absorbed in his own discontent to be aware of his burden. He was surprised to find the Daisy still awake. Going round to the garden door, he saw, through the bead curtain, that Mrs Gunner was at her pianoforte.

He dropped Hugh into a garden chair and Hugh, awakening, asked 'What's happening?'

'She's having a sing-song.'

They listened to 'Daisy, Daisy' sung in a quavering stridor.

Hugh, rubbing the sleep from his eyes, looked in through the curtain and saw that the chairs and tables had been pushed back to give Mrs Gunner a stage. The upright piano had been pulled into the middle of the room and Mrs Gunner was perched on a stool, wound up so high that she hung over the keyboard like a red paroquet on a play-ring. As she sang, she tossed her head about and at the end of each verse she flourished her hands in the air. The audience watched her glumly.

No doubt it had been a convivial evening but now the glasses were empty and the safragis had retired. Everyone, except Mrs Gunner, had had enough. Some of the men lay open-mouthed, asleep in their chairs: the rest had the strained gaze of those who endure too much. And, Hugh supposed, they must endure to the end, for the Daisy was the best the island could offer an official who had to make do on a government salary.

He asked Ambrose 'Does this happen often?'

'No. Once in a while she feels she must let off steam. Now, watch this.'

Mrs Gunner had slid down from the stool and was standing with arms outstretched. She announced: 'I'm going to do m'cart-wheels.' She fluttered her hands at those near to her, requiring them to move back. She pointed her foot at the shrimp-pink man: 'Get back there, Superscale Simpson.' Her manner was humorously domineering but was beginning to verge on to something less pleasant. Her voice was very hoarse. As the guests began a weary pushing back of chairs, she urged them sharply: 'Go on back, the lot of you.'

Satisfied at last, she stood with arms and legs spread, and said: 'Any blighter thinks he can beat me at this game, he's welcome to try.' Having spoken, she dropped down on one hand and flashed round the room, a scarlet Catherine-wheel. There was applause when she finished but instead of responding, she stood with one hand over her eyes and the other pressed to her side.

Ambrose caught his breath, anxious inquiry creasing his face. Inside the room, the guests had risen in alarm and Simpson hurried to her. She pushed him aside and looked about her, all humour gone: 'The show's over, so clear off. If you don't have to work tomorrow, I do.'

The guests, without argument, followed each other up the stairs and Mrs Gunner lit a cigarette. With the cigarette hanging from

35

her lips, she lifted a loaded ash-tray, saying loudly: 'Look at them fag-ends. Filthy lot. Place stinks. Makes you sick.' She came towards the bead curtain and Ambrose jumped away from it, showing an emotion deeper and less explicable than fear. To the consternation of both the men, she put her head through the curtain.

'You can come in now,' she said. 'Lucky the others didn't see you. A nice thing on your first night, Mr Foster, coming home sloshed. Here, you,' she ordered Ambrose, 'get him upstairs.'

Ambrose pulled Hugh up and taking him under the arm, helped him to the upper floor. As they went, they heard Mrs Gunner bolting the garden door and slamming the bar grille into place.

One door stood ajar on the landing and Ambrose whispered into it: 'Mrs Foster?' Kristy at once switched on the bedside light. Ambrose dropped Hugh on to the bed and went before questions could be asked.

Kristy put her questions to Hugh who was blinking at her and trying to rise: 'What were you doing till two in the morning? How did you get in this state?'

'I thought you were asleep.'

'Asleep, with that row going on downstairs?'

Hugh, giving up the struggle to rise, dropped down and closed his eyes. Kristy, furious at his unconcern, shook him, demanding to be told where he had been. When he did not reply, she struck him across the face. The blow roused him. Suddenly excited, he swung his feet to the floor, pulled off his clothes and threw himself naked on to the bed. He rolled on top of her.

She pushed him away: 'I don't want you. I'm tired. Leave me alone.'

'You hit me. D'you remember? You hit me.'

As she fought against him, he slapped her angrily and she replied by catching his ear-lobe between her teeth. She bit so fiercely, he could scarcely stifle his cry of pain. Tugging at her hair, he forced her to release him then, covering her mouth with his own, he held her beneath him. For the first time in years, they made love with an ardour they thought had gone for ever.

3

Down in the main room which Mrs Gunner called the Salon, Ambrose stood by the open pianoforte and touched a single note. He touched it tenderly, feeling rather than hearing the sound. The piano was a Bechstein and well maintained by a Negro tuner who understood the instrument.

When Ambrose came back to the Daisy, nearly eighteen months before, he had spent his days playing the piano. The noise had disturbed the pension and guests complained. His music was not their music, nor was it Mrs Gunner's music and, he suspected, she did not want a rival performer in the house. She said 'That's enough of that' and ordered him to play no more.

Remembering how she had put her hand to her heart, he thought, 'She's growing old at last', not that anyone would believe it. Simpson, when he first arrived from some collapsed Crown colony, had opened his eyes in astonishment when Mrs Gunner turned cartwheels and nudging Ambrose, had said: 'We'd have to shed a few years before *we* could do that.'

Ambrose had been upset but later decided that Simpson, the old fool, was trying to flatter Mrs Gunner. They all flattered her but their flattery, Ambrose felt, covered contempt. Axelrod with his 'Mrs G., you're blooming' and Prince, a Dickens addict, who called her 'Heart's Delight', and Simpson with his 'I'd ask you to marry me if I thought you'd have me', all provoked the same throaty falsetto come-back: 'Do you moi-nd!' The rebuke reassured them. She might be in control, but socially she was below their level. Every word she said, proved it. She had once been Daisy Plimpton, part of a song and dance act called 'Daisy and May'. She and her sister May had been performing on South Parade pier, Southsea, when she met her future husband, Lieutenant-Commander George Gunner.

Ambrose had made sure of one thing: they did not flatter him. They had thought they knew just where they were with Mrs Gunner but the appearance of Ambrose had disconcerted them. His voice, his physique, his stately manners, dumbfounded the lot of them. Had he deferred to them, buttered them up, acted the servitor, they would, no doubt, have extended their patronage to him. He thought: 'Not for me.' Later, when they realized that he counted for nothing in the pension, they ignored him.

This did not worry him. Mrs Gunner, who could be tyrant or entertainer as she chose, enjoyed playing the goat for them, but Ambrose had known greatness. He had been head boy at Tuffington and gained a scholarship to Kings. He had taken a double first.

Bemused by these memories, he forgot Mrs Gunner's ban on his playing and winding down the stool, seated himself before the keys. He intended a little Mozart, a passage from the Piano Concerto K467, a calm subtle passage that would assuage his longing for a different world. Bending close to the keyboard, he began quietly enough but, carried away by the music, he ran into fury.

Mrs Gunner's door opened and one eye showed through.

'Stop that, Ambrose.'

Ambrose stopped. He threw down the lid. As he rose, the front door-bell rang. He took himself into the pension office and half shutting the door, watched through it as the Egyptian safragi, Hassan, hastened out of the kitchen quarters, dressing as he came.

Mrs Gunner had been expecting a couple called Ogden who were arriving on the helicopter from Réunion. Having sold their villa before going on home leave, they had decided to spend their final year at the Daisy. He listened as Hassan opened the door and heard Ogden addressing him with amiable superiority: 'Sorry to get you up. We had helicopter trouble. Hope there's a room ready for us.'

Hassan, gaping at Ogden's six foot four, said, 'Best room. Best room for you and sayyidah.'

Closing the office door, Ambrose muttered 'Opinionated ass. Best room, indeed!' He looked at the place allotted him: the office, cluttered with his bed and all his possessions: 'And here

I am, her only son: crammed into a cuddy no bigger than a jakes!'

Hassan opened a door on the upper landing and put on a light. He stood aside to let the Ogdens see the splendour of the room and the Ogdens looked at Hugh and Kristy wrapped together on the bed. Ogden ushered his wife out and switched off the light. He motioned Hassan to come quietly, and quietly closed the door.

The slight sounds that reached Hugh lifted him a little out of sleep. Someone, he thought, had tried to signal him. Someone, somewhere, was about to tell him the nature of the place in which he found himself.

The place had been familiar to him since his adolescence. In early years he had felt himself hopelessly immersed in it then, gradually, he found he could move through it. What he had never discovered was, how to get out of it. The substance of the place was congested about him. He could feel it but he could see nothing. When he was young the sense of total impasse terrified him: he would fight himself awake. If his stepmother heard him cry out and came to ask what the trouble was, he would say they had been smothering him. But *who* had been smothering him? she would ask.

He still could not answer that question. Later, when he found he could move, he imagined that movement gave him enough air to sustain life and he was less afraid. He began to realize he was occluded not, as he had thought, by a malleable substance but by objects that were unwilling to yield yet were not entirely obdurate. By struggling, he managed to make a way through them. Then the question arose: where was he going? Having no knowledge of the place and no known objective, he could not tell back from forward, and it came to him that there was no-where to go. The place, compacted and unchanging, could go on for ever.

As the door clicked closed, he opened his eyes, expecting a revelation, but there was only darkness. He knew no more than he had ever known. In that night-time dark, he thought the place was infinity and his presence in it was a damnation.

Next morning, when he pulled aside the bamboo blind and saw

the outside world hidden by a tropical downpour, panic came over him. His head ached and he pressed it into his hands.

Kristy said accusingly: 'You've had that dream again.'

He said: 'I haven't' and going into the bathroom, he locked the door against her.

Rain had flattened the garden plants and the lawn was a lake. An awning protected the guests on their way to breakfast. Inside the tent, the sodden canvas was black and the rain, drumming on it, made it blacker. The inner air felt tangible with heat and moisture. Scarcely able to see each other through the gloom, the Fosters did not speak until a lemur jumped on to their table and stared at Kristy, confident that she would feed it. At the sight of it, she gave a cry of joy and putting her hands on its fawn-coloured, woolly coat, she managed to hold it a moment before it leapt away from her. Once out of reach, it stopped again and waited for food.

She said 'The little hands' and offered it a piece of bacon. It showed no interest.

Ambrose, watching from his table, said: 'Try giving it fruit.'

She cut a piece of pineapple and the hands reached out and gently took it.

She asked 'Does it belong to you?'

'No. It lives in the garden. Lemurs are nocturnal creatures and on days like this, they're not sure if it's night or day.'

After Kristy had fed the lemur, Ambrose chose a suitable moment to remind her that he had reviewed one of her books. She raised her dark eyes, that were full of delight in the lemur, and looked at him with equal delight: 'So you are the Ambrose Gunner who used to review in the *Sunday Times*?'

Hugh sighed. He was despondent, knowing he must soon set out to find the Government Offices and face the boredom of a routine job. Ambrose, trying to keep him in the conversation, asked him why he had written only one novel. When did he intend to write another?

'Never,' Hugh said despondently. 'One loses the creative habit.'

'But why let it go?'

'It went of itself. My novel was sold to a film company. They asked me to write the script and the script turned out better than the book. Then they asked me to write another script. I'd written and rewritten the novel three times and made three hundred pounds plus two thousand for the film rights. I got five thousand for writing the script and for the second script they offered me seven thousand. The third script I did brought in twelve thousand. I was good at script-writing and all I had to do was bang the stuff out on the typewriter. No effort at all. I became so slick, I was asking, and getting, fifteen thousand before the end. The story of my downfall. I never had time to write another novel. And now I must take myself to work.'

He was in no hurry, he simply wanted to get away from the subject of writing, whether his own or Kristy's. In the salon, he saw Akbar leaning against an alcove that separated the room from the kitchen doorway. Akbar was waiting for him and without changing his nonchalant attitude, said: 'Sayyidah wan' you.'

'Where is she?'

Akbar waved a hand towards the door of Mrs Gunner's room. Hugh knocked on it and entered to find Mrs Gunner lying amid cushions on a long bamboo chair. She put her hand to her brow and said peevishly: 'It's my quiet time; meaning it's the only time I get to be quiet, not that you'd call it quiet.'

The room, small and ill-lit, looked on to a courtyard and across the courtyard was the kitchen window from which came the clatter of dish-washing and the voices of the servants.

She said: 'I should have had m'quiet time before that started but it's been one thing after another this morning.'

'Is there anything wrong, Mrs Gunner?'

'Yes, I should blinkin' well think there is.'

Mrs Gunner, Hugh realized, was feeling as unwell as he did himself. Her skin looked jaundiced in the dull light and was so puckered that folds half hid her wet little eyes. She gave an exasperated laugh and Hugh felt queasy. Here he was, less than twenty-four hours on the island, and already in trouble. She said:

'I want to know how you got in that room? It was reserved for a very senior chap and his wife.'

'Akbar put us there. You remember I thanked you . . .'

'Oh, he did, did he?' The force of Mrs Gunner's annoyance

was at once deflected from Hugh and her voice softened. She patted her big double bed: 'You can sit here, dear. Now tell me, did he meet you at the boat like I told him?'

Seating himself cautiously on the lace counterpane with its trimmings of blue and pink rosebuds, Hugh tried, from habit, not to tell tales: 'The boat was late so we did not expect anyone to meet us. We took a taxi.'

Facing him there was a photograph of Ambrose as a youth. Ambrose, in his photograph, looked like a white bullock: a prize white bullock, one that should have been wreathed in flowers. Above the bed there was another photograph, that of a man in the uniform of a naval commander. The face was Ambrose's face but the expression was humorous and placatory, and the eyes those of a simple man.

'I'll have something to say to Akbar,' Mrs Gunner nodded significantly. 'And now what about you? We may have to move you. Mr Ogden's very senior: he's retiring next year. Still, not to worry. The other room's very comfortable.'

Hugh jumped up eagerly: 'I'll move our stuff at once.'

'No need just yet, dear. The Ogdens are thinking about it. They like the room they've got because it's at the back. It's quiet. They said they'd take a dekko at the balcony room before deciding whether to make the change. So, dear,' Mrs Gunner sat up, 'you get on with your work and leave me to get on with mine.'

The rain had stopped but the monsoon clouds, black and bloated, lay like a weight on the atmosphere. Hugh, climbing the uphill road, felt his raincoat enclose him like a sweat-bath. The road was sheeted with water and bicyclists, speeding downhill, threw up water-fans so Hugh was soaked outside as well as in.

The Egyptian safragi had told him where to find the Government Offices. Leading him out to the road, Hassan had pointed upwards: 'All government in square.'

Hugh was surprised that he was alone on his walk to the square. He had been told that it was government policy to limit the number of cars on the island so, as an example to the islanders, the officials were encouraged to walk to work. But no one seemed to be walking to work that morning.

Reaching the square where the deposed sultan had reviewed his horsemen, Hugh saw that the tall building, the one that had beamed out unhelpfully the previous evening, was inscribed in letters of gold: GOVERNMENT OFFICES. Standing like an up-ended matchbox, it looked out to sea, five storeys high – the only tall building in sight – and built from coral blocks of a dazzling newness. The square was not a square but a wide semi-circle cut into the cliff-face, overhung by trees and lined with clinging vegetation that conserved moisture so the older buildings had the damp, greenish look of neglected tomb-stones. These buildings – there were three of them – appeared to be unused. Hugh guessed that all departments of government were now contained in the new Government Offices.

Disliking the tall building for its high, blank face, its newness, its penitentiary air, Hugh lingered outside, putting off the moment when he must enter and introduce himself. The building showed no sign of life and no one moved in the square. It was so quiet, he heard a helicopter start up and looking towards the top of the island, saw the machine rise from the grassland behind the Medina. He watched as it flew over him and whirred away to Réunion and, looking after it, he felt the wistfulness of exile. When it was out of sight, he turned and looked at the rock ridge which had at its central point two great peaks. Now, where the peaks had stood up, boldly coloured by the sunset light, he saw only grey and empty air. No shadow, no outline. The peaks had disappeared.

He entered the Government Offices. The hallway was spacious with a chequerboard floor of white coral and ebony. The lower flight of the stairway suggested that no expense had been spared. In the midst of this splendour, a half-Arab, half-Negro porter sat with his bare dirty feet on a desk. A white ledge ran round the wall on which sat a line of people, men and women, of all races and conditions, most of them ragged, who had, by shifting along it, covered the ledge with grime. The porter, manifesting his importance before them, kept his feet on the desk as Hugh approached him. When he heard Hugh speak an Englishman's English, he put his feet down. Hugh asked for a Mr Pedley. The porter slowly stood up. He said: 'All gone.'

'Gone where?' Hugh asked.

The man lifted hands and spread fingers as though to say the English had evacuated the island. Hugh, at a loss, asked for Pedley's secretary, but the secretaries, too, had gone. Hugh asked to be directed to Pedley's office. The porter pointed to the lift: 'You go floor up three.'

The Information Suite on the third floor comprised two rooms. One door was marked 'MR PEDLEY', the other 'RECEPTION'. Hugh guessed he would be in Reception. There were three desks, typewriters on two of them. Beside the third there was a television set and Hugh knew it was his.

The room was very large, made larger by the excessive light that came through three windows. Looking out, he saw, a long way below, the Indian Ocean, dark and stormy under the monsoon sky. He sat at his desk and waited for someone to arrive.

An hour later, finding nothing on the television set, he started out on a tour of the silent corridors, occasionally knocking at a door and looking into a room as sterile as his own, all empty of human life. He went up flight after flight and on the top floor came on richness. The corridor was carpeted in ruby Wilton and the doors, of polished mahogany, were furnished with ornamental brass. Here, apparently, someone was at work. Tracing the sound of a typewriter to its source, he knocked on a door and was called into an office that was floored not with planks but parquet. A young African, sitting behind a portable typewriter, paused to gaze at Hugh.

'I am Hugh Foster.'

As one conscious of duty and power, the young man gave Hugh ready attention: 'You are seeking me, Mr Foster?'

'I am seeking someone. I've just arrived to take up a job here and I cannot find anybody about. Is there some function on somewhere?'

The African took off his glasses and said gravely: 'Yes, Mr Foster, there are functions. Today is St George's Day and so a holiday. The senior officials attend a party to welcome Mr Ogden. So there is no one.'

'Except you. Weren't you invited to the party?'

44

'Yes, I was invited but I prefer to work.'

'Then I must not waste your time.'

The young man smiled but did not detain Hugh. Outside, Hugh looked at the name on the door and saw he had interrupted no less a person than Mr Murodi, Minister for Culture. The name on the next door was Mr Aziz Iver, Minister for Home Affairs; on the next Mr Ogwulu, Minister of Finance. Here, he realized, was the seat of government: here were the men who would take over when the British left the island. One day even this fragment of empire would become foreign to the motherland. Feeling he was on alien territory, he hurried back to his own office.

He was delighted, towards the end of the morning, to receive a visitor.

'So here you are,' said Simon Hobhouse, surprisingly friendly: 'I've called to see if you'd do something for me?'

'Certainly, if it's in my power. I don't know my way around yet.'

Simon seated himself on the edge of Hugh's desk and spoke in a casual manner: 'It's nothing. I need a permit to go to the rain forest.'

'On the mainland?'

'Good heavens, no. Only to the northern half of the island. There's a patch of primeval forest there; the last, or almost the last, scrap of the great forest that once covered the earth.'

'You have to cross the ridge?'

'Yes. That's easy enough. There's a pass which was the old escape route for slaves during the sultanate. I've been before and I'm going over again for a day or two.'

'But why do you need a permit?'

'It's a formality. The area's out of bounds because they don't want amateur explorers getting lost. There's no rescue team and people have to be protected against themselves. But in my case, it's nonsense. I know the area and I can look after myself.'

Simon smiled, his handsome, bearded face candid but amused that he, being the man he was, need explain himself to Hugh. Hugh did not doubt what Simon said but the smile and the in-human blue of Simon's eye worried him. He said: 'I think you should see Mr Pedley.'

45

'Pedley won't be back today. I know these junketings. I'm planning to start at dawn.'

'But I've no authority to hand out permits.'

Simon laughed. 'Anyone can sign these things.' Rising in a single movement that was like the sudden, unpremeditated spring of a cat, he went to a cupboard and came back with a form which he placed in front of Hugh. 'Come on. No more argument. Where it says "Destination" put "North".'

Hugh read through the form and feeling under duress, asked: 'What shall I put for purpose of visit?'

'Research. I'm a botanist among other things. I'm making a study of the Pteridophyta.'

'The what?'

Simon spelt out the word but did not explain it. When the form was filled in, he said: 'Stamp it. You must have an official stamp in your drawer.'

There was no stamp in the drawer so Simon, with his cat-like alacrity, went to Pedley's office and came back with one. Hugh stamped the form but was reluctant to hand it over. As he hesitated, Simon pulled it out of his hand.

'Thanks. That'll do. It's only something to show the goons at the road check.' He pushed the form carelessly into the pocket of his bush shirt: 'No point in your hanging around here doing nothing. Why not walk up with me to the Medina?'

Hugh was grateful for any excuse to get away from the office. The sun was breaking through the mist. As the heat grew, the pools of rain on the road could be seen shrinking and rising in a vapour quiver that caused little mirages above the road surface. When the pools vanished, old women swept the lustrous sand surface. The women were as alike as sparrows, bound up in rusty black, and, standing aside to let the men pass, they bobbed and grinned behind their hands. Hugh smiled on them, discomforted by their servility, but Simon ignored them, hurrying by with his head in the air, taking the steep rises of the road with the stride of an athlete. He had nothing to say till they came to a gate in the long wall that rose above the square. The gate was an impressive wrought-iron double entrance from which a policeman looked out and around which were gathered sellers of ice-cream, liquorice and coconut milk. Evidently the gate was a place for sightseers. As Hugh and Simon approached it, the seller of liquorice clashed his brass measures invitingly.

'In there,' Simon said: 'seldom seen but heartily disliked by all, lives your august governor and his fat donkey of a wife.'

'I'm not likely to meet them, I'm glad to say.'

'Oh, yes, you are! Every official has to make his obeisances at least once.'

Simon spoke with a gleeful contempt that was a challenge to Hugh. Knowing he was being mocked for the demands, restraints and absurdities of official life, he said: 'My appointment is temporary. I don't really belong to the service and I'm not likely to remain in it.'

'You didn't tell me what brought you here.'

Hugh sighed and again went over his history, the rather ridiculous history of a man who had earned more than his due and foolishly wasted it. It would not have seemed so ridiculous had he been by nature a playboy, but he was not a playboy. He was, he sadly reflected, a serious, dull fellow who had gained little or no satisfaction from his way of life.

'So, in the end, I had to find a job.'

'But why four thousand miles from base?'

'Perhaps . . . to get out of sight. It's a dismal situation, being well off one day and poor the next. You become a sort of refugee. People expect from you what you can no longer give. You have to make excuses, you apologize and try to explain. You feel a fool. What happened was not my fault, but I began, somehow, to think it was. So I ran away.'

Simon gave him a sidelong glance, amiable and amused: 'You had a good time while it lasted, I suppose?'

Hugh shrugged and said: 'I'd call it a difficult time. You conform to a standard and then you have to keep it up.' And, he thought, he had rejected the claims of a creative life. And why had he rejected them? He turned from this question, unwilling to inquire too closely into it, and laughed: 'I wasted time, and now doth time waste me.'

'Hah!' Simon threw back his head in appreciation and dropped his bantering tone: 'You may enjoy the life here. Things aren't so bad. The government wants to do what is right. They've preserved the island, so far as any place can be preserved these days. You have to get a permit to build or cut down a tree. Buildings are kept to two storeys.'

'What about the Government Offices?'

'Hah, yes. The Offices are a sore point with a lot of people. The planners decided they were a special case as they're intended for a future House of Representatives. The building is showy but it's a flimsy structure. If there was an earthquake, the whole thing would come down like a stack of cards.'

'Oh?'

'Don't worry. There hasn't been a serious earthquake in the last hundred years.'

'So, on the whole, you approve of British rule?'

'I don't revel in the company of administrators but they've done their best to keep this place intact. God knows what will happen when they go.'

Beyond the wall of the Residency, they came to the steep rise where the trees hung thickly over the road. Here the white sand surface came to an abrupt stop. Beneath it there was a rough track and at one point, where a stream ran across the road, a broad area of mud. African women, in robes of scarlet and indigo, were standing in the stream and slapping their washing against the riverside stones. They shouted and laughed when they saw the men and Hugh paused to watch them but Simon strode on, mounting the last of the slope as though on some mission that demanded haste. At the top they came out on to a wide, open plateau. What, the night before, had seemed a mysterious region of darkness was, Hugh now saw, the sugar plantations. The rows of cane stretched as far as the eye could see, a plain of dark green here and there set with an immense tree.

'What are these trees?' Hugh asked.

'They're forest trees: mahogany, ebony, amkoré, avodiré. The Arabs cleared the forest on this side but when they came on a particularly fine tree, they left it as shade for the workers. But come here! Come and survey the enemy.'

Simon went to the side of the road where there was a drop down to the shore. It was, Hugh saw, less fearful than it had seemed the night before because a rail protected the wayfarer from the chasm. Simon pointed to a long, low building by the sea: 'The Praslin.'

The Praslin, very white against the green of its lawns, was built among casuarina trees on a stretch of land that ran out to the water's edge. It looked to Hugh a simple, inoffensive building and he asked 'Why do you say "the enemy"?'

'You see the swimming pool? The people lying round it will destroy this place. There, on the right, is the basin for their private yachts. At the moment, only a few can afford to come here but if anyone built an air-strip, they'd come in droves. For a long time no one could see where to build an air-strip but, alas, the Seychelles solved the problem for all these islands. They reclaimed land from the sea.'

'Where do these visitors come from?'

'The Rand, Kimberley, the oil states: anywhere where you can get money without working for it. They're mostly South Africans but there are also English people, so rich they can't afford to live in England. And there are always a few speculators trying to get permission to build bungalows and hotels. I call them the enemy because they are, by nature, wreckers. They'll finish this place if it doesn't finish them.'

Hugh laughed: 'How could it finish them?'

'Easily enough. This is the slide area. The last earthquake brought down a chunk of cliff that formed the cape on which the Praslin is built. Look!' Simon traced with his foot a crack that ran from the cliff edge towards the centre of the road: 'And here's another. And another. These indicate a movement in the rock below. Another earthquake could bury the Praslin.'

'Why was it built there?'

'People forget. Or they take a risk because it all happened so long ago. They build under Vesuvius. They build under Etna. And there's a land shortage here. I doubt if there's more than 40,000 acres of good soil on the whole island. And this is good soil.' He crossed the road to a lane that ran through the plantation and picked up a handful of reddish soil: 'It's friable, the texture's fine and it holds water. It has given the Praslin those green and pleasant gardens.'

'I suppose the Praslin's owner knows the danger?'

'I doubt it. Who is there to tell him? I'm the only one who knows what could happen and I'm minding my own business. Are you worried about those people who have nothing but money to recommend them?'

'They've as much right to life as we have.'

'You're a sentimental fellow. Come on.' Simon strode off down the lane but half-way towards the Medina, he came to a stop and stood gazing into the branches of a tree. When Hugh caught him up, he said: 'This is a bird tree. I've noticed that some trees attract birds more than others. This mango is particularly a bird tree.'

The mango had a heavily noduled trunk of a purple-red colour and its crown of leaves was dense and very dark. The leaves were thick and egg-shaped, with a high gloss so they looked like green lustres. The birds flashed in and out, yellow and black, maroon, amethyst, crimson and green. Simon, following their flight with a thoughtful interest, murmured: 'An oriole, a cardinal, a black-headed gonolex, two parakeets, a sunbird . . .'

A group of women were working near the tree, moving slowly between the canes and pulling out the maidenhair fern that grew as a weed here. They were Indian and had none of the Negro ribaldry. When they noticed the men, they bent lower as though to hide from them. They were followed by children of all ages, the older ones pulling boxes on wheels and the younger loading up the fern roots. The whole concourse worked without urgency but with a singleness of purpose that moved Hugh, who saw them as gentle and patient, like those animals for whom life is work. The children, less inured to their condition than the women, paused to watch the tall, bearded man who was transfixed by the sight of birds in a tree.

Simon, lifting his head to follow the flight of a gonolex, gave a shout and pointed towards the mountain ridge. A large bird was sailing above the ridge, catching the light on bronze-brown wings.

'An eagle?'

'Yes, a golden eagle: the last of its kind here; an old bird that must fly alone. The first time I came to Al-Bustan less than ten years ago, you might have seen half a dozen of them in a day's walk. Now . . .' Simon made a gesture of regret and they stood and watched the lonely bird gliding and banking on the air then, suddenly, drop out of sight: 'That's one of the lost, beautiful things of earth, soon to be seen no more.' He looked down and met the curious stares of the Indian children: 'But these we have always with us.'

'You don't like people.'

'I don't like too many of them. I like six, eight, even ten eagles, but if there were so many of them that they jostled each other and fought and polluted everything about them, I wouldn't like eagles, either.'

Hugh was silent, impressed by Simon's certainty in life and having no argument against it. It was true, he supposed, that he was a sentimental fellow, easily confused and no match for a man like Simon Hobhouse, a man who had both knowledge and reason. Giving a glance at the pale, regular, bearded face beside him, Hugh again saw in it the idealized father image that had attracted him on the boat.

Remembering the peaks, he asked Simon why they had disappeared.

'They're hidden by mist. They usually appear, if at all, just before sunset when the air suddenly clears. The Arabs call them Allati Takhtafi al-Mukhtafiyya, the Hills that Disappear, but the Africans call them the Guardians. They guard the pass. It was generally believed that once a slave had got beyond the peaks, he was safe. The Arabs would not follow him.'

'Why was that?'

'Because the other side is a place of ill-omen. There's a proverb: "*Ash-sharr qu'imu wara at-tilal*", meaning "Evil lives on the other side". It was meant to scare the slaves but it scared the Arabs more.'

They were coming up to the Medina that, from a distance, had had a visionary splendour. Now, Hugh saw, its domes, minarets and spires were in a state of decay. The plaster was crumbling and the red and gold paint flaking off. The box-shaped houses, rising one behind the other, were shabby and strung with washing. Balconies had broken and fallen. On all the flat roofs rubbish was piled for the wind to blow away.

'But it was glorious in its day,' Simon said. 'Magellan wrote that the gleam of its gold could be seen twenty leagues out to sea.'

'Then the English came?'

'Somewhat later. In 1810, to be exact. Napoleon was making trouble and they decided Al-Bustan would be a useful place from which to protect our Indiamen. When we turned up, the Arabs withdrew into the Medina and prepared for a siege. Two gunboat crews were sent ashore and the improvident Arabs were starved out in a fortnight. You could call it a Glorious Victory.'

'We did liberate the slaves.'

'That's true, but the plantations fell into rack and ruin until the Governor brought in Indian labour. No Arab would do slaves' work.'

'Who owns the plantations now?'

Simon gave his shout of laughter: 'The Arabs of course. Whatever happened, we never lost our respect for private property. The ex-sultan still owns two-thirds of the island.'

The gates had gone from the archway leading into the city. Through the cracked plaster of the city walls could be seen the grimy dun colour of unbaked brick. There was nothing to halt the two Englishmen as they went under the archway into the dark and narrow street within. The street burrowed like a rabbit run towards a dim interior, rising so steeply that the ground was frequently cut into steps. On either side were high walls that converged at the top to keep out the sun. There was, Simon said, a whole complex of lanes on the city's south side, designed to confuse an invader. There were doors set in the walls, heavy, iron-bound, dusty as though from lack of use. Hugh, with his old dream-fear of being stifled, disliked the walls and asked what was behind them.

'The courtyards of houses, once filled with the riches of the east.'

When they met anyone in the lanes, each party had to press against the walls in order to sidle past. If the other was a man, Simon greeted him enthusiastically, in Arabic; if a woman, Simon looked over her head. The lane ended abruptly and they passed from darkness into a sun-filled market-place that had about it all the main buildings of the Medina. There was an immense tree, a forest relic, at the centre and beside it a drinking fountain. Around about were the mosques, the Catholic church, the Mission school and three Arab hotels.

After the heat and airless dankness of the lanes, the wind in the square was mountain fresh. It elated Hugh who was roused to excited interest in the city and looked for its people, but all, it seemed, were asleep. They took their siesta beside their merchandise. Some lay beneath market stalls, hands over eyes: others were curled round sacks of lentils or coffee beans. A number lay together under the tree that Simon said was an ebony. The ebony, that had a bark crusted and black as iron, was in flower and the small white flowers, almost hidden by the leaves, gave out a scent that overpowered the market scents of cloves, vanilla, coffee, spice and fruit. Through the sleepy quiet of the square came the sound of bees that clouded about the ebony flowers.

Without slackening his pace, Simon moved lightly among the stalls, skirting piles of coconuts and breadfruit, bananas and pineapples, and towering displays of pottery decorated in black, brown and terra cotta. He was making for one of the hotels and said:

'We should get a reasonable meal here.'

Hugh, knowing that Kristy expected him to luncheon at the Daisy, said nothing but followed Simon into the courtyard that, in fine weather, was the hotel's restaurant. The courtyard was screened from the square by vines trained across lattice and over beams hung with brass lamps. In the middle of the courtyard was a small fountain from which the safragis scooped up water for the kitchen. Simon and Hugh were not asked what they would eat but were brought pork kebabs and beans, that being the day's menu.

Charmed by the prettiness and simplicity of the place, Hugh said: 'We should have stayed here. We were told that no European could stay in an Arab hotel but I'd prefer this to the bourgeoise awfulness of the Daisy.'

Simon laughed at him. 'Not for long, you wouldn't. There's no running water, the sani-cans stink and I have my doubts about that fountain. If I didn't have my own flat, I'd stay at the Daisy. That is, if my dear old friend Ambrose didn't kick me out.'

'I got the impression you'd upset him. What did you do?'

'Nothing much. A joke. I used to pull his leg in a gentle way.' At the memory of the joke, Simon began to laugh and became so convulsed, he put down his knife and fork. He said at last: 'It was like this: a poor devil of a lascar was brought into port suffering from smallpox. The hospital couldn't take him because it has no isolation wing and no one on board knew how to nurse him. I suspect they were too scared to go near him. I heard about the case and went down to the harbour in my Land-Rover and persuaded the harbour master to let me bring him up here to my flat.'

'You weren't afraid for yourself?'

'Of course not. I keep myself properly inoculated. Anyway, I never catch anything. Well, our Ambrose, not knowing what had happened, came to pay me a visit and I took him in to see the patient. Smallpox is not a pretty sight. Ambrose nearly collapsed. I could see his knees shaking. He stuffed a handkerchief into his mouth and ran. I looked out of the window and saw him scuttling down the sûk, flapping about like a terrified turtle. Thus we were estranged.'

'I'm not surprised.'

'Yes,' Simon wiped the tears of laughter from his eyes: 'It was unkind, I admit: and I was sorry when he refused to speak to me again. I went down to the Daisy to tell him not to be silly but he was very huffy; told me to keep away from him. He should have been vaccinated before he came out, but, like a lot of people, he'd managed to dodge it. Extraordinary fellow. He's ten years my senior but when I went to Cambridge, they were still talking about him. People said he was the most brilliant man of his year. Apparently it was a toss-up whether he devoted himself to music or to literature. He still hasn't made up his mind.'

Hugh laughed at Simon's irony and said: 'I like him. He's a sympathetic character. I find it sad, the way he lives here. Surprising he's never married.'

'Ambrose? Never married? He's been married at least three times. Strong women have fought over his body for years.'

'And now.'

'He's got a wife somewhere. But look at him! He's ten stone overweight. Probably impotent.'

'He's vague about his past. What did he do in England?'

'I don't know and I've never asked. The English here are a dim lot. If you meet anyone with a mind, he's probably a fugitive.'

'Like me?'

A safragi came from the hotel and whispered to Simon who shook his head and said: 'I don't want to see them.'

'They come with a little one.'

'A little one? You mean a child? God preserve us. All right, bring them out here.'

The visitors were called and came silently, with a portentous slowness: three young English people, two men and a girl, one of the men carrying a child. They wore kaftans of dirty white cotton. They looked to Hugh much like the young drop-outs he had seen in the London streets but one of the men, greenish pale, with auburn hair and beard, had the startling looks of Rosetti's Angel of the Annunciation. They were all pale with the moist skin of ill-health and the smell that came from them might have come from a corpse.

They approached the table and Simon, warding them off with a gesture, said sternly: 'I have nothing for you.'

The man with the child said, 'She made us bring it to you.'

The girl had remained in the doorway, leaning against the jamb with an air of sensuous abandon. Catching Hugh's eye, she smiled and the smile remained fixed on her face as though she had forgotten how to remove it.

Simon took the child, a baby of about three months, and put it down on the table. He sat to examine it. Calling Hugh to observe it, he spoke as to a colleague: 'This child is not only sick, it's been shamefully neglected.'

Hugh looked at the small, grey-faced creature that was rolling its wet, scabby mouth, not having the strength to cry, and turned away, disgusted.

Simon asked the girl: 'Is she yours, madam?'

The girl, still smiling, shook her head and the man who had held the child, mumbled: 'Not our kid. Left by a couple who came here with two others, then had this one and cleared off; left them all behind.'

'Where did they go?'

The man seemed baffled but after brooding on it for some time, managed to say: 'On the boat.'

Simon looked at Hugh with a despairing lift of the brows then gave his attention to the child. Speaking to the man as though he, too, were a child, Simon said: 'She had an infection, possibly bronchitis. If I give you a note for the hospital, do you think you could find your way there?'

The man looked at his friends. When they offered no help, he said: 'We'll try.'

Simon took a note-pad from his hip pocket and said as he wrote: 'You're to ask for Dr Dixon. Do you understand? – Dr Dixon.'

The girl spoke, her tone almost flirtatious: 'Will she die?'

'Not if she receives proper treatment. But what are your plans? When you move on, what will you do with her?'

The three stared silently at Simon, confused by his incisive questions and the anger behind his voice. Obviously they had no plans. They could not answer him but they watched, as though hoping he had more to give. Motioning them to pick up the child and go, he turned impatiently away.

They departed as slowly as they had come. When they were out of hearing, he said: 'What hope for a child like that? The Mission runs a school but not an orphanage. Poor little brat! They'll take her off on the heroin trail and she'll die between here and the Philippines.'

'They're bombed out. Where do they get the stuff?'

'You can get anything here. All the planters raise patches of hemp or opium poppies. Other drugs are smuggled in. With the connivance of the police, needless to say. There's a regular traffic in forbidden goods, like D.D.T., the stuff that wiped out the golden eagle. The government banned it but it's still coming in.' He slapped the table in sudden rage then jumped to his feet: 'Come on. We'll have coffee at my flat.'

'Is the government aware of what's going on?'

'Aware? Of course it's aware!' Simon dodged angrily among the market stalls, making for the northern end of the square: 'It wrings its hands and occasionally sacks the worst offenders, then others take over. The present chief of police, Culbertson, was brought out to reform the force from top to bottom, and for a few weeks he went round like God's Good Man, then you could see him flagging. He'd realized he could do nothing. The system defeated him: now he's part of it.'

'You mean: he's as corrupt as the rest of them?'

'No. I mean he shuts his eyes to what's going on. He has to. It's the only way to get anything done in a place like this.'

They passed from the square into the northern lanes that were wide enough to take small shops on either side. The shops were opening up and people coming out. Simon pushed his way through the crowd with an energy that seemed to amuse the Arabs. He lived above a shop that sold spices. The flat comprised two small rooms full of the noise of the sûk and the smells that came up from it. Sniffing the spice smell, Hugh felt again that by settling into the Daisy, they had shown a dismal lack of enterprise.

'Could we get a flat like this?'

'Would your wife like to live without a bathroom and get her water from the spice seller's pump and defecate in a communal privy where there's nothing but a hole in the floor?'

'I admit those are disadvantages, but, still, it's very pleasant.'

The small rooms, one of which was a kitchen, were clean and ordered with extreme neatness. Simon went about making coffee and setting out the cups and saucers with the economical movements of a man who could expect to find things exactly where he had placed them. He was, Hugh felt, a self-sufficient man, a man who chose to live alone.

The furniture in the living-room was practical rather than comfortable. Simon offered Hugh the only chair and took his coffee standing. He went to the window, cup in hand, and stared intently out then beckoned Hugh and pointed. Below were the three young people who had visited him at the hotel. The child, held up like an exhibit, was still with them and the men and girl were accosting people, not aggressively but with persistence, each holding out a hand and smiling and waiting for what would come to them. The Arabs laughed back at them as though they were a popular show and, more often than not, put something into one of the outstretched hands. Whatever was given went to the girl who hid it in the pockets of her kaftan.

'They haven't tried to find the hospital.' Frowning, Simon watched them as they drifted past, holding up the grey-faced child with its rolling, helpless mouth. 'They'll probably consult a witch-doctor.'

'Are there witch-doctors here?'

'Certainly. Down in the Dobo they do a thriving trade in death-potions, love-potions, cures and the like.'

'They're doing pretty well,' Hugh said.

'Yes. The Arabs are charitable, but there's more to it than that. They see these drop-outs as proof of our decadence and they encourage them. They are regarded as the last ragged remnants of a once great nation: proof that we're down the drain.'

'What does the government do about them?'

'The Medina's a separate world. If the kids go on the rampage, which happens sometimes, the police round them up and put them on the boat. But usually, being restless as well as lethargic, they move themselves on.'

'I meant: does no one try to rehabilitate them?'

'No. There's no centre here. Besides, they're on the run from rehabilitation. They only come to me because they know I'm not a medical missionary. I don't interfere with them.'

'But surely one *should* interfere. If you saw a man taking his own life, you'd interfere.'

Simon laughed: 'Not me. If any man wants to opt out of this overcrowded planet, I'd say "Go ahead. We're grateful to you." '

'You're joking, of course?'

Simon, looking into Hugh's serious face, gave an ironical grin and, lifting the tray, took it into the kitchen. He poured water from a jug into a basin and washed each cup and saucer scrupulously then put it away. Hugh, watching him, said: 'That auburn-haired boy: with his looks he could get anything he wanted and all he wants is to destroy himself. The waste. How can you bear it?'

'There's always been waste. Before the war, he'd have died of T.B. He's a typical T.B. subject. And here, in the graveyard, lie handsome young Englishmen wiped out by all the diseases of Africa: typhus, plague, yellow fever, smallpox, to say nothing of dysentery and malaria. Now they die of despair.'

'Why?'

'Because there's nothing left to kill them. Not even a war. There's too many of them. Some profound instinct prompts them to die and the weakest submit to it.'

Watching Simon's exact movements as he tidied the kitchen, Hugh was impressed again by his imperturbable assurance but said: 'I think you feel more than you admit. What about the seaman with smallpox? And you wanted to help the child.'

'Merely habit. I don't practise medicine but if consulted, I automatically advise. Just habit. But you're right. I should have said: "Let the child die. The world has no use for it." '

As Hugh opened his mouth to expostulate, Simon laughed at him and, taking him by the shoulder, pushed him towards the front door: 'If you don't go, you'll be caught by the dark. I'll walk you across the square.'

Hugh was aware that Simon's amusement disparaged him but, at the same time, he was excited by the fact that this man, who had no friends, was treating him with the affection of friendship.

'Are you really going tomorrow?'

'I can't say. I have to take a look at the Land-Rover. It's been in the car park for the last three months and may need an overhaul. You can go back this way.' Turning right through the awakened and noisy market, Simon led the way to the western sûks and the gate on to the car park. A few old cars stood round the petrol pump, the Land-Rover among them. Simon waved Hugh away: 'If you walk down there, you'll come to the plantations.'

The road was as decayed as the wall beside it but Hugh, who had been dreading a return through the lanes, set out with the light step of the reprieved.

4

Kristy had pushed the desk to a point opposite the balcony door. Finding her seated before a view of the harbour, pen in hand, paper stacked in front of her, Hugh was unreasonably irritated: 'You can't move things around. The room isn't ours.'

'What do you mean?'

Kristy had spent most of the day unpacking and arranging the room so it had for her the sympathetic semblance of a workroom. The balcony, that had table and chairs of its own, delighted her, but she could not work out of doors. The ideal, she felt, was to remain in out of the heat and wind but so placed that she could, if she raised her head, enjoy the view of the harbour and the rock façade rising behind it.

The morning scene had been silvered over with mist, making the foliage more blue than green. As the clouds lifted, the Indian Ocean could be seen crashing in, as fierce as the Atlantic. The look of the island suggested to her an autumnal smell of bonfires and a nip in the air, yet even then, at ten in the morning, the heat pressed on her. She noted the incongruity of the frigid light and the tropical temperature, and wrote a few words on the flap of a used envelope. She did not keep notebooks but liked to collect notes on slips of paper, preferably of an odd shape or colour, and when she went through them, she was stimulated by their variety and disorder.

No one had spoken to her during the day. She knew nothing of the mistake about the room and she faced Hugh with such a look of dismay, he regretted his grudging ill-humour and said: 'Well, it may be ours. It was reserved for a senior couple called Ogden but they may let us have it.'

To make amends, Hugh decided to go at once and ask Mrs

Gunner if the Ogdens had spoken yet. Mrs Gunner was unlocking the bar grille.

'What now, dear?' she asked as though Hugh's importunings were too much to be borne. When, apologetically, he explained his mission, she said in a tone of long-suffering: 'If I'd heard, dear, I'd've told you.'

'I'm sorry to have troubled you. I wonder, could I have a word with Mr Gunner?'

'No one's stopping you, dear. He's in the office, or should be. Over there, dear. *It's clearly marked.*'

Ambrose, calling Hugh to enter, sounded as discouraging as his mother. He was sitting on the edge of a bed, his weight bending the mattress down to the floor, his expression preoccupied. He smiled at the sight of Hugh and said: 'Thank God, it's only you. Sit down somewhere.'

Hugh thought the office a gloomy place. The window was obscured by creepers that had glued their tendrils to the glass. A few rays from the setting sun struck through the leaves and reddened the floor that was cluttered with Ambrose's possessions.

A typist's desk stood by the door and Hugh, unable to advance further, seated himself on top of it. The whole room smelled of Ambrose, whose large, seedy garments hung from every shelf. At his feet stood an old suitcase, a telephone, a wireless set, a portable typewriter and books enough to stock a bookshop.

'This isn't your bedroom, is it?' Hugh asked in surprise.

'You may well wonder at it. I'm her only child. I'm all she has in the world, yet she won't waste a room on me, and even this isn't all mine. Every afternoon, when I could be taking a nap, a girl comes in to do the typing.' Ambrose picked up a cigar box that was filled with small keys: 'I've been trying to open this suitcase. I'm pretty sure it contains my collection of modern poets and I believe the chart's inside Adrian Mitchell.'

'Where did the keys come from?'

'She collected them over the years. Guests leave things, you know.'

Hugh watched as Ambrose tried key after key until one turned in the lock and the case was opened.

'What have we here?'

61

The case was full of objects roughly wrapped up in newspaper. Ambrose lifted one, unwrapped it and disclosed half a brick. He turned it about in a puzzled way then sighed and dropped it back into the case.

'Not the poets after all.' He tried to push the case with his foot but it was too heavy to move.

Hugh, bewildered by what he had seen, awaited an explanation. Getting none, he asked: 'Who would send you a suitcase full of bricks?'

'Oh, some landlady, long forgotten. Mrs G. has more sympathy with landladies than she has with me. When one of them manages to track me down, she sends the scratch and they release the goods.'

'I'm sorry, I still don't understand.'

'It's the usual thing. A heavy suitcase creates confidence. You have to put something into it. You know what it's like! They want something in lieu. You make them up a case, hand it over, say you'll be back and settle up. You must have done it often.'

Darkness came down. Ambrose switched on a lamp and looked at Hugh through sad, bleary eyes. Remembering Simon's statement that on Al-Bustan an intelligent man was likely to be a fugitive, Hugh did not try to know more but said: 'I was wondering if you could put in a word for us. We've been given a room intended for Mr and Mrs Ogden and as Kristy doesn't want to leave it, I thought perhaps you . . .'

'Me? In this place I count for as much as the kitchen cat. Rather less. I wouldn't dare speak to Ogden or Mrs G. Better let them fight it out.' Dismissing Hugh's anxiety with a gesture, Ambrose changed to a subject of more interest to himself: 'Did you get the impression Lomax will, eventually, come across?'

'It's hard to say. He's not an easy man. Where did you pick him up?'

'I dropped into Gurgur's one night and saw him sitting there. I felt his solitude: it was like a sickness. I was moved by it.' An expression of concern came on to Ambrose's face and his eyelids slid down in modest consciousness of his own good-nature: 'I offered to sit with him and we had a few drinks together. I began to wonder how I could rouse him out of himself. He needed, I felt, a spiritual undertaking, a larger window on life, an interest beyond his narrow preoccupation with money-making. I gave myself to helping him. You see how he repays me.'

'And you learnt nothing about his background?'

'I've learnt a little, but not from him. When Gurgur's had a few drinks, you can get him talking.' In his present state of annoyance with Lomax, Ambrose was more willing to disclose the source of his wealth: 'He's the eternal middle man and speculator. And he started young. He reached Cairo during the war – God knows where he came from. Scarcely more than a boy, he was a refugee, penniless; but not for long. He offered himself as a contractor to the army and was put on several building jobs. He paid his men the minimum and chalked up the maximum, and, what's more, half the names on the pay-roll were imaginary. At first he employed fifty men and charged for a hundred, but by the end of the war he was employing five hundred and charging for five thousand.'

'How did he get away with it?'

'I'm told you could get away with most things in those days. The ordnance officers didn't care, they were too busy feathering their own nests. Lomax got the work done and saved them trouble. That's what they wanted. Once he had money, his money made money. He settled in Beirut and became a professional middle man, doing nothing but just sitting there, passing things from his right hand to his left. He was a broker between enemies. Or friends. If one friendly country wanted to export the wrong thing to another friendly country, they used Lomax. Gurgur says you could find his name on the dockets of some pretty strange things.'

'What sort of things?'

'Rhino horn, cantharides ...'

'Drugs?'

The telephone rang. Ambrose, who had been sprawling, indolent with grievance, sat upright. He lifted the receiver and said in a coldly businesslike tone: 'Yes?' Listening to the caller, he sank down again, smiling a smile of great charm. 'I think we would be delighted,' he said very warmly.

He looked across at Hugh and winked. Hugh whispered

'Lomax?' Ambrose raised his chin and dropped his eyelids meaningfully. Hugh laughed, knowing that he was, and always would be, on Ambrose's side.

Putting down the receiver, Ambrose said with satisfaction: 'Well, that's very nice! He's off to Beirut for a few days and when he comes back, he means to invite us all to the Praslin for a meal. You, me and your missus. Really, he's not a bad fellow. What were you asking me? Whether he dabbles in drugs? No, no. Most certainly not. Not his line at all.'

The dinner-bell sounded and Ambrose, ready for food, said, 'See you in the tent.'

As Hugh passed the bar, Mrs Gunner called cheerfully to him: 'I've heard from the Ogdens. They'll let you keep the room.'

The lemur, coming in at supper-time, fixed its expectant stare on Kristy who fed it pineapple, saying in a cooing voice that irritated Hugh: 'Look at it! I love it. I love its hands. I love its ringed tail. It's my lemur.'

'It's not your lemur. It's a wild creature. It doesn't want love. It wants pineapple.'

The lemur was not the Fosters' only visitor that evening. A man and a woman, on their way out of the tent, paused beside their table, looking as expectant as the lemur. The man, very tall, bony and red-skinned, smiled down on them but the wife, a plain little woman, self-consciously reflecting the power vested in her husband, kept a step behind him and saw no reason to smile.

The man said: 'We are Mr and Mrs Ogden.'

'Oh!' Hugh leapt to his feet, realizing that the Ogdens expected what was outside the lemur's scheme of things: gratitude. He stuttered in his effort to express it: 'We must thank you . . . we were so pleased . . .'

Ogden silenced him by lifting a hand: 'Mrs Ogden and I talked it over, and we decided we'd leave you where you are. When we looked in last night and saw the pair of you, curled up like puppies in a basket, I said to my lady wife: "Let the young people stay put." I admit I had to talk her round, but now we're agreed. The room is yours and we hope you enjoy it.'

'It's enormously kind of you.' Hugh looked at Mrs Ogden who

gave a minimal stretch of the lips. She, he realized, had taken some talking round, but Ogden was affable for both of them. He said 'Say nothing of it' and nodding from his great height, he put a hand to his wife's shoulder and steered her away.

'There!' Hugh spoke with relief: 'Someone has spoken to us.'

'Mrs Ogden was careful not to speak to me,' Kristy said. 'She's not going to be the one who lets me into the girls' club.'

'If you don't upset them, they'll accept you in time.'

That evening the Ogdens gave a little party in the Lettuce Room. The only guests invited from the Daisy were the Axelrods, Princes and Mr Simpson. The rest were villa-owning officials who looked to Kristy and Hugh exactly like everyone else. The uninvited inmates of the Daisy tactfully kept their backs to the glass door of the room and pretended that nothing was happening behind them. The Fosters, in their obscure corner, could look without being seen to look. Remembering London parties where the guests sorted themselves into couples and made love on the floor, the Fosters thought this party not so much formal as static. When Ambrose joined them for coffee, Kristy asked: 'Are all Al-Bustan parties as dull as this?'

'Duller, I'd imagine. This lot's the service upper crust. Most of them can afford to own villas and villas aren't cheap.' A couple passed through the salon to the Lettuce Room. Though indistinguishable in dress and appearance from the Daisy couples, they managed in a very decorous way to convey their superiority. Ambrose raised an ironical brow: 'Still, they're not as grand as the island Smart Set.'

'Is there a Smart Set?'

'A small one: an exclusive, moneyed little group that circulates round the Chief Secretary.'

'Are we likely to meet them?'

'Not likely, no. You see, you'll probably never meet anyone who is in a position to introduce you.'

Hugh had secretly consulted his contract and found that he was of the middle rank. Conscious of his demotion in the world, he realized that if Kristy could not make friends among the Daisy women, she would get little chance to make them elsewhere. He wondered how long she could remain here, an isolated figure in the midst of social tedium? And if she decided to return home, how would he feel? It was strange that he could not answer that question.

5

Hugh shared his office with an Indian girl who was his secretary and a half-Arab girl who was Pedley's secretary. The noise of their typewriters rattled through the television news but he could not bring himself to ask for a respite. And there was another distraction: Pedley, in the room next door, had a habit of shouting when on the telephone and his pinched military voice penetrated the wall behind Hugh's desk.

Pedley was Assistant to the Minister of Information. In his youth, he had been an officer in the Guards and he still wore an army moustache, but now he was fat with the general dilapidation of the addict. Wherever he went, he trailed after him a fruity aroma of stale alcohol. Pedley, expressing surprise that the Fosters had not come by helicopter, said briskly, 'Thought Ogden'd look after you. If I'd known y'were on the boat, I'd've met you.' It was evident he, like Akbar, had been remiss and, later, Hugh wondered if Pedley had been too drunk to meet the boat. Still, he was sober enough to say on their first encounter that he saw neither use nor purpose in Hugh's appointment.

'This news-sheet's a nonsense. If you want it to be read, stick to rape and murder, keep off politics.'

'But that's not the idea at all. I'm supposed to get the ministers interested in the problems of government.'

Pedley sniggered: 'Rather you than me', and left him to it. Hugh thought Pedley was a friendly fellow, tolerant of Hugh's work even while disapproving it, but later in the morning, he heard Pedley shouting on the telephone: 'Guess what they've sent me this time! A long-haired type who thinks he can teach me m'job.'

Hugh feared there was more to Pedley than first appeared, and the more was not friendly. Later, recovering from the remark about the 'long-haired type', he decided that Pedley had been drinking and did not mean what he said. He was, most likely, a sick man, for the whites of his eyes were dotted over with tiny yellow growths, like yolk crumbs from a hard-boiled egg. Repelled and fascinated by these growths, Hugh attributed them to a liver disorder that would account for Pedley's unreliability.

The thing that irritated Hugh most was Pedley's interference in his work. One of his tasks was to pick news items from the Reuters sheets and collate them with island politics. Hugh would have found this simple enough had he been left to do it on his own. Pedley, however, was always wandering in with a brooding expression and picking up the sheets that came each day by helicopter, would mark the items he thought significant and say: 'Put those in.' Hugh, who was paid to make these decisions himself, looked at the growths on Pedley's eye-balls, and excused when he should have remonstrated.

During his early days, he was flattered as the supplicants in the hall crowded round him, assuring him, 'You, only you, Mr Foster, can understand my case.' Feeling that at last his life here was taking on depth and purpose, he hurried to ask Pedley whom he should approach in order to help this one or that.

Pedley discouraged him wearily: 'Go away. They're only pestering you because you're a new face.' And this, alas, proved to be true. Before the week was out, the supplicants ceased to see Hugh as he passed through the hall.

On the same day that he lost the sense of personal consequence they had given him, he heard Pedley shout: 'A pass? Who the devil issued a pass? What's the signature? God almighty, that's the new man.'

Hugh grew cold. He pressed close to the wall, his whole body become an ear, but he heard no more. Pedley threw down his receiver, crashed his way out of the office and could be heard ringing for the lift. When the lift did not come, he kicked the gate and bawled down the shaft: 'Bring that bloody lift or else.' The lift came and Pedley was carried to the floor above.

Hugh shifted his Reuters' sheets, unable to see the print. The telephone rang and the Indian girl in her soft, plaintive voice told him he was to go and see Sir George Easterbrook. For some moments Hugh could not move. He was held in a paralysis of apprehension such as he had not known since, long ago, he was summoned to the headmaster for punishment. When he managed to rise, he saw the Indian girl was looking at him. He thought she pitied him and he would, if he could, have expressed his gratitude. He went up by the stairs, slowly, seeing his life here in ruins. Still, he reminded himself, if his contract were terminated, they had to give him a year's salary and repatriate him and his wife. That would mean a free year in which to do his own work. He could write a novel. He ought to be elated by the thought but all he could feel was a sense of failure. He had started a structure of life here, a new beginning and new friendships that would, if he went, never be developed or brought to maturity.

He passed Pedley in the corridor. Pedley ignored him. Sir George was a heavy man nearing the end of his service. He had a big, square-chinned face of an even raspberry colour, that might have been carved from old red sandstone. He half rose in his seat and offered Hugh his hand, saying in a bland sing-song: 'Happy to meet you, Foster. Hope you'll enjoy your stay with us. Now, I gather you've made an error of judgement. Could happen to any one of us. Pedley's a good chap, inclined to fly off the handle. Don't let him worry you. Sit down, do.'

Hugh sank down, stupid with relief.

'Now, about this pass. You were not to know that the back of the island is out of bounds. You'll ask me why? I can only say, we have our reasons. Among them is the fact it is a forested area, very dense. The slaves who went there, never came back. We don't want to lose Dr Hobhouse, do we? And if he is lost, we've no rescue team to send after him.'

As Sir George smiled broadly, Hugh felt sufficiently restored to try and defend Simon. 'He said he had experience of the forest and knew his way around.'

'He said that, did he? He's a bit full of himself, is Hobhouse. Thinks the rules don't apply to him. He took advantage of your ignorance of conditions over there. And your ignorance of service rulings. Not very nice, Foster, not very nice.' Sir George stood and again held out his hand: 'Remember in future, it's not your job to issue passes.' He smiled his broad smile and said in a pleading tone: 'Don't do it again, Foster.'

Hugh's response was heartfelt: 'No, sir, I certainly won't' and he was outside the door before he realized he had said 'sir'. In a London office, Easterbrook would have been 'George' to the staff, at most 'Sir George', but who could impose the idea of a classless society on these people? And oddly enough, Hugh was not wholly displeased by the fact he had left behind him the freedom of maturity and was back in the world of school.

The Fosters had left behind them not only casual manners but casual weather. When Kristy complained of the sticky heat and the difficulty of writing with a pen that became so wet, it slipped from the hand, Ambrose said 'The Monsoon is a lazy time. When the Trades settle into the south-east, it will be cooler and you'll be invigorated and feel the will to create.'

'How can you be so sure?'

Ambrose laughed: 'The powers that be organized the weather in this part of the world so we know exactly what will happen next.'

They discovered that people on Al-Bustan did not speak of winter and summer but of winds and transitional periods. Hugh and Kristy had arrived in a transitional period. The storms that swept the island were not freakish or haphazard: they resulted from the North-East Trades giving way to the South-East Trades. Rain was not a nuisance but a blessing. Rain all the year round prevented the island from turning, at certain seasons, into a dust heap.

The clouds that piled themselves over the sea, rising in gigantic curves that slowly swelled up like inflating balloons, black on grey, grey on white, white on black, were not, as they had first seemed, an ominous sight. They brought refreshment for man and beast, foliage and flowers.

Kristy, at her desk, looked down on the harbour and saw the Arab dhows loading up with island produce and preparing to return home. They would sail away at the end of the North-East Trades and later, when the wind veered south, they would return with merchandise from the Arab world. The same dhows, the same produce, had been blown back and forth for centuries. She realized that the winds were named not, as she had thought, for the British and their tea clippers but for the Arabs with their little dhows. She noted it, as she noted everything, and saw it was a matter for wonder. At the moment she found Al-Bustan as formless as a map held too close to the eyes; but one day, when she had left it, she would remember it complete, like a sphere, and brilliantly strange. Meanwhile, she was roughing out what she called to herself 'the suicide story'. She saw something peculiarly pertinent in the fact that Hugh's father and his second wife had both been medicos, and she worked on the fact with enthusiasm. The first draft of the book was going so well, she had quite forgotten the annoyance of Mrs Axelrod and Mrs Prince. When she could work, the world had no defects. Secure in her creative retreat, she brushed aside a card that required them to luncheon at the Residency and meet Sir Beresford and Lady Urquhart.

'I can't interrupt my work for that. You go without me.'

Hugh refused to take this seriously: 'You'll have to come with me. Look, it's so important, they've given us three weeks' notice to get into training. You'll feel different when the time comes.'

'I won't.' Unable to imagine anything being of importance outside her own afflatus, she said: 'I don't want to go, and I'm not going. There's only one way to live: by doing what one wants to do and not doing what one doesn't want to do.'

'That's all very well in London, but you chose to come here so once in a while you must do what you don't want to do.'

'Why?'

'For my sake. You should back me up – not, I may say, that you ever have backed me up.'

'*Never backed you up?* Did we go to that bloody club to please me? Do you think I had anything in common with the pretentious, limited show-offs we met there? Do you think I wanted to put on a jolly act to be one of them? If you do, you must be mad. It was all for your sake. I would have been just as happy eating a hamburger and getting on with my work. The trouble was, you'd gone the wrong way and someone had to help you through it.'

'What do you mean: "I'd gone the wrong way"?'

'You know what I mean. You went outwards instead of inwards. You hadn't the courage to look into yourself, you were afraid of what you might find.'

Hugh had a painful sense that Ambrose was not the only one listening in to this quarrel. He glanced to one side and saw Ogden leaning back in his chair with an intent expression. He said quietly: 'Come to please me, Kristy. We're already marked down as a couple of eccentrics. Don't make things more difficult than need be.'

Ambrose, having seen Hugh's desperate glance round, felt drawn into the argument: 'You shouldn't miss the Residency,' he said. 'It used to be the sultan's winter palace, and I'm told it's charming. The garden is quite famous. I must say, I'd jump at an invitation.'

Kristy, in exasperated acquiescence, said: 'Oh, all right.'

6

The rains were dying out in brief morning showers. Between the showers, steam clouded up from the soaked ground and the island was a *grisaille*, the Indian Ocean a ghost sea, its long, monotonous waves rolling in, blue as buttermilk.

On the day of the Residency luncheon, the sun, like a thirsty dog, had licked up the moisture by breakfast-time and was blazing at mid-day. Hugh said: 'We'll take a taxi and arrive cool and composed.'

The taxi, when it eventually appeared in answer to Akbar's telephone call, was the very one that had abducted the Fosters on the night of their arrival. The driver seemed not to recognize them but they recognized him.

Hugh said: 'I don't want this one. Get me another one.'

'Not any other,' said Akbar. 'Only one, two taxi at harbour. Him best.' Contemptuous of the Fosters' complaints, Akbar waved them off in his lordly way and they realized there was no time for argument.

The driver remained impassive until he was stopped at the Residency gates by two policemen, an Arab and a Negro, who had to check the Fosters' right of entry. They went very slowly through the guest list and the driver picked his teeth more and more fiercely as the wait was prolonged. When, at last, the gates were opened and the taxi allowed through, he leant out and spat, shouting 'Bastard men' then drove at a furious pace down the long curving drive. The first sight of the Residency, its domed Oriental façade rising amid palm trees, was lost on the Fosters who clung to their seats, certain the driver intended to rush the taxi up the steps and crash in through the open doorway at the top. A man standing on the steps seemed to think the same thing.

73

He jumped back as the taxi approached but the driver, turning the wheel, managed to come to a stop. As the man came down the steps to welcome the Fosters, the driver bawled at him: 'Bastard men. All English bastard men.'

Smiling imperturbably, the man introduced himself: 'I'm Cyril Millman, aide to the Governor. *So* pleased to meet you.'

'I'm sorry to arrive as part of a demonstration,' Hugh said.

'Oh, these little incidents occur. Don't give him more than five rupees.'

The driver accepted this sum without comment and Millman, placing a hand lightly on the shoulder of each of the Fosters, led them up to the central hall of the Residency. This act of kindness so surprised and reassured them that Hugh was about to tell the hilarious story of their first taxi ride on Al-Bustan. Before he could get going, Millman, having delivered them into the hall, turned and hurried back to his watch on the steps.

Eighteen or more other guests were standing about, bored and constrained, awaiting the Urquharts. The arrival of the Fosters seemed to cause a diversion and Hugh, looking at Kristy, realized how extraordinary she must seem to them in her yellow Pucci outfit and her Gamba shoes. As she walked down the length of the hall and stopped at the doors that opened on to the rear gardens, she looked serene but Hugh, nervously following, knew it was in just such a situation as this that she could be outrageous.

As at Gurgur's, the air was over-conditioned and struck chill. The hall was distinguished by a ceiling that imitated the quadpartite roof of a tent and rose into a miniature dome made of green glass. The dome gleamed like a cabochon emerald and the sun striking through it, cast a little lake of green light on to the ebony blocks of the floor. This fantasy was all that could be seen of the hall's sultanic past. What else there may have been was buried under the Urquharts' trophies of empire and the faded medley of chintz-covered sofas on which no one was brave enough to sit.

A terrace outside was covered by an awning and beyond, its colour heightened by the awning's shade, was the garden. So resplendent was it that Hugh, fearing she would be drawn out to it, caught Kristy by the elbow.

A safragi carried round lime juice and Tiger beer. Kristy said: 'What miserable drinks. It's not much of a party. You can see we're a makeshift lot.'

Hugh had to agree that the guests were not distinguished. Apart from three who were strikingly different, they might all have been inmates of the Daisy. The three were Murodi, an Arab who wore the gold algol of rank, and an elderly Englishwoman who was almost hidden in pink chiffon. Apart from Murodi, the only persons known to Hugh were the Ogdens. Mr Ogden was talking in low tones to a wan, thin woman who wore the dress uniform of a hospital matron. The woman was smiling the distracted smile of one who thinks only of her own face. It was, sadly, a plain face and no longer a young one. Ogden alone had the temerity to talk. Everyone else seemed to be subdued into silence.

Murodi crossed over to Hugh: 'We have met before. You remember?'

'Of course. You are Minister for Culture.'

Murodi seemed pleased that his title should be known. 'Would you, one day, perhaps, discuss a matter with me? Yes? Then shall I come to your room, or you to mine?'

'I would prefer to come to yours. Please tell me, who is the handsome Arab?'

Murodi grinned: 'The ex-sultan, Yusef Abubakr, the once and future king.'

'Was he ever a reigning sultan?'

'Yes, under the British, but for two years only. As a young man he tried to make a revolt and failed. He was deposed. Now, you see, he is a tame dog. He comes to eat at the Governor's table.'

'You said "once and future": do you mean, you think he will be restored when the British leave here?'

'No, I think not. I made a quotation only. This island is part of Africa. The Arabs will not rule here again.'

The Urquharts now made their entry. The hall, that had been quiescent before, sank into a hush as thick as blotting-paper. Even Murodi seemed to hold his breath.

Without speaking or showing any recognition of their guests, the Urquharts took up their stand in the centre of the hall and stood there. A safragi hurried to them, holding on a tray what appeared to be a very large whisky. Sir Beresford took it and gulped it down, grimacing as if he were swallowing cascara, then looked for another. Another was brought to him.

He was a thin man, not old but bent like an old man, his chest caving in and his shoulders hunched over it like the hubs of wings. His expression was mordant. While he took his second drink slowly, his black eyes shifted about, viewing the company as though the occasion had been sprung on him and he greatly disliked it. His wife, standing patiently a step behind him, was dowdy and stout and seemed nervously aware that more was expected of her than she could give.

The second whisky finished, Sir Beresford, for the first time, raised his twanging, nasal voice: 'Come on, then.' He swung round and led the way to the dining-room.

By the time the Fosters reached the room, the Urquharts were seated at either end of a long dining-table. Their high-backed chairs, of regal design, were notably larger than the chairs of the guests and each was over-hung by a green feathered punka, much trimmed with gold, its golden cords looped up, perhaps never to be used again. Sir Beresford, watching as the others were seated, showed a sullen boredom at having to share his meal with such people. Millman, seating-plan in hand, put Murodi at Lady Urquhart's right and Ogden on her left. Mrs Ogden, uneasy but pink with gratification, was placed on Sir Beresford's right and the matron on his left.

These four settled, Millman rapidly sorted the rest, displaying a geniality intended to divert everyone from Urquhart's lack of it. A flurried young woman, so like Lady Urquhart, she could only be her daughter, came in late and Millman seized on Hugh as a suitable neighbour for her.

When all were seated, two large Nubians entered from opposite ends of the room, each bearing a vast silver tureen. One went to Sir Beresford, the other to Lady Urquhart and the Fosters, ignorant of protocol, looked away from the astonishing sight of host and hostess being served before the guests.

Kristy, assuming a light and worldly tone, said to the elderly clergyman beside her: 'I suppose this isn't much of an occasion?'

The clergyman, who had introduced himself as the Reverend

Pierce, said in a voice weak with surprise: 'Why should you think that?'

'The Urquharts being served first. I suppose that means there's no one here more important than they are?'

'Of course that's what it means. The governor represents the British sovereign so how could there be anyone present who was more important?'

The Reverend Pierce sounded exasperated at being drawn into this conversation. Kristy laughed while Pierce and Hugh – and who else? Hugh wondered – looked at her in dismay. She tried to re-establish herself: 'Ridiculous, keeping this up with the empire down the drain.'

The clergyman turned away from her and gave his attention to his other neighbour.

The soup was turtle soup. Kristy who had pitied the turtles, having seen them, tears running from their eyes, carried in carts from the harbour pool to the canning factory, now spoke to her other neighbour: 'I'm beginning to hate this stuff.'

The man on her other side, large, strong-bodied, red-faced, with police buttons on his khaki drill jacket, answered her brusquely: 'It's excellent soup. You're lucky to have it. The Residency's got its own turtle pool. Wouldn't get better at Buckingham Palace.' He, too, sounded exasperated and Hugh, catching Kristy's eye, gave her a slight admonitory shake of the head.

He saw she had been unfortunate in her neighbours while he had been fortunate. On one side he had Miss Urquhart, a pleasant, simple-looking girl; on the other, the elderly woman in chiffon. The woman told him she was Aggie Hampton, widow of a past chief secretary. Her husband had died in office and she had decided to stay on Al-Bustan where she had a villa and 'my own darling garden'. She was, Hugh realized, a vivacious relic of an age when to be entertaining was a social duty. Leaning across to Miss Urquhart, she said: 'I think we've done well, having this beautiful young man between us. Look at his golden hair.' Miss Urquhart blushed. Mrs Hampton, dried out by the tropical sun, was like a flower pressed in a book. With the unselfconsciousness of the aged, she touched Hugh's hair, saying: 'Really, it's lovely' and he, too, blushed, and was captivated.

77

The fish came in small portions, one for each guest: but someone had the audacity to take two. Ogden, when the safragi reached him, was presented with an empty dish. He shook his head and while the others ate, sat with his hands in his lap. Lady Urquhart, who had seen all, tackled her own portion as though fearful of losing it.

At the other end of the table, the matron leant towards Sir Beresford and said in a very genteel way. 'The garden's looking ever so lovely.'

'What's that?' Sir Beresford fixed her with his black eyes as though trying to account for her presence.

Mrs Ogden, firm in support of the matron, spoke out: 'Yes, indeed. The garden's truly lovely.'

Sir Beresford shifted away from the pair of them and his chair, like an aristocratic pew, hid him from their sight. A dry white wine had been served with the fish but he would have none of it. He frowned at his Nubian who, understanding his master, went away and returned with a whisky bottle from which Sir Beresford helped himself during the meal.

Kristy could see that Hugh was having an amusing time with Mrs Hampton. Mrs Hampton, in a large transparent hat, a chiffon rose at her throat, threw up her old eyes and gazed ardently at him whenever he spoke, and once or twice placed her skeleton hand on his arm. Miss Urquhart, watching them, was like a nice bull terrier observing human speech and trying to have a part in it.

Who, Kristy wondered, would she have chosen for a neighbour? She looked down the table and paused at the ex-sultan who sat with his handsome face bent meekly over his steak and kidney pie, quite unaware of her.

Mrs Hampton was saying: 'Do you know why the Arabs called this island Al-Bustan? *Bustan* is a garden and desert people see paradise as a garden. The island seemed a garden to them and they thought it must be paradise.'

'Would that,' Hugh asked, 'be a sequitur or a non-sequitur?'

'Oh, naughty!' laughed Mrs Hampton and Miss Urquhart, pressing closer, whimpered at so much wit.

Mrs Hampton asked eagerly: 'Tell me, who have you met on Al-Bustan? Anyone remarkable?'

'Yes, you.' When this had been appreciated, Hugh added the names of his two new friends, Ambrose Gunner and Simon Hobhouse.'

'Oh, Hobhouse! He's quite, quite lunatic.'

'He struck me as unusually sane.'

'That's the form his lunacy takes.'

'And I met some young English people with a dying baby.'

'*English?*' Mrs Hampton was astounded that death, prevalent enough among the infants of Al-Bustan, should dare to threaten an English child. She exclaimed so loudly that those about her stopped to listen. She asked: 'Whose baby did you say it was?'

Hugh described the two men and the girl who had brought the child to Simon, and Mrs Hampton held her hands up in horror: 'How do such people get here?'

Finding himself the centre of attention, Hugh was inclined to retreat but Mrs Hampton, with every eye on her, expanded. She shouted across to the large man with police buttons: 'Come now, Mr Culbertson, tell us all about them.'

In a solemnly matter-of-fact tone, Culbertson gave a little lecture: 'They make their way here from different places. Usually they hitch-hike to Afghanistan or Turkey and we get them when those countries throw them out. They trek down to Zanzibar one way or another then beg or steal enough to make their way here.'

'But why *here*?'

Culbertson shrugged and helped himself to the pudding that was going round. Mrs Hampton turned back to Hugh and raised pleading eyes. Hugh, who had long ago accepted drug addiction as a fact of life, answered happily: 'They say this is a likely place to get hash or heroin or some other fix.'

There was immediate commotion. Hugh, shocked by the protests to which he had given rise, realized he had upset almost everyone around him. He looked at Murodi and there met with understanding. The ex-sultan, his head bowed, was smiling at so much dissension among his deposers. For the rest, Culbertson was the most enraged. Hugh had grown red but Culbertson was redder. His voice rose: 'Who told you that? I heard you speaking of Hobhouse. That's just the sort of bunk he'd put about.'

Catching Kristy's delighted gaze, Hugh tried to speak and could not.

Culbertson's hoarse voice grew hoarser: 'Those kids are kept under strict surveillance. If one puts a foot wrong, he's out on the next boat.'

'Then where does he go?' Kristy asked.

'How do I know?' Culbertson snatched up his table napkin and scrubbed the sweat from his face: 'And why should I care? Those kids are a bloody nuisance, if the ladies'll excuse my French.' He threw the napkin down angrily then, remembering where he was, picked it up and bowed to Lady Urquhart.

She gave him an uncomprehending stare and returned to her pudding.

The solace of food, Kristy thought; not a happy woman.

'Newcomers,' muttered Culbertson. 'Ignorant busybodies' and Kristy turned on him.

'The fact is,' she said, 'you neither know nor care what happens to them. They're our own young people yet you do nothing to help them.'

Hugh, glancing round to see what effect this was having, saw the matron had lost her vapid gentility. As she observed Kristy, her washed-out face lit with the malicious hope that Kristy would talk herself into trouble.

Culbertson, awkwardly turning in his chair, looked directly at Kristy. He was indignant and she was indignant but she had an advantage. In her indignation, she had smudged her mascara and her face was softened by what Hugh called her 'panda look'. Culbertson, disarmed by it, gave a laugh! 'What do you want me to do? Put them in prison? There's a clink up at the barracks but I don't recommend it.'

Mrs Hampton said fiercely: 'I'd put them in prison.'

Mrs Ogden, heated but vague, also spoke up: 'It's disgraceful: it really is. I've heard they actually beg for drugs in the market. What sort of impression does that give?'

'The worst possible, mem,' Culbertson said.

Kristy, looking towards Mrs Ogden, asked: 'Have you asked yourself why they beg for drugs? They want dreams or oblivion.

Why? Don't you ever ask what's wrong with the world when the young try to opt out of it?'

Culbertson gave a sardonic snort: 'I wonder what's wrong with *them*?'

'You don't wonder what's wrong with yourself?'

'Really!' Mrs Ogden looked about her. She was not the only one aghast at Kristy's pertness. Even Sir Beresford had been jolted from boredom and thrusting his head out, he stared at Hugh. Realizing he was about to speak, the guests were hushed.

'If I'm not mistaken,' he said, 'you're the chap who hands out passes to the forest area?'

Kristy, who had not heard of Hugh's misdemeanour, was startled by this accusation while Hugh looked as though he wished he were anywhere but where he was. When he did not reply, Sir Beresford, having reduced the Fosters with a sentence, shouted down the table to Ogden: 'Well, Ogden, how did you find the fishing in Devon?'

'First class, Your Excellency.'

The women sat in respectful silence while the men talked of fishing, a diversion that on Al-Bustan came second only to alcohol. When there was a pause, Lady Urquhart got to her feet and, without signal or warning to the other women, bolted from the room. Millman lifted a finger to Mrs Ogden then hurried into the hall. When the women came out, he indicated to Mrs Ogden that behind a certain door there was a cloakroom. This done, he returned to the dining-room and she tactfully passed the information on to everyone except Kristy. Lady Urquhart, who had gone upstairs, reappeared and still with nothing to say, led the women out to the terrace where the safragis waited with coffee.

The women guests gathered about their hostess, carefully excluding Kristy who, realizing she was outcast, went to the edge of the terrace and stood where the lawn began. The lawn, that had the spacious grandeur of parkland, sloped from its enclosing crescent of cliff down to the edge of the lower cliff which was masked by a spinney of trees. Within the curve of the upper cliff flowers and flowering trees were massed with dramatic effect.

All over the lawn were hoopoes, that played under the water-jets, and cranes that walked like men on stilts, and Kristy saw no reason why she should not walk with them.

When the men came out, Hugh looked for her and could see no sign of her. He was beset by the possibility that Lady Urquhart had asked her to leave. He, too, went and stood by himself and Millman, seeing him alone, came and talked to him about the garden which, he said, had been laid out by the wife of the first governor.

Millman pointed to the trees and flowering creepers under the cliff: 'Some of those are very unusual for these parts. Different people have added to the garden, bringing plants from the new world or Australia or South Africa. The scent at night is unbelievable. The house is full of it. There are several species of gardenias and these large trees on the lawn are different sorts of bombax. You see how the seeds hang down on strings; *rather* nice! And we have a night flowering cereus – a particular treasure. Note how it has spread along the cliff. The hospital, that big building on the top, must get the benefit of it. And here, near the house, is a lemon vine, the perskia; very sweet-smelling. It's interesting to see how non-native plants adapt to this climate. The cereus, for instance, blooms, on and off, all the year round.' Millman turned towards the under cliff and pointed to the spinney: 'Those trees are all chinaberries.'

Hugh, for a frightful moment, thought that he could see, among the blue flowers of the chinaberries, the yellow of Kristy's dress. Unable to bear more, he whispered: 'Can you tell me, what has happened to my wife?'

'Isn't she here? Dear me! I'll inquire.'

Millman went to Lady Urquhart and returning, said in a concerned voice: 'She's over there among the trees. You really ought to bring her back. The Chief Secretary lives just below the cliff and I fear it's not done to look down upon him.'

Hugh set out at once. As he crossed the lawn, the water sprays drenched his trousers and his feet squelched in the soaking grass. Passing through the belt of trees, he found Kristy unashamedly gazing down at the scene below.

'Come away from there.'

'No, come and look. If the island was named for paradise, then I think I've found it.'

Before he could pull her away, Hugh glimpsed, in spite of himself, a large white villa amid palms and a small enclosed bay. The sand was of a dazzling whiteness, the sea in translucent bands of blue, violet and green. A motor-boat was speeding across the water pulling after it a man on water-skis. Backed by the cliff, shut in by rocks at either end, the scene suggested to him an impregnable privacy. He said severely: 'It's not done to look down there.'

'Don't be absurd. See what I've found.' Kristy pointed to the branch of a tree where a large reddish spider sat, still and suspicious.

'For God's sake, don't touch it.'

'I lifted it up. It was down there and I was afraid someone might tread on it. It wasn't at all frightened.'

'Sometimes I think you're insane. Why did you leave the company?'

'No one would speak to me, so I went for a walk.'

'And ruined your shoes.'

She took them off. The guests were departing but those still on the terrace were entertained to the sight of young Mrs Foster walking across the lawn with her shoes in her hand. Millman intercepted her as she stepped, wet-footed, on to the terrace, and conducted the pair of them out of Lady Urquhart's sight. He was still so good-humoured, Hugh felt a wild hope that, in spite of everything, Millman might prove a friend. At the front steps, he paused and shook hands with each of them, saying 'Good-bye. We may run into each other at the club.'

Hugh said eagerly: 'Yes, and thank you,' but he knew that the club, a shabby sort of place, was scarcely a resort for such as Millman.

Kristy sat on the steps to put on her shoes just as the Ogdens appeared at the top. Hugh, wandering ahead of her, wishing he could disown her, was disconsolate, and not even able to reprimand her because he had suffered reprimand himself. He felt, nevertheless, that his annoyance was justified. He had defaulted by accident while she, he felt, had been deliberately troublesome.

They walked in silence down the hill to the Government Square. Though it was still early afternoon, Hugh decided to go back to his office: she could, if she wished, take this as an intimation of his disapproval.

'And,' he said, having said nothing before: 'You ought to stop putting that black stuff on your eyes. In this sticky climate, it smudges badly. Now it's half-way down your cheeks.'

She took out her glass and said, 'Why didn't you tell me before?'

He realized she was agitated and under strain, and said contritely: 'As a matter of fact, it's rather fetching. Culbertson was quite bowled over. His wrath subsided before it.'

Her mouth quivered as she tried to wipe the mascara from under her eyes and he squeezed her arm: 'Why worry? What do we care about those people?'

'I'm not worried about them. I don't feel well. I don't think the food here agrees with me.'

'You'll soon be conditioned to it.'

She gulped and as she turned to go, she shouted: 'Go to the office, if you want to,' and ran to get away from him.

As she reached the front lawn of the Daisy, the official wives, smirking under the dominion of Mrs Axelrod, came out of the front door, carrying swim-suits, knitting-bags and Japanese sunshades, and sighing and grumbling about the heat.

Now, having observed Mrs Axelrod, Mrs Prince and the lesser women over the weeks, Kristy had decided that Mrs Prince was a harmless creature who did what was expected of her, but Mrs Axelrod had individuality of sorts. Though she was sedate, even severe, when upholding her official status, she had a touch of grotesquerie in her make-up. While the other women would have been happy to spend the afternoon indoors, Mrs Axelrod demanded action. She would appear on the stairs and, taking a theatrical pose, would shout in a threatening way: 'Girls!' If she did not get immediate attention, she would call 'Girls, girls' until every eye was on her. She seemed about to make a sensational announcement but at the end it was only: 'I vote we go for a swim at the club!' or 'Let's all off to the hairdresser's, girls!'

If she had not roused them, the other women, become lackadaisical in the heat, would have remained indoors, in the salon or their own rooms, lying about in a stupor of nothing to do. It was Mrs Axelrod who kept them alive. At times, instead of her 'Girls, girls', she would run down the stairs, spring into the salon and dance round, clapping her hands, forcing them out of their chairs and on to their feet. Though they moaned at the effort, they obeyed, proud to be included in her regard, and knowing that to survive, they must combat their own lassitude. One woman, already overweight, called her 'the voice of conscience' and all of them, behind her back, laughed at her energy. When she had driven the last of them out into the sunlight or the hot, heavy rain, silence came down on the pension.

'Blessed silence,' Kristy thought and she told herself she could be thankful that Mrs Axelrod ignored her. She had the freedom of the excluded and need neither obey nor find an excuse for her disobedience.

Yet, lately, she had felt she had less cause for self-congratulation. Her malaise, whatever it was, had slowed down her work and was gradually bringing it to a stop. The impetus of the 'suicide story' was dying on her. Sitting down to her desk, she was threatened by boredom.

But she still had the habit of work and would try to drive herself, telling herself to 'get on with it'. Her irritation did not carry her very far. Her mind was like a lazy horse that refuses to be driven. She had lost her enthusiasm for the novel, feeling that brilliance had gone from it. At other times, her memory, like a bottomless lucky dip, had offered her entrancing pieces of the past from which she constructed a personal mosaic that always worked out. This way she transmuted reality and made it bearable. She could almost claim she got the better of it. But now, for Heaven's sake, when she ordered her pen to move, she wrote 'just like everyone else'.

In England, having to give so much of her day to shopping and housekeeping, she had jealously conserved the time put aside for her writing. And even here, where she could write all day, she was so confirmed a time-saver, she had on Ambrose's advice, asked Akbar to do her shopping.

Ambrose had said: 'He has to go to the Harbour every day to

buy stuff for Mrs G. If she ordered everything by phone, she'd be thoroughly gypped. Akbar's such a power down there, they always give him the best. Just tell him what you want and slip him a few rupees now and then. He'll bring up whatever you want.'

Ambrose was mistaken about this. Akbar's importance was such, he would not diminish it by the purchase of trifles. Kristy had given him the money to buy soap but the soap did not arrive. Asked for it, he said: 'Me no remember. Too much busy.' Next day, he swore that soap had disappeared off the market. She then told him to spend the money on toothpaste. When asked for toothpaste, he said '*Bukra*' which was supposed to mean 'To-morrow' but which, Kristy was beginning to realize, meant any time between now and eternity. For the next three days he shrugged her off in a lofty way, saying each time '*Bukra*' then, on the fourth day, he said: '*Madha Yahihm?*' Knowing that the toothpaste would never be bought by Akbar, she asked for her money back. He looked over her head and said '*Bukra*'.

Thinking she might find a more reliable messenger, she approached the Malay whose job was to polish the landing floor, using half a coconut shell which he gripped under his foot. Her request seemed to terrify him. He hung his head and whispered: 'No speak me. Speak Akbar.'

Now, sitting at her desk, looking out at the view with a bleak sense of mental emptiness, it occurred to her she might do her own shopping. *And* she would get her money from Akbar.

She found Akbar where he usually was: lolling in the short passage that separated the salon from the kitchen. This was a place he had made his own. His kaftans, too valuable to be left in the servant-quarters, hung in a row with his prayer-rug rolled up beneath them. He had an old, lop-sided basket-chair where he dozed, or pretended to doze. He was dozing now but when Kristy spoke his name, he was instantly on his feet. Rolling out his prayer-rug with a single skilled movement, he dropped down to his knees and gave himself to prayer. His devotions must not be interrupted. By the time she reached him, he was inviolable.

She stood and watched as he put his brow to the floor, straightened himself, lifted his arms to heaven and then went down again, muttering all the time. He had his back to her. He had kicked off his heel-less leather slippers and she saw the soles of his feet, their rosy colour meeting the upper brown in an exact line all round the sole and the pads of the toes. The feet of a colossus.

As the ritual went on, she felt she was being exorcized. He would not rise till he had rid himself of her presence. She turned to go. A door opened beside her and Mrs Gunner, coming out, asked her: 'Want anything, dear?'

Kristy explained why she was there and Mrs Gunner considered Akbar's gigantic backside with a quizzical smile: ''Fraid this could go on quite a while. Why don't you cut along and get what you want. I'll make him cough up the money.'

'I'd like to go to the Medina.'

'I don't see why not. You can get most things in the market, but be careful in them lanes,' Mrs Gunner was in a pleasant mood. She smiled on Kristy and her smile, that was not seen every day, gave her face the mischievous gaiety of a little girl: 'Arabs are funny people, dear. It comes of their women being shut up in that unnatural way. It's this religion of theirs,' she raised her voice and addressed Akbar's posterior: 'I don't hold with it. What happens, in those lanes they push against you: but don't you stand no nonsense. Be quite polite, of course. Just say, very dignified: "No jig-a-jig here." That shakes them, I can tell you.'

'What does it mean?'

'Never mind what it means, dear. They'll understand.'

Thus armed, Kristy thanked her and set out to walk to the Medina.

The evening hours at the office were five o'clock to seven, but on the two afternoons when Hugh had to monitor a programme at four, he was free to leave at six. The first time Pedley found Hugh making his early departure, he said: 'You've got jam on it: walking home in the sunset.'

Hugh had come to realize that Pedley thought him not only inessential but overpaid. Temporary and without pension rights, the appointment carried a special salary nearly as high as Pedley's own. Pedley's resentment, usually hidden, would manifest itself suddenly, when he seemed at his most affable. The result was that Hugh was never certain of Pedley and never on guard. When least expecting it, he would suffer Pedley's scorn.

Pedley said: 'A junior like you, living at the Daisy! I don't know what things are coming to.'

'Why? Where should we live?'

'Don't ask me. We haven't had any juniors for years. The last lot took rooms in an Arab lodging-house and, even then, couldn't make ends meet.'

'You should be glad things have improved.'

'I don't know about that.' Pedley's sullen tone seemed to suggest that no good could come of the Fosters' affluence. So fixed were the rights and wrongs of service life that Hugh brooded a long time, wondering exactly what Pedley had meant.

On the evening of the Residency visit, Pedley said: 'You're off again, are you?' as though his earlier resentment should have proved to Hugh the unwisdom of leaving before seven.

Hugh, who rejoiced in the sunset, made no reply but walked thankfully under the brilliant light that glistened through the pepper trees and reddened the sand of the road. He rejoiced, too, in the scents of evening.

There was a bookcase in the Daisy salon where the inmates put books they did not want to keep. Hugh had found there a Victorian book of African flowers and had begun to name the flowers and distinguish the fragrances about him: the clove tree, the lily flowers of the white bauhinia, and the true lilies, arum and madonna, that grew everywhere, and gardenia, the red jasmin called frangipani, the white cleordendrum, the mahogany bean, ebony flower, African peach. He paused to single one from the other and would breathe them in until he was faint with scent.

On some evenings, Kristy would walk up to meet him but that evening she did not come. Reaching the Daisy as darkness fell, seeing no light in their window, he expected to find her in the salon. She was not there. He went upstairs. Switching on the room light, he knew at once that something was wrong. Akbar had not pulled the blind against the night-flying insects but that was nothing new.

He could see no immediate cause for unease and yet he stood in the doorway, unwilling to go into the room. Feeling the onset of his old suffocating anxiety, he threw up his head, attempting to resist it, and saw a black mark on the cornice. He could not remember whether it had been there before. It was the size of two clenched fists held together, and so intensely black, it looked like a hole through which the night could be seen. He suddenly realized what it was and darting out, slammed the door on it.

Kristy was coming up the stairs. He caught her as she went to the door and held to her: 'No, don't go in. There's a bat in the room. Where on earth have you been?'

'I went for a walk. I've decided I can't stay here. The place makes me ill and I can't write. I'm going back to England.'

'You don't mean it. What about the fare?'

'I've got a bit in the bank.'

Her seriousness appalled him: 'So you'd leave me alone here?'

She gave an irritable laugh: 'You didn't want me to come: now you don't want me to go. You don't know what you do want. I'm sorry. Life here is futile. It's a waste of time.'

'How would you manage in London? You know what it costs to live there now? You'd have to stay with your parents.'

Realizing he had jolted her, he adopted a tone of indifference: 'Oh, well! If you must go, you must. What does it matter? You left me long ago.'

'What do you mean by that?'

'You ought to know. You're the successful one. You're the one that's praised for sensitivity and insight into character and all that jazz. We've always been saddled with your bloody writing. We could never go away for any length of time because you're always starting a book, or working on a book, or finishing a book, or beginning another one. You've never been any sort of companion because you live in a private world. You don't know what's going on outside, and you don't care. You've never given me the affection I need.'

'And what have you given me?'

'You've had everything you want.'

'So you think. You're so wrapped up in your deprivations, you can't see beyond them. That business of your mother . . .'

'Shut up. Don't you dare mention my mother.'

As Hugh's voice rose, the Ogdens came out of their room and went to the staircase. Mr Ogden turned his head away from the Fosters but Mrs Ogden stared at them with lifted brows.

Kristy whispered: 'All right. I won't go.' She squeezed his hand to reassure him then opened the door of their room and called out cheerfully: 'The bat's gone. The light has driven it away.'

7

Kristy was drawn to the Lettuce Room yet hesitated to enter.
Though the door was unlocked, the room had an aura of privacy.
She noticed that the only guests who went into it were Mrs Axelrod and Mrs Prince, and they went only in the company of Mrs
Gunner. Except when in use for a private party – the Ogdens'
party had been followed at intervals by similar parties – the room
was unlit after dark, and the outside lights, shining through walls,
reflecting and re-reflecting in glassy surfaces, gave it the depth and
glimmer of a pond at night. Kristy was astonished one evening
to find that phosphorescent lights had come on over the lettuce
boxes and, looking through the door, she saw the small delicate
plants glowing viridian green. The lights stayed on for three nights
then went out. Six weeks later, they came on again.

When the sun shone, Hassan pulled bamboo blinds over the
glass roof and walls. It seemed the lettuces had to be protected
against tropical conditions just as maidenhair fern, the bane of
Al-Bustan, was cosseted and protected in English conservatories.

One afternoon of heavy cloud, Kristy, depressed and solitary,
wandered into the Lettuce Room. It disappointed her. It was
smaller than she imagined and the slatted shelves took so much
space, a party, she thought, must be a congested occasion. The
atmosphere, cool and moist, had a chemical smell of artificial
fertilizers. There were garden chairs set round a wooden table on
which stood a box made of inlaid woods. She opened the box and
found needles and reels of silk. She had never seen Mrs Gunner
sewing in here but she knew it was Mrs Gunner's work-box.
Outside on the lawn, Mr Simpson had measured out a cricket
pitch and having put up a walking-stick for a wicket, was bowling
a cricket-ball at the trunk of a pepper tree. While she watched

him through the glass, the sun came out and at once Akbar entered and, with an air of importance, pulled the blind down in front of her. Blind-pulling was ordinarily too menial a job for Akbar. She knew he had been watching her as she entered the room and now would urge her out of it.

Catching her eyes, he said severely: 'Lettuce Room belong Mis' Gunner. Yo' no come in only with Mis' Gunner.'

Kristy retreated and it was a long time before anyone invited her in again. She did, however, hear Mrs Gunner asking Mrs Axelrod and Mrs Prince to 'come and see the lettuces'. Mrs Gunner had a habit of snuffling her laughter back up her nose, intended to convey a gamin good-fellowship but its effect was insinuating. The invitation was always given with a snuffle and Kristy guessed it meant an exchange of all the gossip of the Daisy.

The pension's evening life centred on the bar. Some of the guests played bridge, others tried to follow the long-drawn-out dramas on Indian television, but for all of them, drink was the thing. They seldom went out. The Praslin was beyond their income level and Gurgur's beyond their experience, but they needed no other resort. The Daisy gave them everything. Occasionally officers from a visiting ship, or old Dr Dixon, or the half-Indian harbour-master, would drop in for an evening's drinking and the residents knew themselves privileged, living, as they did, at a centre of island entertainment.

The Fosters, though they drank less, lived much like the rest. Ambrose, anxious for Lomax's return, constantly begged Hugh to go with him to Gurgur's where he pestered Gurgur for news of Lomax. Gurgur, his mind on other things, could only hunch his shoulders and say: 'What do I know? He has big affairs in Beirut. When he comes, then you will see him.'

Ambrose grumbled and threatened to take himself back to London but always, in the end, told Hugh: 'Might as well wait till the old thing turns up.' He once persuaded Kristy to go with them but the place disgusted her. She had been promised a night club and found herself in a brothel. Hugh, who liked the place no more than she did, refused to go more than once a week. At the end of the month he found that all Ambrose's triple whiskies had been set against his account and he owed rather more than his month's salary.

Kristy had lost her taste for alcohol. Watching the Daisy's guests pass from dull sobriety to alcoholic elation, from elation to alcoholic stupor, she saw the futility of the process. Tomorrow they would be sober again. At times, when Hugh was out with Ambrose, she would wander into the garden but the outdoor air was hot and heavy and few people passed on the road. The Indians kept to their quarter round the harbour and the blacks to a suburb called the Dobo. Only a few Arabs and mulattos commuted between harbour and Medina and, at night, they went by at a trot, heads down, fearful of the night spirits that the Arabs called afreets and the mulattos gris-gris.

The outside world was so quiet, she could hear every word of the film being shown at the open-air cinema at the harbour. If she went to the edge of the road, she could look down on the harbour lights and the phosphorescent water shining like quicksilver. Once in a while, the richer officials went visiting and a couple, passing from one villa to another, might nod at Kristy as she stood on the lawn, but they did no more than that. Their silence, no doubt, was prescribed social behaviour yet she found herself oddly dashed by it. It was as though she had come out to find something and could find nothing. The outside world was as empty as the inside, and her own mind was emptier than either. At a loss, she would return to the salon where, if there was nothing else, she might hope for a row between Mrs Gunner and Akbar.

These rows were a feature of the pension. Hugh deplored them and like the other guests, would move his chair in an attempt to repudiate sight and sound of the contestants bawling insults at each other. When the voices reached the highest pitch of acrimony, Mrs Axelrod might frown or click her tongue but the rest, with their ability to be unaware of what they chose not to see, behaved as though they heard nothing.

The rows were occasioned by Akbar's bills. The pension's main items of food and drink were charged to an account at Aly's. The small daily needs of the cook and cleaners were bought by Akbar who maintained his power by shopping around. This freedom required him to pay in cash and each evening he expected to be repaid. Mrs Gunner would leave the bar to check the bills and she dealt with them according to mood. If she laughed, saying 'you're a right old scoundrel, Akbar, but you don't fool me', Akbar would recognize her humorous intent with a tolerant smirk. But Mrs Gunner had another sort of laugh, a laugh of venomous anger and Akbar, when he heard it, would stiffen indignantly and prepare for a fight.

The first of these rows overheard by the Fosters concerned a new baking tin. Mrs Gunner wanted to see the tin. With experienced cunning, she did not send Akbar to fetch it but sent the nervous, simple Malay who knew little English. The price on the bottom of the tin proved to be two rupees less than that on Akbar's bill. Akbar was angry but his defence was weak: 'You try make thief of Akbar? Yo' no sense, no little sense, sayyida. Akbar best man in market. Akbar save money, all time.' Mrs Gunner insisted on an explanation and Akbar accused the Malay of writing the price on the tin. The Malay, it turned out, could not write. Akbar then accused the shopkeeper of writing one price and charging another: 'Why you go Indian shop? Indian cheat all time. Indian no good people. Indian bring malaria, bring many bad thing. Yo' go Arab shop in Medina, you get good men. Yo' too big fool, *sayyida*.'

'You call me a fool and I'll kick your fat arse.'

'You tell Mas' Gunner he kick Akbar arse? That too, too funny. Akbar kick Mas' Gunner arse.'

'I didn't say Mr Gunner. I said I – *I* – would kick your arse.'

'Yo'? Yo' kick Akbar arse! Ho, ho, ho, ho, ho, ho . . .' Akbar's basso profundo laughter rolled round the salon walls: 'Yo' little, little,' Akbar indicated with a hand that Mrs Gunner's height was about two foot from the ground: 'Akbar knock yo' with one finger. Yo' no fit speak Akbar. Yo' fool woman, sayyida.'

This final impertinence stirred Mrs Axelrod who, looking at Mrs Prince with lips tight shut, jabbed a cushion with her crochethook. Thus would she deal with Akbar! But Mrs Gunner had her own methods. Coldly dismissive, she said: 'That's enough from you, you Egyptian bastard. Take your clobber and go.'

Akbar threw back his head and walked to his domain and

there, turning, he surveyed Mrs Gunner, his eyeballs standing out and stretched downwards so he could see her without lowering his head. He said firmly: 'Me no Egyptian bastard. Me Soudanese man,' then, gathering up his kaftans and prayer-rug, he flung open the kitchen door, admitting a smell of drains, salt fish and rancid coconut oil, and departed.

That, the Fosters thought, was the end of Akbar and they felt no regrets. But, no. Next morning he stood at his usual place beside the serving-table, a composed and splendid figure, ruling the servants with an inclination of the head or a movement of a finger.

Kristy said to Ambrose: 'I thought he'd been turned out bag and baggage.'

'Oh,' Ambrose laughed, 'Mrs G. would never let him go. He's the Daisy's pride and joy. Every large household wants its Akbar, and there aren't so many of them here. He's a pure-bred Nubian, directly descended from the blacks pictured in Queen Hatshepsu's tomb. On Al-Bustan, where blood is so mixed, he has the authority of pure breeding.'

8

In the past, Kristy had been given to late nights but now, at ten o'clock, she was as sleepy as the salon's hard-drinkers. She slept heavily and so long that, more often than not, Hugh would leave the breakfast-table before she came down. Ambrose, with no more occupation than she had, would remain at his table until she appeared.

A few days after the Residency luncheon, seeing her push aside her breakfast coffee, he asked: 'What's the matter?'

'I don't know. I think I'm sickening for jaundice or something. I can't write and if there's nothing to distract me, I'm usually half-asleep.'

Ambrose sighed his sympathy: 'Same here. It's this bloody climate. If I were in better nick, I'd be writing myself. I've had it in mind to do a piece about island superstitions; a *feuilleton* only.'

'The gris-gris?'

'Yes, indeed, the gris-gris. The Dobo's the place for them. If you go there at night, you find all the windows shut because of the gris-gris. We might get a taxi and drive round there. I'd show you the turtle factory.'

'No, no, I don't want to see the turtle factory. I couldn't bear it.' Without warning, she burst into tears but talked fiercely as she cried: 'I can't bear the things human beings do to animals. I can't bear cruelty to anyone, but especially animals or children. I loathe vivisection and experiments on living creatures. I can't bear animals being hunted and killed by human imbeciles and show-offs. I hate the sight of the English papers. There's always something in them to make you sick.'

Ambrose's gaze became luminous with sympathy: 'I'm sorry.

I should not have mentioned the factory. I did not know you felt so deeply.'

'I do . . .' But Kristy, too, had not known she felt so deeply. Lately it seemed, she had become unendurably tender in her feelings about small creatures, human or animal. Reported cruelties that before had roused in her a normal anger, now inflamed her with an agonized rage.

Having started to cry, she could not stop. She cried because children were ill-treated and because animals were killed for their fur or used in futile experiments or wantonly tormented or wantonly hunted. Between her sobs she spoke brokenly: 'You'll scarcely believe what I heard: some accursed French scientist, in American pay, caught dolphins and cut them up alive. The idea was to discover how they breathe. He said they had to be conscious so he strapped them down and cut into the living, conscious flesh. Dolphins! Creatures that have always trusted and befriended human beings . . . saved human beings from drowning . . . Our friends, betrayed.' She broke off, unable to go on for her tears.

'Who told you that?'

'A young man. They went out on a yacht to catch dolphins. He was employed as a sailor. He saw it all. He told me.'

Ambrose, who had watched her enticing the lemur until she had persuaded it into her hands, now watched her as she wept. When her sobs had subsided, he said: 'You have no children, have you?'

She shook her head.

'Why is that?'

'Hugh didn't want any. He feels that his mother failed him and he thinks if he had children, he would fail them. It's a neurotic fear, of course, but real to him. And I'm not mother material. I have my own work.'

Ambrose said: 'Of course' and left it at that.

9

Hugh went several times to the top floor but the room of the Minister for Culture was always empty. Then, on Coronation Day, he saw all the ministers setting out to pay their respects to the Governor.

He came into the hall as they descended the stairs, slowly, like a religious procession. Stately of mien, self-consciously prestigious, the seven men appeared from above, each wearing the robes of his ancestors. The lift would have held them all but, for the sake of effect, they had chosen the stairs.

At the first glimpse of the leading figure, the porter jumped to his feet and alerted the supplicants. The supplicants, as eager as he was, roused themselves from the dirty white seat and crowded together at the bottom of the staircase. The ministers took their time but as soon as they were within reach, the supplicants held up their hands and the ministers stretched down to shake them and entered the press of supplicants with a show of sympathy and delighted good-fellowship. They were embraced like relatives. Exchanging greetings, giving to even the dirtiest of the crew assurances of friendship and love, the ministers gently disentangled themselves and crossed the hall to the door.

Murodi, noticing Hugh, twitched his mouth as though deriding the whole charade but at once regained his solemnity and continued his part in things.

Pedley, in joking mood, referred to the ministerial floor as 'the nursery', a sobriquet that, in Hugh's opinion, betrayed the official attitude towards the whole idea of Al-Bustan's self-government. As the Arabs despised British concepts of government, the two Arab ministers had less standing among their kind than the Negroes had among the Africans. The five Negro ministers were highly conscious of their tribal cultures and their awakening to power. They were figures of supreme importance both to themselves and to the blacks, and were careful to maintain their image. English officials walked to the office. The Arabs might stroll down from the Medina but four of the Negro ministers journeyed everywhere in the official Daimlers. The fifth, the Socialist Diddar, made a show of being the exception to this rule.

Now, though the Residency gates were less than two hundred yards up the road, the ministers, Diddar among them, packed into the two Daimlers and were driven to their appointment.

Hugh, watching them go, decided that they had grasped the privileges of their position but wondered what they knew of its responsibilities. He was also surprised by the inequality of representation. Two Arabs and five Negroes seemed to him an unjust division of power and he decided, when next he found Pedley affable, to question him about it.

Hugh was learning Pedley's moods as he was learning the weather. Pedley in a nice state of insobriety, would let him sort the Reuters' sheets unsupervised. A few more pulls at the whisky bottle and he was so eupeptic that he was liable to spill over into an outburst of distrust and violent rage. Caught as he balanced on this emotional ledge, he could be informative and even at times critical of his kind.

Hugh found him critical a week after Coronation Day when it had been noted that cracks were running up the north wall of the Government Offices.

'Bloody awful building,' he said. 'We've needed an administrative block for over a century and they rush this place up just as we're thinking of pulling out. Always the same. They did it in Aden. Chucking away tax-payers' money.'

Hugh saw his chance to ask why there were only two Arab ministers.

'Policy of H.M.G.,' Pedley briskly said. 'We decided to make a black majority. The chaps we put in were selected three years later by popular vote and have been re-elected since. Chiefly, I may say, because the Arabs are too damn indifferent to come to the polls.'

'But why instate five blacks in the first place?'

'We favour the blacks as a safeguard against the return of

slavery. It exists, you know, in the Arab world. If the Arabs regained power here, there's no knowing.'

'So the blacks, having come as slaves, will end as rulers. Rather like the Memluks.'

'If you want to be fanciful, yes.'

'And the Indians? Why aren't they represented?'

Pedley, teetering on the edge of ill-temper, grunted twice before he said: 'Good question' as though surprised that a good question should come from Hugh: 'They're a minority. The plantation workers are indented labour: they come and go, so don't have a vote. The shopkeepers have Dr Gopal who looks after their interest. He's not a minister but he's a deal more powerful. *And* active. He's the government planning officer.'

'I don't know him. But what, in fact, do the ministers do?'

'They don't do anything, but they have very advanced ideas. They all, to a man, believe in higher wages, better social services, improved housing, and jobs for all. These desiderata will automatically come about as soon as the British leave.'

Hugh laughed: 'And what *will* happen when the British leave?'

'God knows. I expect the Indians and blacks will fight it out.'

'And the Arabs?'

'They're a spent force. They'll retreat into the Medina and stay there till the others rout them out.'

'And when will this happen? I mean, when will the ministers be ready for independence?'

Pedley sniggered. 'Never, at the rate they're going.' He paused to grin into himself then with one of his sudden changes of mood, he said in a disagreeable tone: 'And here endeth the first lesson.' Leaving the room, he slammed the door furiously after him.

The only minister, apart from Murodi, with whom Hugh came into contact was Mr Diddar. Diddar, a bent, elderly black, was Minister for Internal Affairs and when the first edition of the news-sheet was ready, he came in person to collect his copy, saying: 'I thank you, Mr Editor, for this fine work. I assure you, I shall read it with avidity.'

He had since called in on Hugh whenever he felt inclined. Every time he picked up a copy of the news-sheet, he said: 'I thank you, Mr Editor, for your fine work. Every copy I read with avidity.'

Hugh was gratified, feeling that in Diddar, if in none of the others, there was the political consciousness which he was paid to nurture. He discovered that Diddar lived at the Dobo and when he came to the office, he walked the three miles to Government Square. Diddar, too, was pleased by Hugh's regard for him.

'I see you are a man of broad vision,' Diddar said, smiling his constant, happy smile: 'So you will understand how I live and where I live. It is that I may identify with my black brothers. I, also, for the same reason, walk on my feet. I am – you will respect me, I know – a left wing.'

Mr Diddar, who seemed to be bent by constantly plodding up the steep hill road, had a round nose and a projecting jaw between which there was a very wide mouth that he kept stretched in almost continuous laughter. Even when speaking seriously of his political beliefs, he laughed all the time.

'I am building up among my brothers an understanding of the policies of Mr Foot and Mr Mikardo. I hope you will lose no opportunity to quote from those great men.'

Hugh, who suspected that Diddar was his only reader, promised to keep Mr Foot and Mr Mikardo in mind.

Diddar said: 'Naturally, I am preparing a revolution but there are elements here who do not want a redistribution of wealth. They could prove obstructive. There is, for instance, Dr Gopal. A dangerous man.'

'I have not met Dr Gopal.'

'No, he does not come to this office but,' Diddar bent confidingly towards Hugh and whispered, 'Mr Pedley goes to his. They talk very much.'

'What about?'

'Many things. Many and various.' Diddar nodded as though he could tell more but would not. 'And now I must go and consult with Mr Axelrod.'

'May I ask how you work in with Mr Axelrod?'

'It is done *very* well. I go to Mr Axelrod and I say: "Mr Axelrod, explain this thing to me" and he says: "Mr Diddar, you learn *very* fast." Yes, I am a very fast learner, and I work in well with Mr Axelrod. He has said to me, "You are a man to government born."'

'What about Mr Murodi. What are his policies?'

Diddar made a face and stretching out his thin, old hand, palm downwards, tilted it this way and that to express the ambivalent nature of Murodi's policies: 'But he is young. His thoughts are not formed. When he is older, I trust he will be with me. I intend to be leader; Mr Editor. Believe me, when I take over this island, things will be very different.'

Mr Diddar's admiration for the news-sheet heightened Hugh's sense of responsibility. He felt it necessary to understand, as far as he could, Diddar's political ideals and when Diddar next dropped in, he tried to discover what reforms, apart from the redistribution of wealth, Diddar wished to see introduced.

Diddar could only say: 'They are yet to be formulated.'

'And when do you expect to take over?'

'That, Mr Foster, remains to be seen.'

Hugh next saw Murodi when he was waiting for the lift. Murodi came across the hall wearing the African tobe, its whiteness enhancing the smooth, rich darkness of his skin. At the sight of Hugh, he raised his arms, lifting the white linen so he seemed to be winged: 'Ah-ha, Mr Foster, I see you again!'

'I have been looking for you for a fortnight.'

'True, I have been absent from my office. At times, when I am much inspired, I work at home.'

'You are like Mr Diddar. The science of government inspires you.'

Murodi, with the same gesture as Simon Hobhouse, put back his head, showing the pink roof of his mouth and all his fine teeth, and was still laughing when Hugh got out at the second floor and watched him ascend like a black seraphim to the august company above.

'Come and see me. Come and see me,' he shouted as his feet passed out of sight.

During the morning coffee break, Hugh hastened to the top floor. Through the silent, carpeted corridor, came the sound of Murodi's typewriter.

Murodi stretched out a hand to Hugh: 'Sit here, Mr Foster. In a minute I will be with you.' He touched his brow to show that, meanwhile, his thoughts were elsewhere. He typed rapidly to the bottom of the page, plucked the paper from the machine, then smiled at Hugh: 'Imagine my joy and surprise when I learnt that we had a famous writer in our midst!'

'Oh. I don't think I'd call my wife famous.'

'Now, Mr Foster, let us not be facetious. We all know you are a famous writer. The news was overheard at Gurgur's club and here such news travels fast.'

'I'm afraid Mr Gunner was joking.'

'You are too modest.' Murodi opened the drawer of his desk and took out a manuscript: 'When I heard of your fame, I said to myself: "Here is one who can give the true opinion of writing." I have here the romance of a young Swahili prince captured by Arab slavers and brought to Al-Bustan to work on the plantations. With your permission, I will read a little.'

'I'm afraid I'm not a critic, either.'

Murodi smiled and propping his feet on a ledge under his desk, tilted back his chair and began to read.

Hugh, acutely unwilling to listen, stared from the window at the vast, pale brilliance of the sea. From this height, and at this distance from the window, he could see only the earliest forming of the long wave that rolled slowly towards the strand, carrying on its back a line of sunlight. For how many centuries had that wave formed itself and travelled in exactly as it travelled now? He decided to be generous about Murodi's writing. He would be kind, but not too kind. Murodi was no fool. He would know if the plaudits were false.

Murodi read like an actor, every now and then throwing out an arm or shaking the manuscript to enhance the passion of the work. Soon, Hugh was listening in earnest. Murodi's story had the simplicity of a Celtic legend and his inexact English gave it a vigour that disturbed Hugh out of any thought of being kind. Another emotion filled him: not, of course, envy. He rejected any possibility of envy: a profitless sin and one that did not even give pleasure.

Looking up and meeting Hugh's intent frown, Murodi anxiously asked: 'You do not like it?'

'I do, I do. It is very good. It is more than good: it has poetry. How does it end?'

'Very well, I think. The prince runs away over the mountain to join with other escaped men. He gathers them beneath his banner and he tells them they will march back to the Medina and kill the sultan. He will be their king. They set out but – here it is very sad, very tragic – one by one they die of blig-blig.'

'What is blig-blig?'

'It is an illness. There is a belief among the Africans that on the other side of the mountain, people sicken and die. I think it is an invention of the Arabs but, still, you must admit it is an exciting device: the army coming over the mountain to seize the sultan's throne and all dying one by one.'

'It is a traditional story?'

'It has traditions. The deaths I thought for myself, but there *was* a prince among the slaves and they talked of killing the Arabs and making him king, but nothing came of it. The Arabs had guns; the slaves did not. Still, there could be such a king.'

'A king who is also a poet?'

'You are laughing at me, Mr Foster.'

'I am not. Do you think a poet could not be a king?'

Putting his feet on the ground and sitting upright, Murodi gazed gravely at Hugh: 'I will be honest with you, Mr Foster: I have asked myself the same question and this is my answer: A poet could be a king, but a king could not be a poet. Do you understand me?'

Feeling he understood only too well, Hugh said he had better return to his television set.

'No,' Murodi put out his hand to detain him: 'Stay, I beg you. You have listened to me and been very kind. Now it is your turn. Tell me, please, the things you have done.'

Hugh, at a loss, stared at the long roll of the distant sea, then at Murodi: 'Mr Murodi, when your work is finished, you will have overcome a number of problems. The effect will have been noted, the elusive cause caught, the characters given substance, made to move and meet each other in telling circumstances; their development mapped; each, in contributing to the story, will have worked out his own fate. This you will have done yourself. Isn't that so?'

Murodi beamed: 'You, Mr Foster, have a true understanding of the writer's exertions.'

'I suppose I have. Now, you asked what have I done? I will tell you. I spoilt other men's work. I would take the completed book and extract the plot and change it to suit the producer. I would use the dialogue but omit any conversation or situation too subtle or profound for a mass audience. For doing this, I would be paid so much more than the author of the book, you would laugh if I told you. That sounds unjust, but perhaps it wasn't. You see, I had no joy in my work.'

Murodi, realizing that Hugh was serious, stared at him in alarmed dismay as though watching a man in acute pain. But Hugh did not betray any pain. He spoke without emotion, his face was expressionless.

Murodi shook his head slowly: 'But, why? You understand so much. Why did you give yourself to this work?'

'Perhaps it was all I could do. I don't know. I wrote a novel. Sometimes I think I could write another, but I am frightened. After all, one can only do what one can do.'

'I understand.'

Hugh saw retreat on Murodi's face and, reminded of Kristy, thought: 'They are all the same. Their work is all that matters. They can make contact only with another like themselves. They are useless as friends for, in fact, they are not here. They are in another place.' He rose and went quickly to the door. Murodi, hurrying after him, held out his hand: 'If you have suffered in this way, then your kindness is the more kind.'

Smiling, Hugh took Murodi's hand then went, aware that the minister would not seek him out again. In spite of this, he suggested that Kristy meet Murodi. Kristy was not responsive.

'I thought you'd be glad to know you have a fellow-writer on the island.'

She said despondently: 'I've stopped writing.'

'I don't know why you ever started. I suppose you were imitating me.'

This roused her. She laughed: 'You think I can only imitate. What an ass you are. Women can do anything, but they're lazy. Mentally, they're bone lazy. They want someone to do their thinking for them. But you did nothing for me. You threw me out on my own, so I started using my own brain.'

'What are you getting at?'

'You didn't want the things that make for a combined effort: a family, a proper home. I should probably have settled down quite happily to domesticity. There's nothing women like better than to be in a sort of mish-mash of nappies and brats and kitchen-sink squalor. It calls for no mental effort. The efforts are all being made by the chap who brings home the bacon.'

He could not tell whether or not she was laughing at him, so he said sharply: 'Do you want to meet Murodi or not?'

'Not at the moment.'

'If you don't want to see people when they are there, you'll find when you do want to see them, that they're not there.'

'Yes, that's the artist's dilemma.'

'I sometimes wonder if you have any feeling for anyone. You told me once about your leaving home when you were sixteen. Just walking out without a word or a message. You stayed away for weeks and when the police tracked you down, you were surprised to find your mother crying. You said: "What was she crying for? We always disliked each other."'

'Subject for a short story.'

'Exactly.'

10

Awaiting the resurgence of her creativity, Kristy behaved much like the other women. In the past, to save time, she had washed her own hair but now, glad of any sort of diversion, she went down to Aly's hairdressing saloon. She was delighted by it. She had often wondered what women found to do with themselves in the afternoons and now, as though on a holiday from herself, she was discovering another order of existence. She went round Aly's large rambling shop that sold, not only food, wines and spirits, but Indian silks and jewellery, toys, hardwear and newspapers. Here newspapers and magazines lived for ever. Some of the copies of *Vogue*, *Harper's*, the *New Statesman* and the *Spectator* were three years old but they had not been reduced in price. There was a corner where customers could sit and study catalogues from the big shops in Nairobi. The goods, when ordered, arrived promptly by boat and the customer was at once telephoned and advised of their arrival.

In the saloon above the shop, the floor with its long flexing boards sloped down from east to west. Around the walls were old-fashioned washbasins and chairs like dentists' chairs. In the centre of the floor there was a large table where the women could take coffee and read magazines and sit out the long process of Aly's permanent wave. The two young male hairdressers, one Indian, one mulatto, each, at different times, told Kristy how he longed to work in the Praslin's hairdressing saloon. The mulatto said: 'There you find many beautiful ladies.'

Kristy laughed: 'So you don't find the government women beautiful?'

The mulatto gravely replied: 'The government ladies are beautiful, it goes without saying, but the Praslin ladies are rich.'

Coming out of Aly's, Kristy walked along the shore road and went across the white strand to the edge of the Indian Ocean. The strand was deserted and she felt it was deserted for some reason unknown to her. She asked Ambrose who said it was a haunt of water-snakes. She hated the small lukewarm pool at the club and wanted to bathe in the sea, but Ambrose said the sea was infested with sharks. Then, she asked, how was it the Chief Secretary and his friends were able to water-ski?

'He put up a shark net, and the water-snakes haven't found his cove. It's not a private beach, but if you went down there, you'd get a pretty cool reception.'

'It's monstrous he should have that place to himself. I'm surprised the others put up with it.'

'They understand perfectly. The Chief Secretary and his friends are charming, but they have their own games. You'd need a lot of money to play with them.'

'You mean, they gamble?'

'I believe that's their chief diversion.'

The diversion of lesser men was fishing, a diversion that Kristy greatly disliked. The giant game fish were coarse eating and she had noticed that after one had been put on show in the dining-room, the safragis, more often than not, took it out and buried it in the garden. The destruction of these creatures was killing for killing's sake.

One day, meeting Simpson coming up from the harbour, an Arab boy, at his heels, carrying a blue marlin, she came to a stop in front of him. 'That's a disgusting sight,' she said.

Simpson flirtatiously asked: 'What is, young lady?'

'That fish. What *point* in killing these harmless creatures? It's slaughter. Savagery. It's degrading.'

Simpson, his brows and moustache a-twitch, could not speak at first, and then broke out brusquely: 'What's it to do with you?'

'Everything. The creatures of the world belong to all of us. When you kill them, you rob everyone.'

Simpson's mouth gaped but he had nothing to say, and Kristy walked on.

News of this encounter reached Pedley before it reached Hugh. Hugh, hearing Pedley on the telephone, shouting: 'I can't believe it. I absolutely can't believe it', realized that someone had committed some heinous social trespass but knew no reason to relate it to himself. He was alarmed when Pedley rushed in on him and said: 'Well, Foster, your wife's really done it this time. She'll be excluded from the club.'

'I don't know what you're talking about.'

'She hasn't told you she bawled out Simpson for catching a bally fish? Well, she did, and there's a lot of feeling about it. She'll have to apologize.'

'Kristy?' Hugh, resentful of the fear that Pedley had roused in him, laughed scornfully. 'She wouldn't apologize to God.'

'If you aren't careful, she'll wreck your career.'

'I haven't got a career.'

'Yes, that's the trouble. You think you're free to do what you like. I can tell you, the people you go around with aren't the right people. That fellow Ambrose Gunner, he's not liked. He thinks he's a cut above his mother: he's a bally snob.'

'Nothing he's ever said or done has led me to think so.'

Hugh was sorry that Kristy had picked on Simpson who sometimes seemed almost on the point of speaking. That evening, catching the man's eye, Hugh realized he was more hurt than resentful. Hugh would have apologized himself had an apology not been a disloyalty to Kristy.

While he was considering what to do, Mrs Gunner and Akbar started to quarrel and Kristy's peccadillo was forgotten.

The quarrel began mildly enough with Mrs Gunner giving a loud, critical sniff and saying half-humorously: 'Crikey, old cock, you know how to lay it on.' She tittered and it seemed all would be well, but suddenly, her cordiality was jolted by a mysterious item on Akbar's list: 'What's this, I'd like to know?'

'Pick-lees,' Akbar said firmly. 'Today I buy pick-lees.'

'Pickles? It's not your job to buy pickles. What sort of pickles?'

Akbar, his eyes rolling in search of an answer, said: 'Pan-Yan.'

'Go and get them.'

'Not any more. All pick-lees in soup.'

'You don't put pickles in soup. And you didn't buy none, neither. Pan-Yan, indeed! You saw that written up in the shop.'

Anger was mounting on both sides. 'Me buy. Me buy,' Akbar

cried in anguish, striking his breast. 'Why Akbar write pick-lees, if Akbar not buy?'

'Because Akbar's a shifty bastard, that's why.'

'Yo' say Akbar "bastard", Akbar break yo' in two. Akbar tear out yo's eyes. Akbar break yo's neck like chicken.'

As the uproar grew, Ogden, sitting near the bar, looked appealingly towards it but the adversaries had no eyes for him. Threats were met with threats, insults with insults, and in the midst of the row, the telephone started ringing. Ambrose, who had come out of the office, went back to answer it.

Akbar, describing how he would put a rope round Mrs Gunner's neck and pull it tight, tight, tight, broke off in mid-sentence. There was a silence during which Ambrose, his voice very musical, could be heard in charmed agreement with his caller. The silence went on so long that people turned to see what had caused it. Mrs Gunner had fallen to the floor.

Akbar was bending back in a pose of theatrical astonishment, his great eyeballs starting from his head. He remained fixed until Ogden jumped to his feet, saying: 'Good God, man, what have you done?'

'Me not done. *Ya sayyidati* stan' there. Next time, *ya sayyidati* fall down dead.'

Mrs Axelrod, very excited, pointed at Akbar: 'He's murdered her. I knew it would happen sooner or later. I knew it. I knew it.' She shouted: 'You'll pay for this.'

Akbar fled to the kitchen as Ambrose returned to the salon. Seeing his mother on the floor, Ambrose said crossly: 'Really, mother, what a time to choose!' and bending over her, he caught her hands and pulled her up. When he let her go, she fell down again.

Ambrose's behaviour shocked everyone.

'Have you no consideration?' Mrs Axelrod asked. 'Can't you see your mother's unconscious?'

Ambrose made a flustered attempt to defend himself: 'When I was a child, she was always doing this to frighten me.'

'You're not a child now,' Ogden said, 'and she's not trying to frighten you. Go and ring Dr Dixon. Better still, get the hospital to send the ambulance.'

Ambrose returned to the office. When he had made the call, he came to the Fosters and muttered: 'This would happen just as Lomax comes back.'

Hugh and Kristy did not try to reply and Ambrose, looking aggrieved, went and stood alone near the piano. After a while, he furtively lifted the lid and, sitting down, brooded over the keyboard then, with a rapture that startled the room, he began to play the last movement of the 'Eroica'. He played on as the ambulance arrived and the men lifted Mrs Gunner on to a stretcher, but as the front door was propped open and they were carrying her out, he came to an abrupt stop and hurried after them.

Next morning, he was at his table, eagerly awaiting the arrival of the Fosters. 'I have splendid news for you,' he said.

Kristy said: 'So Mrs Gunner is better?'

'Oh, that? Yes, she was coming round when I left. She's as tough as an old boot. No, that's not the news. Lomax plans to entertain us *en prince*. In two days' time, on Sunday, he's sending the car for us and we'll take a trip to Morgo's Bay where the treasure lies. We return to drinks on the Praslin terrace and then! – what do you think? He's booked a table for the great opening spread in the new dining-room, the Salle Verte. There'll be a special cabaret show to mark the occasion. All the quality and gentry will be there. A real treat, eh? Don't tell me you aren't delighted.'

Hugh said: 'It seems a bit heartless to have all this fun while Mrs Gunner's ill in hospital.'

'Would it help her if we refused the invitation?'

The Fosters had to agree it would not help and Ambrose was so excited about the projected party, they realized it would be even more heartless to disappoint him.

It was unfortunate that the Fosters and Ambrose, dressed for the occasion, were awaiting Lomax's car just when the churchgoers returned to the Daisy. Entering the salon, they stared, astonished, at the three of them. No sooner had the churchgoers settled down to their pre-luncheon drinking than the ardent Catholics, who attended the mission church, returned by taxi from the Medina and the surprise and disapproval was renewed.

Akbar had disappeared and Hassan was struggling with the bar grille when Ambrose, his chin tilted up in an attitude of extreme hauteur, led his fellow guests out to Lomax's Mercedes 600. The day was brilliant, the wind cool.

'A perfect day for a picnic,' said Ambrose who, having placed Hassan in charge of the pension, felt he had done enough.

But Hassan was not Akbar. Hassan had no presence. He was a small, sallow, pock-marked peasant from a poor village on the Upper Nile and though he was eager to excel, he lacked Akbar's authority. Already there was disorder among the servants and Aly, unsupervised, had that morning sent up a consignment of frozen mutton so poor that Hassan came running after Ambrose.

'Cook say only for stewing,' Hassan cried.

'Then let it be stewed,' said Ambrose, who had no patience with the humdrum details of office.

The Fosters sat on the wide, broad back seat of the car while Ambrose, on the centre seat, sprawled in an opulent way, aglow with the munificence of success. For him the trip to Morgo's Bay meant only one thing: the treasure project was in hand.

'And this is the merest beginning,' he said. 'Once the treasure is secure, I mean to ease Lomax into publishing. That, after all, is my *métier*.'

'I didn't know you were in publishing,' Kristy said.

'Oh, dear me, yes. I did a couple of years in the army during the war. Rose to be lieutenant. When I was demobbed, I got a little gratuity in order to set up in publishing. I did a few choice books: poetry, essays and so on. The firm didn't last long but the experience is there.'

Ambrose's massively noble appearance had become more massive, more noble, in view of his prospects. As was usual with him when he felt satisfied with life, he assumed, as by right, the rôle of guide and mentor. Though the Fosters had come to know the Harbour as well as he did, he pointed out its sights as they drove past Aly's and Gurgur's and reached, at the end of the quay, the private houses of the Indian shopkeepers. The houses, of wood and ornamented like the shops, had balconies where the women lay in hammocks gazing lethargically at nothing. After the houses came tumbledown huts where the Malagasy women sat under canvas awnings doing embroidery, and the men, working on small pieces of ebony, carved elephants, giraffes, leopards and other denizens of a continent they had never seen. The huts and houses, backing against the cliff, were overhung by palms and fruit trees. Picking on one tree that was weighted down by large, noduled fruits, Ambrose said with imposing solemnity: 'A bread-fruit tree.'

There was a fish-curing works at the farthest end of the quay and the whole district stank of fish and toddy. It was a relief to bump down on the sandy shore road and drive under the palms with the sea wind blowing through the car. Here there were no buildings, only the cliff on one side and the shore on the other. They drove in a silence that was shattered whenever the wheels struck a fallen coconut. The shell would break with a watery crackle that unnerved Kristy who feared they had gone over a landcrab.

The long white strand flashed between the palms. The sea, for once almost motionless, appeared to be banked up, coloured like a water-ice, a glassy wall in layers of violet, pistachio and indigo. Kristy meant to make a note of this but, drifting into a near-sleep, she forgot.

Ambrose gave them a dissertation on water-snakes: 'A lovely shore,' he said, 'yet, as you can see, deserted. Once it was a play-ground, and fishermen would hang out their nets to dry, then, one day, two people were bitten by water-snakes; next day, two more were bitten. Then five were bitten. They all died. Men, wearing gumboots, were sent to dig out the snakes but as they dug, the snakes slid deeper into the sand. The men were unused to boots so took them off. One of them was bitten and died. The rest downed tools and now the water-snakes have the place to themselves. Look, look!' Ambrose pointed to where a small sil-very torpedo was launching itself from the water: 'Things are so quiet now, the flying-fish have come back.'

One after the other, the winged fish rose and flashed like bows of light, a-dazzle in the dazzling air.

Kristy murmured: 'How sad!'

'Why sad?'

'Sad that we had to go before the fish could come back.'

113

As the heat grew, drawing up moisture, mirages appeared on the road ahead: illusory lakes in which a stone or a piece of stick appeared to be a tall bird. When the long building of the Praslin could be seen through the palms, it, too, seemed like a mirage, fluid and wavering, with the intense whiteness of light.

The sight so excited Ambrose that he pulled himself up as though, like the flying-fish, he were about to launch himself into a more inspiriting element.

As the car stopped at the hotel steps, he opened the door and jumped out, saying to the Fosters: 'You stay there. Don't let us delay. I'll fetch him out and we'll drive straight on.' Ambrose's voice fluted with satisfaction and his hands patted the air as though shaping circumstances to his desired design. He went importantly through the dark glass doors. As they opened before him, the Fosters got a glimpse of the interior, shaded and dappled over with spots of gold.

The chauffeur put his head down on the wheel and went to sleep. Waiting, Kristy watched the sea-wind stirring the leafless, plumy filaments of the casuarina trees and the birds that darted in a worried way, whistling from tree to tree. The lawn sprays hissed and slurred as the wind caught them and hoopoes, running this way and that, tried to bathe in the caracoling water.

Hugh remembered what Simon Hobhouse had said about the cliff that overhung the hotel. Leaning from the window, he looked up at the weight of rock and earth that could be brought down by an earthquake. The cliffside was matted over with maidenhair and thorn-apple but there were no heavy bushes. He wondered if the earth were too friable to hold them. Something moved under the fern and seeing the claw of a crab, he twitched in disgust.

The doors of the hotel opened and Lomax came out with Gurgur. Behind them was an Indian and a light-skinned mulatto. Ambrose, bringing up the rear, had lost his air of importance.

The Indian knew who the Fosters were and, getting into the centre seat, he smiled back at them with an appearance of brilliant interest. When he was seated, he held out his hand to Hugh: 'I am Dr Gopal. It is with great pleasure, Mr and Mrs Foster, that I meet you at last.'

114

Gurgur and the mulatto got in with Gopal while Lomax took the seat beside the driver. For Ambrose there remained only a space on the back seat between Hugh and Kristy. Diminished by the unexpected size of the company, he lifted an uneasy brow at Hugh. Why, he seemed to ask, were these interlopers coming with them to Morgo's Bay? Hugh was wondering the same thing.

Lomax introduced the mulatto as Reaney, the producer of the evening's cabaret. The girls, it seemed, were to be Gurgur's girls. At the moment, the girls were resting before the show, and the two men, finding themselves at a loose end, had accepted Lomax's invitation to join the picnic. That accounted for Gurgur and Reaney, but why was Gopal there?

Whatever the reason, Gopal had all the confidence of a much wanted guest.

They drove past the yacht basin. Beyond that the road lost its sand surface and dwindled into a track. The cliff sank gradually until there was no cliff but, instead, a long slope up to the western end of the plantations. Above the plantations, the police barracks, a crenellated square like a little fort, stood alone on a plateau that was, Gopal explained, the helicopter landing-ground. On the sloping ground between shore and plateau were the villages of the workers. The first was the Dobo.

Dr Gopal tutted when they came to it. 'The name means mud,' he said. 'During the monsoon, the whole place is a sea of mud.'

No one else made any comment on the Dobo. It was as though the place were a canker better ignored, though no one could ignore the smells from the factories. A row of buildings, one of them the turtle factory, stood, iron-roofed, down by the loading quay. The whole village seemed to be armoured with corrugated iron but between the shacks vegetation had forced its way so that even here there were creepers and palms and bread-fruit trees. Beside the road there were dumps of indestructible plastic containers, so many of them that it seemed, in the end, the waste must take over. People too old to work were picking about among the bottles and egg-boxes, and at the sight of the great car, they stopped to stare while dirty, naked children came running at it, screaming, 'Rupee, rupee.'

Kristy said: 'Even in paradise, I suppose there must be a reservation for the poor.'

'What sort of people live here?' Hugh asked, abashed by this aspect of Al-Bustan.

Dr Gopal looked round: 'Every sort. The Negroes came first, when they were released from slavery, but many have joined them. Here you will find Arabs, Malays, mulattos, even poor whites.'

'But no Indians?'

'No, the Indians have their own community. They live apart. The Dobo is where people come when they can sink no further. Here they are all one colour. They are not brown or white, they are grey.'

A heavy stench of urine came from a line of communal privies, then the Dobo was left behind. The road turned. The shore, running into the remote distance, was fluted with small bays. Between road and shore there were old coconut groves where dying palms, like worn-out feather dusters, bent to touch the ground. Between the groves, old adobe villas were falling into ruin.

'Arab villas,' said Dr Gopal. 'Once very pretty but now, you see! The district calls for much development.'

Kristy was disturbed by the word 'development' but it was clear that a way of life had ended here and, whether she liked it or not, something would take its place.

This western side lacked the flamboyance of the island's façade but it was made remarkable by the distant prospect of the mountain ridge coming down to the shore. On the eastern side, the ridge had been cut through by some cataclysm, leaving an escarpment that dropped sheer into the water. Here the ridge fell in humps, like the spine of a dinosaur that, entering the sea, gave rise to a trail of rocky islets.

Gopal, leaning forward, murmured to Lomax: 'What do you think? A lot to be done, eh?'

Lomax nodded without looking at him.

They had reached another group of houses and Gopal said: 'Here you see the Indian community.'

The houses, that covered the hillside, were of adobe and surrounded by vegetable patches, palms and screens hung over with vines.

Gopal said: 'As you see, they are well kept, but there is no sanitation, no drainage and there are many diseases. I am pressing for a clearance scheme.'

'But what would happen to the people?' Kristy asked.

'Oh, Mrs Foster, don't worry. They will be well cared for. We would build them block houses up beside the police station. No doubt there are some who would be against it, but good sense must prevail.'

'And if the people themselves don't want block houses?'

Gopal turned to smile at Kristy: 'Why should they not want them? They would be fine buildings, very clean, very hygienic.' He held her with a bold, almost amorous, gaze and Hugh saw that with his confidence, his vitality, his large eyes and his silken black hair, Gopal could be attractive to women.

Hugh would have been more irritated by Gopal had his mind not been on another thing. The approach of the mountain ridge reminded him that on the other side there was the rain forest, the mysterious back half of the island to which Simon had journeyed and from which he had not yet returned. Following the line of the ridge up to the point where the peaks stood, he thought he could see them, a shadow on the air. The track was so rough now that the big car rolled like a porpoise. As it bumped over a protruding stone, the occupants were jerked out of their seats. In the moment of rising, Hugh thought that he had seen over the ridge, that he had glimpsed, for an instant, the forest, like a section through black fur. Whether he had seen it or not, he felt a frisson of fear and exhilaration: and a longing to see it again.

Gopal was saying: 'These slopes were cleared of trees, but the Arabs made little use of them. The rain washed the seedlings down to the littoral and the farmers, ignorant of our new methods, rented the land to the workers.'

Gurgur said in his neutral voice: 'Waste land; of no great value.'

Kristy, looking out at the Indian settlement, asked: 'Why do so many houses show the Nazi sign?'

Gopal, with his smile and his large admiring eyes, jerked round

117

again: 'Oh, no, no, no, no, no, Mrs Foster, not Nazi. Do not be mistaken about that. The swastika is an Indian sign. It is the sign of good luck.'

Reaney sombrely added: 'It is also the sign of the Jan Sangh, the Indian party that would like to take over our island.'

Gopal laughed: 'Come now, Mr Reaney! The Jan Sangh is formed of idealists: a little group that could take over nothing. All young people have their ambition, and all of them talk: but, in the end, they do no more than the rest of us.' Gopal laughed again, apparently amused by Reaney's remark but he was quick to change the subject. Turning again and this time looking at Ambrose, he said: 'This is your fabled shore, Mr Gunner. You have not yet shown us where your treasure lies buried.'

Ambrose, who had been held in dispirited silence, now looked annoyed: 'It is not a buried treasure. It was lost on a ship at sea.'

'Of course. So I heard. Forgive me. There were rumours of a chart. Is the chart in your pocket, Mr Gunner?' When Ambrose did not reply, Gopal went on: 'You are doubtless aware that they have invented a new kind of submarine that can locate ships lost at sea. From it you look down on the sea bottom and pick out all sort of objects, such as ships, cannons, amphora and treasure chests.'

This news so startled Ambrose that he gave an indignant squeak: 'That's not true.'

'Oh, Mr Gunner, believe me, I do not tell lies. Why are you angry? Such a submarine would make your search more easy.'

Lomax, as though to discourage this baiting of Ambrose, called from the front seat: 'Come on, Ambrose. Where is Morgo's Bay?'

Ambrose looked uneasily out at the small sandy inlets: 'It should be about here. My father once drove me round to show me the bay. At least, he thought it was the one.'

The track was disappearing into scrub. When he could go no farther, the driver stamped on the foot brake, threw up his hands and shouted: 'Intaha.' The rocks of the ridge were a few yards ahead of them.

At once, as though by pre-arrangement, Lomax, Gurgur and Gopal got out of the car. Lomax had a picnic basket which had been at the front and he handed it to the three on the back seat:

'All for you. We have already had our little snack,' then, with Gurgur and Gopal at his heels, he started walking back the way they had come. Their purposeful departure made evident that they had some business in this forsaken region. Ambrose looked out of the rear window, saying in an injured tone: 'What are they up to?'

Reaney may have known but he was silent in the middle seat, staring out through the window as though he wanted no dealings with those in the back. Kristy, opening the basket, offered him chicken sandwiches and a glass of white wine, cold from the Thermos flask, but, without turning round, he said he had already eaten.

Ambrose, too upset to consider Reaney's presence, said: 'I might have guessed Lomax had some ploy on. He told me once he only bet on certainties. My quest – a quest for the Holy Grail, in a manner of speaking – is outside the scope of such a man. He has no imagination. What is he, after all? A rogue, a chiseller, a gutter-rat . . .'

While Ambrose's small, suffering voice went on, Kristy sat half-asleep in her corner. Hugh was alert, but not to Ambrose. He was considering the rockfall, the only barrier between him and the forbidden territory on the other side. It looked an easy climb. He slipped off his silk jacket and put it on the back shelf of the car. Then he edged forward on his seat, preparing for action, but cautiously, knowing that what he wanted to do would seem odd and be impossible to explain. He murmured 'Must have a piss' and jumped from the car. Pushing his way through the scrub, too excited to fear the insect life, he came out to the shore. The sand was littered with rock pieces broken from the ridge. When he reached it, he found the headland was higher and more complex than it had looked from the car yet, having reached it, he felt compelled to climb it. His exhilaration carried him so, making his way up, he did not miss a foothold or the possibility of a foothold but when he came to what had seemed the top, he saw only rock and more rock; a waste of rock all riven through with crevices he could not hope to cross. There was no forest, no answer to his own confusion; only a louring heat mist that darkened the lower sky.

Seeing nothing, he was unsure if he had, in fact, seen anything. What he had taken to be forest might have been one of the black cloud lines that, as the monsoon died out, formed on the horizon and dispersed; a storm frustrated.

His shirt was soaked. He stripped it off and held it against the wind to dry. From where he stood, he could see Lomax, Gurgur and Gopal standing under a tree some three or four hundred yards down the road. The tree was one Hugh had noticed, an old breadfruit that had dropped fruits as big as footballs.

Amused by his vantage point, from which he could view the inception of events, he sat down to watch what they would do next. A green van came round the corner and stopped by the tree and three more men came out of it. The newcomers seemed to be Arabs: two wore dark clothing but one had the white kefia and kaftan of the Medina Moslems. When he moved, there was a glint of gold about his head.

A rendezvous, no doubt of it; a ploy, for which poor Ambrose's project had been no more than a cover.

Ambrose drooped into sulky silence while Kristy, waking up, started to talk to Reaney. As soon as she said 'Mr Reaney', he jumped round and his delicate, nervous face turned pink.

'Did you study theatre production in London?'

'In London, madame?' he laughed: 'I have been nowhere. I have not even been to Réunion or Mombasa. But I see all the films at the cinema. You might say I have studied them, for every time I have said to myself: "Ah, yes, I see how they do it." In this way I have learnt many things.' In his eagerness to explain himself, he put his arm along the back of the seat and gesticulated with his long, fine hands: 'And it is the only way to learn here if one has no family and no money.'

'And when you have learnt, where do you go?'

Reaney lifted his hands as though to say 'Where indeed!' He said: 'I am of mixed blood, madame, which means I am not Arab or African or Indian or English. I am none of those things. Some of us are clever fellows. In another place we might be doctors or solicitors or grow rich in business. But here, what is there for us?'

'When the English go, there will be more opportunities?'

'I don't think so. We are a little island in a big world: what does independence mean to us? It means we are pushed out like a small boat on a big sea. We do not know how to sail ourselves. The only thing for us is tourism, but we must have more hotels and diversions. So, we need money and we must look for people from the big world to give us patronage. Do you understand?'

'I'm afraid I do.'

A silence fell and Reaney, realizing he had told Kristy all he had to tell, let his arm drop and slowly, by stages, turned in his seat until he was looking out of the windscreen again.

Ambrose said indignantly! 'Do you realize: Lomax and his cronies have been gone half-an-hour. It's extremely rude of him to treat you like this.'

'Why me, in particular?'

'Because you are a lady.'

Kristy laughed and Ambrose bridled with annoyance. Lomax, returning a few minutes later, looked into the window and apologized for his absence.

'We had to discuss a little matter of business. And now, Ambrose, are we to see Morgo's Bay?'

Ambrose mumbled: 'I've forgotten which it is. I need the chart. If you flew me home, I could put my hand on it at once.'

Not replying to this new suggestion, Lomax took his seat by the driver while Gurgur and Gopal got in beside Reaney. The driver at once backed the car to a space where it could be turned.

Hugh, coming out of the scrub, saw the car running away from him and thought he had been left behind. A cold exultation came over him. He said aloud: 'Even Kristy. Even Kristy!' and it seemed to him he had discovered the worst in human nature. Then, as swiftly as it had departed, the car returned for him and he burnt with shame at his own suspicion.

'So you have been exploring, Mr Foster?' Gopal said gaily: 'Tell me, what did you see? Did you see Mr Gunner's treasure ship at the bottom of the sea? That would be useful for he has forgotten where it is.'

Hugh watched for the bread-fruit tree but the Arabs had gone.

The sun was setting when the party reached the Praslin. The glass doors stood open and the windows of the main room had been opened so that, for a little while before night fell, the wind could blow through it, bringing in the scents of wet grass and frangipani and flowering trees, and dispelling the dull atmosphere of the day.

Lomax was a formal host. Leaving the men to follow, he escorted Kristy into the room and paused with her as she gazed at the walls, darkly covered with rich, chocolate-coloured silk, at the intricate lacings of the bamboo chairs and the gold metal of the tables. The glass of the windows had the same dark tinge as the walls and in daytime, she thought, the whole place must be as dim as an oubliette. The floor was of coral scooped out here and there to accommodate fish pools and fountains, and everywhere there were orange trees planted in wire baskets. When she had seen it all, Lomax took her out to a terrace where the awning had been pulled back to reveal the sumptuous colours of the sky.

Lomax led the way to a group of chairs at the edge of the coral floor so they might look over the rear lawns towards the blue fog that was the sea. A tulip tree, planted in the lawn, dropped its flowers on to the terrace where they lay crumpled like swabs soaked in arterial blood.

Lomax, when he had ordered the drinks, devoted himself to Kristy, asking her conventional questions about her sojourn on the island. In the uncertain light, his biscuit-coloured skin, smooth yet not young, looked to her like the skin of an embalmed corpse. He was amiable with an artificial amiability that made her want to get away from him.

After they had had a drink, Gopal, Gurgur and Reaney left the party: Gopal to make a telephone call, the other two to attend to the cabaret. Ambrose, seeing Lomax's attention fixed on Kristy, whispered to Hugh: 'Walk down the garden with me. I want to show you the mangosteen trees.'

Hugh followed him beneath the casuarinas that wavered like horse-tails in the wind. The lawn ended in a ha-ha with steps down to the star-shaped pool where the bathers lay in long chairs drinking drinks served from an outdoor bar. As Ambrose, in his old tweed suit, descended among them, they stared at him in amazement. The pressure of his belly had caused a slit down the

122

side of his fly but so lofty was his mien that no one laughed or smiled or did more than glance at this revealing hole.

Ambrose passed among them, apparently unaware of them, and descended more steps that brought him to land's end. The screen of mangosteens stood at the very edge of the cape. Hugh began to praise their glossy foliage and purple fruits but Ambrose had forgotten them. Standing between two of the trees, he gazed out to sea and said: 'At times, I can tell you, I'm bloody sick of this bloody paradise.'

'You aren't really leaving, are you? If you went, we'd have no one to talk to.'

'What do you think he intends to do?'

'I don't know. Why didn't you show him the bay?'

'Because of those other bastards. I don't trust Gurgur. And what about Gopal with that submarine contraption? Why should I show them where the treasure is? If Lomax wants information, let him put his money on the table. The least he could do is fly me back to find the chart.'

'It's an expensive trip.'

'What's a few hundred to him? Chicken-feed. You'd think he didn't trust me.'

'Do you trust him?'

'I do – in a way. He's a rainbow. You know what I mean? Some men are as crooked as corkscrews and others are bent like rainbows. He's bent, but if you follow his line, it's consistent. Length without breadth. Why I brought you here: would you do something for me? Have a word with him. Say I'm ill with worry. Tell him about Mrs G.'s attack. Say I'm under strain and he ought to let me know what he intends to do. Rouse his sympathy. Pin him down.'

Hugh promised to do what he could then they stood together in friendship. The sunset was almost at an end. The western sky, a mackerel of glowing red and purple, was reflected in the east. The long incurl of the wave carried on its back a line of crimson. When, in a moment, in the twinkling of an eye, the spectacle was switched off, Hugh said: 'There is one thing you must tell me: has Lomax ever led you to believe he might invest in this venture?'

'He did. He most certainly did.'

'Very well. I'll try and pin him down.'

When they returned past the pool, the bathers had gone. The awning had been pulled down over the terrace and a beaded fringe, hanging from roof to floor, protected the guests against the night insects. The bathers were crowded into this enclosure and the air was heavy with their exposed flesh. Hugh, remembering what Simon had said of them, observed them critically. Some of the women were young but the men were all in the prime of early middle-age. They looked to him big, strong, brute creatures, noisy but perhaps too noisy to be as satisfied as they seemed. The men, muscular, sunburnt, manifestly virile, clearly had everything and wanted more. The women were blonde or red-haired, and even the youngest was raddled by the sun. Several of the women had come bare-breasted from the pool and the inexperienced safragis stared, thunderstruck, while the old hands grinned and dodged about the women like randy dogs. The women, knowing that no harm could come to them, were amused by the excitement they caused.

Hugh told himself that Simon had been right. These people were the devourers, the enemy. They made a ruthless demand on life. For them the world was being squandered, its resources used up, its wildlife decimated, its seas polluted, the sea life destroyed and the seabirds in their thousands killed by their accursed oil-tankers.

Considering all this, Hugh felt such rage that the smell of their bodies sickened him. Ambrose, walking in front, pushed his way through them as through a herd of cattle. They did not give way readily but his weight defeated them and Hugh followed in his wake.

Lomax and Kristy had retreated into the room. Hugh, seated among the fountains and orange trees, knew his reaction against the holiday-makers had been unreasonable. If those people were guilty, was he not guilty, too? Even Simon, angry because of the lost, beautiful things of the world, even Kristy who suffered for them, had a part in destruction. They were all guilty but he was the most guilty because, more often than not, he chose to put the destruction out of his mind.

Gopal came hurrying back to the party and seated himself beside Kristy. Kristy, obviously weary of Lomax, turned to him, animated by his admiration. Lomax, who had been looking for Ambrose, got to his feet and going to him, asked: 'Where have you been?'

Overhearing the question, Hugh was surprised by its urgency, but before he could give much thought to it, Ambrose walked away, leaving Lomax to him.

Dutifully, Hugh said: 'I enjoyed the drive but it was sad, wasn't it, not finding Morgo's Bay?'

'Did you expect to find it?'

Hugh, fearing his question would irritate Lomax, nevertheless asked what he had promised to ask: 'Do you really mean to invest in this treasure hunt?'

Lomax took a gold cigarette-case from his pocket opened it slowly and looked at its emptiness. He said: 'You're fond of him, aren't you?'

'We both are. He's the only person at the Daisy who has even bothered to speak to us.'

'But you know nothing about him?'

'Not much, no.'

'Excuse me, I must get some cigarettes.' Lomax walked away.

Gopal, who had been entertaining Kristy with some of the island gossip, suddenly touched her on the hand and said: 'I've seen you before, you know! One day you were in the Medina and you looked into my shop. I saw you through the glass, but you did not see me.'

'An antique shop? – with swords and carpets and silks?'

He was pleased that she remembered: 'When I saw your face, I said to myself, "A remarkable lady." She is someone.'

'Everyone is someone.'

'There, you see! You are a philosopher. But I also asked myself: "Why is she alone and sad?" For you were sad, were you not?'

'Yes, I suppose I was. I was trying to decide whether or not to return to England.'

Gopal's eyes opened in astonishment: 'But how could you return to England if your husband works here?'

'I can move about on my own. I have a separate existence.'

Gopal laughed as though at an uproarious joke: 'So you

thought you would return all by yourself? But why, why? The ladies here live pleasantly. I think they do nothing at all.'

'Yes, they are like oysters.'

'Oysters? You mean they are shut up this way?' Gopal put his hands palm to palm.

'No. I mean they have never developed. Oysters have remained the same for millions of years. They exist only to reproduce another generation of oysters identical with themselves. What point in it?'

'You mean: what point in living to produce another generation? What else should a lady do? The rest they can leave to the men. We do everything and ask only that they have their children. In this they are fortunate, I think. Life is so easy for them.'

'It may be easy but it turns them into a destructive force. The world is full of narrow, frustrated women eating up their children. In the end, they will eat up the world.'

Gopal wiped tears of laughter from his eyes: 'Oh, Mrs Foster, you are a funny lady. I am happy to talk with you. We must talk another time. Will you come again to my shop? Have you time?'

'I have all the time in the world.'

Lomax returned to his party. Ambrose, weary and inert, sprawled in his chair with eyes half-closed. He yawned: 'I'm off as soon as my old mum's better. My friends want me in London. I've had offers.' Ambrose's small voice tailed away as though he were already in flight.

'What sort of offers?' Kristy asked.

'I have, among other things, been asked to edit a magazine of the arts. A lavish affair, covering not only poetry, prose, painting, sculpture and music, but architecture, interior decoration and . . . film.' Inspired by the idea of this magazine, Ambrose sat up and looked about him. His eye lit on Hugh: 'I want you in on this, Hugh. You're the very one to do a piece on film. I'd like a survey of the most significant directors: Pasolini, Borowczyk, Pontecorvo, Antonioni, Visconti, Louis Malle, Rohmer, Vihanová, Chabrol . . .'

As Ambrose paused, Hugh added: 'Zeffirelli, Antonini?'

'Indeed, yes. No doubt you'll think of a few more – but only the Great. Only the truly Great.'

Hugh, compelled by Ambrose's small, dulcet voice, discussed the film article with enthusiasm. He began to think that writing about films might be exactly the sort of writing he was meant to do.

Lomax who, at first, had had the air of a man not easily deceived, was obviously shaken by the fact that Hugh could not only accept but augment Ambrose's litany of names. His expression seemed to say: 'So they are real names? – the names of real people?' Then, becoming conscious of his own ignorance with regard to them, he looked uneasy as though he were not only excluded but criticized. He broke in contemptuously, saying:

'There's no money in art magazines.'

Ambrose returned his contempt: 'We are not seeking money. Our purpose is to discover. Anyone can buy a Renoir: all you need is cash. It's another matter when you lay out a few thousand on a Rothko or a de Kooning. There you're exploring a dark continent. You must have instinct.'

Lomax, as though impressed against his own judgement, turned his face from Ambrose and again took out his cigarette-case. It was still empty.

He stood up and said to Hugh: 'I think I left some Gauloises in the Rain Room. Perhaps you would walk through with me?'

Feeling that some revelation was about to be made, Hugh followed Lomax down the length of the main room into a large domed glass-house filled with flowering plants. It was not air-conditioned. Fans blew the air about but it was very warm and filled not only with flower scents but a wet, earthy smell that verged on decay. The room, Lomax explained, was intended as an indoor garden which could be enjoyed when the rain kept guests indoors.

In the centre of the floor there was a large pool filled with many coloured fish. Lomax sat on one of the chairs beside the pool and asked Hugh to sit beside him, then he pulled a blue packet from an inside pocket: 'So my Gauloises were here all the time. Shall we stay a little minute and have a smoke? Now! I see you feel I am unjust to our friend Ambrose?'

'I feel you have teased him enough.'

'So, what am I to do next? Give him money and say good-bye to him?'

'Why "good-bye"?'

'If he could get away, do you imagine he would come back here? I am fond of Ambrose, and so are you: but are we deceived by him? Would you call him an honest man?'

Hugh reflected on this and wondered what he would call Ambrose. Remembering the suitcase packed with stones, he thought: 'A leg-puller, a persifleur, a practical joker?' and in the end, said lamely, 'I would not call him a crook.'

'When I first met him, I asked myself what is such a man doing, marooned on this island? I wrote to my London agents and ordered them to make inquiries and I found that in the world he had left, he had destroyed himself. He owed money so he dared not show his face in places he had frequented. More than that, with his persuasive tongue, he had won confidence and betrayed it.'

'How "betrayed it"?'

'This magazine he was talking about a short time ago: a fantasy. He was always projecting such fantasies. He had such enthusiasm for a time that he could persuade people to invest money in almost anything. Then, when the money was spent, his enthusiasm died and that was the end of it. He was made bankrupt. He ran up debts in a different name. Someone else tried to bankrupt him and, of course, it all came out. To save him from prison, his mother sent him his fare and he came here; and here he has to stay.'

'I knew none of this.'

'So, what would you have me do? Give him money? Risk losing him for ever?'

Bewildered, Hugh asked: 'But why do you care whether he goes or stays?'

Lomax stubbed out his cigarette then rubbed the base of his palms into his eyes. He stood up, sighing, and said: 'Because I love him.'

Dr Gopal, keeping his hold on Kristy as they went to dinner, explained that a real *salle verte* was a temporary structure made of bamboo and palm leaves: 'They make them in the Seychelles for weddings and parties, but the Praslin's Salle Verte is a permanent room so the palms are of plastic. The owner here named the hotel after his birthplace: a small, not important island but certain people have called it the Garden of Eden and perhaps the hotel is an Eden of sorts. Tonight, the food will be excellent. There is to be a special buffet with a hundred sorts of sea-food. Are you tempted by such food, Mrs Foster? Here we say you must eat it before it eats you.'

Had it not been for Gopal, Kristy thought, Lomax's table would not have been very vivacious. Gurgur, his bleak head hanging, had returned to the party but contributed nothing. Hugh, disconcerted by all he had heard about Ambrose, avoided his eyes and Ambrose, knowing himself avoided, went down in sulks.

The table, which Lomax had chosen earlier in the day, was beside the cabaret floor but separated from it by gardenia shrubs in pots. The heavy scent of the gardenias blotted out the flavour of the food but Lomax seemed satisfied that he and his guests were on the threshold of events.

The cabaret floor was raised and steps went up from it to a small stage. They were all reminded of Reaney and Gopal asked where he was.

'He cannot eat,' Gurgur said. 'He suffers from tension. The entertainment is highly cultural.'

'Cultural!' Ambrose gave a laugh of bitter contempt.

Gopal also laughed: 'Ah! I hear Mr Gunner slip the safety-catch of his revolver.'

Ambrose gave a snort.

The women who had been undressed on the terrace were now, in Kristy's opinion, over-dressed. Only a few of the men wore dinner-jackets but the women were all gowned and jewelled as though for a court ball. There were three parties of officials from the villas and Dr Gopal said he espied the Chief Secretary. Hugh had seen the Chief Secretary once in the office lift but for Kristy he was still a fabled character. Cautiously looking in the direction indicated by Gopal, she saw, for the first and last time, a plump, fair youngish man who had the peculiar serenity of inherited wealth.

'The one like a cream-fed pussy?' she asked.

Gopal pretended to be shocked: 'Oh, you must not say that, Mrs Foster. He is a charming man.'

Mrs Hampton, on her way to join a party, paused to speak to

Ambrose just as the ceiling lights began to dim. Leaning towards him in a cloud of scented chiffon, she earnestly asked: 'How is your mother?'

Shuffling and grunting with gratification, Ambrose managed to get to his feet as she said: 'Oh, *please* don't get up. I heard that Mrs Gunner had gone to hospital. Not *terminal*, I hope?'

'Dear me, no. She'll be up and about in no time.'

'I'm thankful to hear it. She's still a young woman.'

'She's eighty-three.'

'No age at all. Younger than I am.'

When Ambrose gallantly protested that she still looked a girl, she pushed him skittishly from her and disappeared into the dark.

'Charming woman!' said Ambrose, gazing longingly after her as she made her way to more elevated company.

A blue light flooded the floor and Reaney was discovered with a ghostly face, rolling his handkerchief between his hands. He opened and shut his lips several times before coming to the point of speech.

'Ladies and gentlemen,' he said: 'Our cabaret is designed to honour the world's great writers. Therefore, the artistes will represent for you Dante, Cervantes, Shakespeare, Voltaire and Goethe. They are in chronological order and Dante is first. From such a cultural feast, I will not detain you.'

Reaney walked backwards and took his place near the steps. The stage lit up and from somewhere behind it came the deep and awe-filled strains of the *Adagio assai* of the 'Eroica'. A young woman came from behind the back curtains.

'Dante,' Reaney spoke as though from underground.

The woman, a big, full-bosomed, brown-skinned girl, posed in the centre of the stage. She was wearing a red Renaissance head-dress, but for the rest she was naked except for three red diamanté stars, one on each nipple and one on her navel. A narrow diamanté strip half hid her pubic hair and her shoes had heels four inches in height. A red cloak lined with frills of lace hung from her shoulders, throwing into relief her heavily powdered flesh.

The diners, that had been bemused by the mention of great writers, applauded Dante in clamorous relief.

Severe behind her make-up, she came down the steps with a

solemn high-stepping walk, crossed the floor and stood a few yards from the gardenias.

There was a pause in the music while Reaney announced: 'Cervantes.' The music banged on and Cervantes, a stout African girl with a green cloak, made her appearance wearing a helmet and carrying a lance.

Shakespeare, like Cervantes, was identified by his most famous character. Wearing a lace-frilled black cloak, the Shakespeare girl carried a skull.

'My God,' muttered Ambrose: 'The gloomy prince.'

Candide, in purple, carried a garden rake and Faust, in brown, with a white wig, held up a phial that possibly contained the elixir of youth.

When they were all in line, the girls put down their props, and stood straight-faced until the 'Eroica' faded; then, taking off their cloaks and draping them skirt-fashion from the waist, each girl lifted a leg into the air. Offenbach's *Can-Can* was heard at top pitch and at once the girls swung into a furious routine of high kicks, cartwheels and swirling skirts that caused the audience to rise, stamping in delight at this comment on the world's great writers. Shakespeare and Dante, becoming over-excited, began to make reverse V-signs and Ambrose twitched in disgust.

'*Rather* bad taste,' he said to Kristy but Kristy was laughing too much to reply.

Reaney, after he had taken his bows and thrown kisses to the audience, moved about among the tables collecting the congratulations that were shouted at him. Flushed and elated, he seized on the hands held out to him and turned his head this way and that as though searching for some further triumph that must surely be due to him. But where was it? How could he ever find it? Kristy noticed that the women, especially the older ones, touched him familiarly and when he bent to their hands, they ruffled his hair with contemptuous affection. She could imagine that the better-looking mulattos were fair game at the Praslin and, thinking of his talent wasted, his ambition lost in the rôle of amorist, she said to Gopal:

'Something must be done for him. If he gets the chance, he might do remarkable things.'

'*If* he gets the chance.'

'But surely Lomax will help him?'

'Every clever young fellow thinks the rich exist to help him. It is my experience, dear Mrs Foster, that the rich help only themselves. And now let *us* help ourselves. I insist you must try a mangosteen.' Gopal took up a purple fruit and opened it to show her the segments of brilliantly white flesh: 'Try it. The flavour is cool and delicious.'

The evening was ending and even Dr Gopal was beginning to flag. When his talk ceased, Kristy realized how sleepy she was and wished she were in bed. A giant moth had managed to get in through the bamboos and after blundering about among the lights, dropped down to the table in front of her. Its body was as large as a large cigar and the long closed wings of fawn and grey were delicately netted over with black. It sat, stunned by the fall, and she put her hand down beside it, gradually edging closer until she could feel the powdery wing filament against her skin. As she bent over the creature, Hugh saw that her face, though pale and peaky with tiredness, was transformed by a tenderness that she had seldom shown to him.

The moth turned its long antennae to explore the object next to it and as it touched her, she bent to breathe on it, thinking to communicate with it. At once, it made off, its heavy body hitting against the table things as it searched for its natural world of night. Its wing touched Gurgur on the face and he jumped up in anger and slashed at it with his table napkin.

Kristy, also leapt to her feet and snatching the napkin from him, shouted: 'Stop that. Do you want to injure it?'

'Why not?' Gurgur turned his anger on her. 'The thing makes a nuisance of itself.'

'It's confused. It's frightened. You should help it, not torment it.'

'What do I care for such creatures?'

'Then you should care!' Kristy stared at Gurgur in a fervour of rage at his indifference. 'Then you should care. Cruelty begins with animals and ends with concentration camps.'

Gurgur gave her a malign stare from oblique eyes that were, Hugh noticed, of a reddish-brown flecked with grey. They reminded him of a medicine – brown with a grey precipitate, blandly distasteful – that he had been given at school. So much menace came from the man that Hugh pulled Kristy down to her chair and patted her hand.

Gurgur said quietly: 'Do you imagine I am a Jew?'

'I doubt whether the Jewish race would own you.'

Gurgur caught his breath then, letting it out, looked down at Hugh's hand on Kristy's hand and said: 'If this lady is your wife, you should control her.'

Hugh laughed at the idea of controlling Kristy but said: 'Come now, Kristy, the moth's unharmed. We can put it outside. Don't be upset.'

Hugh's mildness was more than Gurgur could bear. He said to Lomax: 'I go now,' and he went off with the stance of an outraged funeral mute.

'So much for the vulture,' said Ambrose. Cheered by the incident, he turned to Lomax: 'A brandy would go down very nicely.'

When the safragi placed the brandy on the table, Ambrose filled his glass and lifted it: 'What shall we drink to?'

'Your magazine of the arts,' said Lomax.

His tone, cold and cynical, caused Ambrose to put his glass down and stare at Lomax like a disappointed child: 'Are you trying to tell me you've decided against the treasure project? You won't fly me back to find the chart?'

Lomax smiled a smile that afflicted every part of his face. Even his ears seemed pained by it. It was perverse and yet sheepish, and had in it an element of cunning. He glanced at Hugh as though to say: 'You will understand' but Hugh did not want to understand. He said to Kristy: 'You look tired. Do you want to go?'

'I must rescue the moth.'

She found it among the gardenias and cupping her hands over it, she went to release it in the garden.

Ambrose had subsided in his chair as though sinking into himself, his huge body going down like a dying dirigible. As he collapsed, his face oozed sweat which seemed to be squeezed from him. He muttered to himself: 'What is left for me now? Where can I go? What can I do?'

Distressed by his suffering air, Hugh tried to rally him: 'This is absurd. You could do anything you wanted to do. Simon Hob-house said that at Cambridge you were regarded as the most brilliant man of your year.'

Ambrose, reflecting on this statement, began slowly to reflate. He said: 'I don't know that I'd've said exactly that. There were at least two other alpha-plus brains up with me. Really,' he sat up and his voice took on its full beauty, 'I think the most remark-able thing about me is, that I am a squire.'

The modesty of this claim caused Hugh to laugh aloud. Am-brose gave him an indignant glance and lifting his chin and brows, he said with some hauteur: 'The Gunner estates carry the squire-ship of a wide area. The Gunners are a very old Catholic family.'

'But you've been married three times,' Hugh protested, 'how did you fix that?'

'A godson of Montini can fix anything.'

Lomax, who had been listening to this conversation with a strained expression, asked: 'Who is Montini?'

Ambrose eyed him with scorn: 'Montini was Secretary of State under Pacelli. He is now Christ's Vicar on Earth.'

Dumbfounded by the audacity of a man who spoke of popes by their surnames, Hugh and Lomax stared in silence as Ambrose emptied his glass and refilled it with an appearance of consider-able satisfaction.

When Kristy returned, Lomax walked with his guests to the hall where he sent the Nubian porter to call his car. As they stood together by the door, Ambrose gazed, in an abstracted way, at a vase filled with Leopard orchids.

Lomax said: 'They're brought from Kenya in the ship's re-frigerator.'

Ambrose did not speak. The vase, an immense artifact of gold-veined Venetian glass, stood on an elaborate, gilded table: a welcome and earnest of the hotel's grandeur. Ambrose, like one under a spell, began to move towards it.

The Nubian, throwing open the doors, called: 'Mis' Lomax car' but Ambrose did not change direction. Reaching the vase, he lifted his arm and gave it so violent a blow, the whole structure of glass and orchids rose into the air before dropping to the ground. The glass shattered and shot in every direction. One piece passed like a razor blade over Lomax's left cheek. The Nubian bawled: 'What you do, *sáyyid?* What you do?'

Hugh hurried to Ambrose and seizing him by the arm, rushed him out of the hotel to the waiting car. Kristy followed. They packed into the back seat and the chauffeur stamped on the accelerator. Before anyone thought to pursue them, they were speeding away from the scene of the crime.

PART TWO

The Bird Tree

1

Ambrose, at breakfast a week later, announced to all present that Mrs Gunner was much recovered and would like to be visited.

'And when will she be back at the helm?' Ogden asked.

'Any day now.'

'That won't be a day too soon,' Ogden said.

Kristy set out for the hospital that very morning. Everyone knew where it was for it stood, stark and isolated on the road above the Residency. Its isolation had been deliberate as it had once housed patients with infectious diseases. In those days, Ambrose had told her, the hospital had been notorious for the fact that whatever disease a patient went in with, he or she had come out – if he or she did come out – with another: malaria.

Now it was a general hospital and would not accept cases of smallpox or bubonic plague, and patients no longer came out with malaria.

There had been a shower that morning and the rain pools were evaporating. The old women were out, smoothing the sand with brushes made of twigs. Along by the Residency, the road had been cleared of every leaf and fallen branch and the surface was patterned over with delicate twig marks. When Kristy came to the rough ground above the Residency, a shudder passed through the island. She found these small earthquakes unnerving. They seemed a manifestation of the quivering mirages above the pools and she saw why, in this unreliable world, the English held to their conventions as their only certainties.

The lane to the hospital ran eastwards, with a cliff face on one side and a cliff drop on the other. Eucalyptus trees had been planted on either side and these had sucked dry the marshy soil and left no breeding place for mosquitoes. The eucalyptus trees had shot up tall and slender. Their leaves, trembling and shaking off the glitter of the rain, reflected the azure of the sky. Massed against the upper cliff were bourgainvillaea covered with papery mauve and reddish-purple flowers that were so long lasting, they collected dust.

The hospital stood in a coign of the rock. It was a plaster-fronted building, its grey-white paint flaking off on to the grass at its base, looking more like a relic of empire than did the Government Offices below it. Kristy, when she reached it, saw that the coign was much deeper than it appeared when viewed from the lower roads. Behind the hospital building there was room for an extensive walled garden, a jungle garden – except, she realized, it was not a garden: it was a graveyard. She was shocked by the sight of it. It was too convenient.

She went to look in through the gate that was padlocked to keep the dead in, or the living out. The gate was ornate but heavily rusted. Peering between the rusty iron curlicues, she saw the stones were almost hidden by weeds and creepers. In the middle of the path stood an ancient tree that bore both flowers and fruit. The flowers were purple – their colour may have been thought fitting for this place – and the fruits, like giant sausages, hung down to touch the ground. Though the area was enclosed by cliffs, a wall had been built round it, so old a wall that its bricks were held together only by mosses.

The nearest memorial, a broken column that had become still more broken, commemorated John Cookson, aged nineteen, dead of dysentery in 1871.

The graveyard, alerted by her step, had fallen silent except for the hum of bees, but she stood so quiet that a lemur swung from the sausage tree and dropped to the column to observe her. She whispered to it and put her hand through the ironwork but as she moved, it flashed away.

'Ladies upstairs,' said the hospital porter. If there were male patients downstairs, Kristy saw no sign of them. The hospital was as silent as the graveyard. On the upper floor a passage, as wide as a ward, ran from one end of the building to the other. Rooms led off on either side. In the centre of the passage stood a long table at which three Arab women sat playing cards. They were fat, their fat breasts rolling out of nylon wrappers, and they put the cards down with a lingering slowness of ennui. Fearing that the newcomer might be a man, they began to cover their faces but seeing Kristy, they sighed and continued their resigned and desultory movements. When Kristy asked them where she might find Mrs Gunner, they pointed to a balcony at the farthest end of the passage. There she found Mrs Gunner lying under an awning, on a bed, her crêpey little face as yellow as saffron.

'So it's you, dear,' she said: 'Well, it's nice to have a bit of company, whoever it is. That son of mine's been up only once. He says the walk kills him and he's the cheek to ask me to pay for a taxi.' Mrs Gunner gave her hoarse, snuffling laugh: 'I said: "No, dear, I don't want to see you that much."'

Kristy sat on a chair beside the bed and looked down on the Residency garden: 'At least, you've something to look at.'

'Not bad, eh?' Mrs Gunner propped herself on her elbow and surveyed the bower of trees and flowers that was still lustrous from the rain: 'In the old days of dip and scarlet and yellow jack, this door was nailed up. They wouldn't have anyone out here then, and now . . .' she made a little grimace of social knowingness: 'You only get out if you're a cut above the others. I know her nibs, the matron, so I'm all right but ornerily they only let government wives out here. It was the war changed things. When they had naval officers and suchlike here, the Governor felt he had to let them out. There, look!' Mrs Gunner's face lit with sardonic glee as Sir Beresford appeared on the Residency terrace: 'Smoking a cigar, eh? The old bugger. All right for some, eh? I bet your hubby's stewing in his office. Her nibs don't like me calling him "old bugger". There's a snobby bitch if you like! And hand in glove with that pair at the Daisy.'

'Mrs Axelrod and Mrs Prince?'

'Who else?'

The confiding note of criticism in Mrs Gunner's voice induced Kristy to speak what she had in mind: 'I'm very worried about something, Mrs Gunner. I was wondering if you could help me?'

'You're worried, dear?' Mrs Gunner settled back with a glow of interest on her cheeks: 'What about?'

'I'm afraid I'm pregnant.'

Mrs Gunner's interest began to fade: 'That's nothing to worry about. You've got a ring on your finger.'

'That's the trouble. If I were the only one concerned, I wouldn't be worried. But my husband doesn't want children.'

'Doesn't he, dear?' Mrs Gunner's renewed interest raised her voice to a delighted squeak: 'He's a funny one.'

Seeing in Mrs Gunner's gaze more curiosity than sympathy, Kristy feared she had said too much. But, having said what she had said, she had to say more: 'He lost his mother when he was a child. She died and he has the feeling that, by dying, she abandoned him and he, if he had a child, might do the same thing.'

'Ree-lee! I never heard the like.'

'The thing is, Mrs Gunner, I wanted to ask you: is there an abortion clinic here?'

'A what?' Mrs Gunner laughed at the question: 'You won't find nothing like that here. You'd have to go . . . Well, I don't know where you'd have to go; Durban or Cape Town, I s'pose. But how far gone are you, dear?'

Too far gone, Kristy feared. She could already feel her dress stretched taut over her stomach. 'I didn't realize. I thought the food had upset me. . . . It didn't enter my head. After all, we've been married eleven years. But now I remember, I was so tired the evening we reached Al-Bustan, I forgot to take that damn pill.'

'If it was as long ago as that, it *is* too late, dear, unless you want a major op. I wouldn't recommend that, dear. You be a sensible girl and go and see Dr Mueller. Don't go to old Dixon, he's past it. Mueller was trained in Johannesburg: he's right up to the minute. And you tell your hubby if he don't like it, he can lump it.'

'That's not so easy. I feel it's unfair to him. I promised him it wouldn't happen.'

'Well!' Mrs Gunner eyed Kristy all over and it was clear she thought the Fosters a freakish couple.

Kristy had come to her as the only woman to whom she could speak, and now she realized her error. She was on the point of making a desperate appeal to her to say nothing to anyone, when footsteps echoed down the passage.

Mrs Axelrod and Mrs Prince were coming to visit Mrs Gunner.

'Why, look who's here!' Mrs Gunner propped herself up to welcome them. In spite of her previous remarks about 'that pair', she looked as joyful as a little girl who finds her playmates at the door.

Kristy said with breathless urgency: '*Please* don't tell them what I told you.'

'Me, dear? As if I would! You know *me*.'

Holding out a hand to each of the new arrivals, Mrs Gunner gave Kristy a vague 'Bye, bye,' while Mrs Axelrod and Mrs Prince seemed not to have seen her.

When she reached the main road, Kristy turned right and went on up towards the plantations. She had decided to visit Gopal in the Medina. 'A last jaunt,' she said to herself, feeling she was a doomed woman.

Up among the plantations, a whole field was on fire. The workers, surrounding it, were fanning the flames with palm leaves and the smoke, rising in yellow clouds, drifted upon the wind. It had settled into the plantation path as into a gully, lying so heavily in places that Kristy could not see the feather tops of the sugar plants. She could feel the heat of the fire and the smoke smell, that was sweet like a compound of honey and nuts, made her feel sick. She should have turned back but refused to give in to her condition. She had mislaid the dimension that fed her imagination but she would not be defeated by her physical self. She ran till she was out of the smoke then, reaching the mango tree, she dropped down beneath it. Propping her elbow on her knees and her head in her hands, she waited for her sickness to pass. It went slowly but when she opened her eyes, she was too dizzy to rise. Her weakness was unlike anything she had experienced before. She felt resentful, believing that the foetus inside her was drawing the life from her, draining her as a cuttle-fish drains its victim. Several minutes passed before she could attempt to rise.

She shuffled across the ground and turned so she sat facing the tree. Looking at all the nubs and nodes and blebs of its red trunk, at its great crown of glossy dark foliage, at the constant coming and going of the coloured birds, she thought of her previous visit when there had been women gathered beneath its shade, making curry on a primus stove. She had tried to talk to them but they were shy and even the children had been disinclined to smile. Having no success with them, she had wandered on, deciding that she would return to England. In the market square, she had observed everything with the detached attention of a temporary visitor. Gopal had said she looked sad. Perhaps she had felt the sadness of impending departure that would, she supposed, have ended her life with Hugh. But sad or not, she had been a free woman who took her freedom for granted.

Now, all was changed. She felt herself hobbled like a nursing cow whose function is to give suck.

'Good God,' she thought. 'No wonder the female sex was left standing at the post. We didn't stand a chance.'

Drowsy in the heat, she felt mesmerized by the movements of the birds. One of them, an inconspicuous grey, black-spotted bird, kept darting out from the tree trunk, fluttering in the air then darting back again. Once settled, it clung close to the bark and crept upwards, making quick, efficient head movements as it picked up insects. When its beak was full, it took off into the dense foliage above it. Looking to see where it had gone, Kristy saw a nest like half a coconut propped on one of the lower branches. As the bird settled on the rim, the nest showed a fringe of movement, the uprising of infant beaks, all open to be fed.

She waited while the bird disgorged the insects and returned to creep again up the trunk and search and gather what it found. 'A mouse bird,' she thought then, as it took off, darting and fluttering: 'A mouse that becomes a butterfly.'

She sat for several minutes, enchanted by the bird's selfless search for food, its assiduous devotion to the greedy beaks above. Kristy was deeply moved by it yet asked: 'What is it for? Next year the bird would be feeding another set of beaks and this year's young would be forgotten. And why did the bird do it? It did not know itself.'

'We are tricked,' Kristy thought: 'However you dress it up, we are tricked.'

She managed to get to her feet and turning her back on the tree creeper, she went on into the Medina.

Dr Gopal's shop, on the eastern side of the square, pressed back against the city wall and seemed to become part of it. He had told her that it was the first 'western style' shop to be set up in the Medina. He had converted it himself from an old grain store, putting in the plate-glass window which was now being copied by other forward-looking shopkeepers. It had, however, no window display; only an inner ledge holding Damascus blades and antique pistols. Looking in, Kristy saw a half-lit cavern of a shop filled with carpets and embroidered hangings. Gopal, too, was inside but he was surrounded by young men. Feeling it would be indiscreet to enter just then, Kristy was moving away when Gopal came running out to detain her.

'Oh, no, no, no, no, no, Mrs Foster, you must not depart from us. Come in, come in. You have arrived at the very moment to meet some young friends with modern ideas. You think too badly of us, Mrs Foster. Now you can tell for yourself how advanced we are in the Medina.'

'But I do not think badly of you.'

'You do. I know you do,' Gopal was playfully flirtatious and eager to show her off to his friends: 'Enter please. My house is yours. Here is Musa, the son of Yusef Pasha. He had an English tutor and is infused with up-to-date opinions. Now I introduce you to the others: Khalil, Nimr, Farih, Zarbay and Sayyid. They have all been students at Cairo and Beirut so are greatly advanced, as you will see for yourself.'

The young men, who had been lying around on Gopal's divans, rose uncertainly as their names were spoken and stood hanging their heads before the English visitor. Gopal saw to it that she shook hands with each of them. Musa was the only one who looked directly at her. Unlike the others, who wore the lightweight suits fashionable among westernized Arabs, he was in Arab dress and wore, as his father had, the gold algol of princes.

When the introductions were over, Kristy was placed in the position of honour on the central divan. The others sat around her.

'Now we must talk,' said Dr Gopal, but whatever they had been discussing before she came in, the young men had nothing to say now. They shot her inquisitive glances from beneath their eyelids but whenever she turned to one of them, he was looking

142

the other way. She tried to break their constraint by speaking herself:

'When I came through the plantations, one of the fields was on fire.'

The boys tittered and Gopal explained that the old canes had to be burnt off before new ones could be planted. One of the boys muttered something in Arabic which led to laughter and a general chatter which Kristy could not understand.

'English. Only English,' Gopal commanded and the silence returned. 'I fear these boys are shy. Why so modest?' Gopal laughed at them and said to Kristy: 'I will send my shop-boy to buy coffee and sweetmeats. That will make them find their tongues.'

While Gopal was briefing the boy, Khalil, a thin small youth with bold eyes, looked at Kristy and said: 'Answer this, if you please: three holes in the floor.'

Kristy shook her head and Khalil answered with satisfaction: 'Well, well, well.' The riddle was riotously received and Khalil said: 'I have many such jokes. I drop them into parties: they keep things going.'

The others, too, had many such jokes and told them, one after the other, until Gopal returned and said: 'Enough. We must speak seriously.' He turned to Kristy and said: 'We are a remarkable gathering, you know. I am an Indian, a Hindu. Nimr here is a Christian, the others Moslem, yet we are all good friends.'

Musa looked up through his eye-lashes and observed Kristy with an expression of challenge and ridicule. He resembled his father but where Yusef Pasha had appeared muted by defeat, the son had about him an aura of vitality and dissatisfaction. He spoke in the sort of richly cultivated voice that in England could be found only among the very old.

'And,' he said, 'we fight for the same thing.'

Kristy was surprised: 'What is that?'

'We fight to rule ourselves.'

'You soon will. It is declared British policy that, as soon as they are ready, you will have self-rule.'

The boy, returning with coffee and Turkish Delight, deferentially offered the tray to Musa who, with a casual, rather sulky movement, waved him away. Gopal spoke and the tray was brought to Kristy, the boy grinning insolently in the belief that she could be there for only one purpose. All the Moslem boys refused the hospitality offered and when Gopal protested, Khalil explained that it was Ramadan, the month when the daylight hours must be spent fasting. Gopal, looking disconcerted, said he had forgotten. Musa, impatient for this interruption to end, sat up and broke in as soon as he could.

'You think it is British policy that the Arabs should have self-rule?' He gave a laugh of derisive anger and threw himself back on his divan.

'Surely you know, Mrs Foster,' said Gopal, 'the British want power for the Africans? They say: "The Arabs are dead, the Africans not yet born." The British, who put down slavery, see the Africans as their children and so they have a pro-African policy.'

Musa, pulling a row of amber beads agitatedly this way and that between his fingers, asked: 'Why should the British make policy here? Why should they be here at all?'

The other boys hissed slightly at this discourtesy towards an English guest and Kristy laughed.

'I see no reason why they should be here. And no reason why the Arabs should be here, either.'

'We are here by right of conquest,' Musa said.

'I don't recognize that right.'

Musa, his head down, gave her a sidelong glance: 'Then, tell me, Mrs Foster, why are you here?'

'First, you tell me why the Africans are here.'

The young man looked down, abashed, and Gopal, perhaps feeling this question was too advanced, broke in to make peace: 'I wish, Mrs Foster, that you could meet Musa's sisters. They are so beautiful and they have been educated. So advanced is the family, that they are permitted to receive visits from men who are not relatives. *And*, you will scarcely believe it, when I had the privilege of meeting them, they were not veiled.'

Nimr said eagerly: 'I too.'

Khalil gave a splutter of laughter: 'As you said, you are Hindu and Nimr is Christian. You do not count.'

Gopal, again disconcerted, looked towards Musa who was smiling. Musa shrugged his shoulders: 'It is true you are not Moslem.'

Nimr had become very red and the others, sorry for his embarrassment, rallied him with jokes about his professed passion for Musa's younger sister. Khalil said daringly: 'You must be watchful, Musa, or Nimr may run away with her.'

Nimr, delighted, giggled wildly and, bending backwards and forwards, hid his face in his hands, crying: 'What would you do, Musa, what would you do?'

Musa answered sombrely: 'I would kill her.'

'And me,' Nimr insisted. 'Would you kill me?'

'I'm not sure. It may not be necessary.'

The Moslems, drawn together, argued whether or not convention would call for the death of Nimr. Kristy, having no part in the discussion, stared into the depths of the shop to see what was there. A skylight, cracked and very dirty, admitted a glimmer of blue light that fell on to a pile of carpets. The carpets covered most of the floor and the walls were hung with prayer-rugs and embroideries. Beyond this twilit area, there was a formless darkness that seemed to go on for ever.

She looked up and saw above her several dozen glass oil lamps, pink, mauve, green, yellow, blue, of different sizes, but all shaped like a cow's udder with the teats filled with oil.

When she looked back to the company, she noticed that Gopal was no longer with them. He returned a few minutes later carrying a pink water-lily which he presented to her. The young men applauded this gesture that suggested to them the end of politics and a change to the light-hearted gallantry proper to female company. Musa alone frowned and said: 'You bought that in the market? It was, I think, stolen from the Praslin.'

'Surely not,' said Kristy who was wondering what to do with the large, heavy flower.

'The servants steal all the time from the Praslin but,' he shrugged, 'what does it matter? It is an immoral place; and an insult to Al-Bustan. A hotel on two floors! Who ever heard of such a thing? This is how the English keep us poor. They may build their offices five floors high, but we! We are to stay close to

145

the ground. It is policy. They wish to keep us primitive.'

Now that Musa, their leading spirit, had broken the barrier of courtesy, the others felt free to criticize British rule. Khalil shouted: 'Why do they not develop the forest area? It is policy. Why do they say there are sea-snakes on the shore? Who has seen these snakes? It is policy. Why can we not have an airfield? It is policy.'

'Where would you put an airfield?'Kristy asked.

Zarbay, a slow, serious, bespectacled youth, answered her: 'It is a simple matter. You build on the sea.'

The others began excitedly to plan what they would do once the tourists could arrive in numbers: a Casino in the Residency, a hotel where the Chief Secretary now lived in seclusion. Khalil spoke the words 'high rise' and the others took them up with enthusiasm. Everything would be 'high rise' when they were free from the oppression of the British.

Their excitement, Kristy thought, was childish, yet they were not children. Their plans were day-dreams but what else had they on this small island, stagnating, they felt, under British rule.

She said: 'All this would cost money.'

'We have friends,' Musa said. 'We could find investors. Even now a rich man wishes to build hotels but the British obstruct him.'

'I suppose you mean Lomax?'

Gopal broke in now: 'Wait, wait. Soon the British must go and we will see.'

'What?' Musa scornfully asked: 'We shall see our island ruled by the blacks. Soon a black dictator will rise. The Arabs will be sent into exile and our women – my sisters, my beautiful sisters – will be married to old black men.'

Kristy laughed: 'I can't see that happening.'

Khalil shouted: 'Can't you? It is happening now. It has happened in Zanzibar. The Arab leaders have gone into exile and the girls were seized and given to old men. The beautiful city is deserted because everyone is afraid. That is life under African rule. That is what the British wish for us. Why should you hold power here? Your young people are dirty; they worship nothing; they are un-moral: they stand in the market-place and beg for hashish.'

146

'That is enough,' Gopal said firmly. 'You have forgotten that Mrs Foster is our guest.'

Khalil rose and looking towards Kristy but not at her, said soberly: 'I regret my rudeness.'

Musa, also making amends, got slowly to his feet and bowed: 'If Mrs Foster would visit my sisters, we would be honoured.'

'Why, that would be very nice,' Gopal delightedly patted Musa's arm though to Kristy the invitation sounded more sullen than contrite.

When the young men took themselves off, it was arranged that Kristy should visit the sisters that afternoon. Meanwhile, Gopal invited her to eat at the Bird of Paradise. 'A restaurant,' he said, 'that is singular for kebabs.'

Kristy had not intended to spend the day at the Medina but she agreed to everything, having little else to do. She was, she thought, becoming like the women she had despised, who, lacking initiative in life, were content to tag along after their men.

Gopal, mistaking her silence, as they crossed the market-place, said: 'Do not be cross with the boys, Mrs Foster. The Moslems, in Ramadan, get a little irritable. But let us forget these arguments about government and I will show you the northern suburbs. All the important people live up here. It is so high, when the north-east trades blow you can smell the sea.'

But not see it. When they were beyond the sûks, they came into lanes that were wider than the southern lanes but enclosed by higher walls. Turning a corner, they met a camel – the first camel of Kristy's life – led by a cameleer and carrying a howdah on its back. The camel was arrayed in a tasselled saddle-cloth and bells and the howdah, its curtains closed, was richly ornamented. The cameleer held a long stick which he used to keep the camel away from the walls and passers-by away from the camel. Kristy and Dr Gopal were required to press against the wall while the camel, planting its feet like suckers, went grunting past.

As its bells jangled away into the distance, Dr Gopal said respectfully: 'Ladies visiting.'

'Who do they visit?'

'Other ladies, of course.'

The lane ended at a river that came down from the mountain,

flowed a short way through the town and then, Gopal said, had been diverted to water the orchards. Here it was trammelled, like a canal, between the backs of houses. The restaurant, that had a balcony overhanging the water, was the only one that seemed to have use for it. The balcony was wired in and thickly screened with creepers. They went by a winding flight of stone steps cut between houses and entered a small, bare room that was both dining-room and kitchen. The proprietor was cooking kebabs over a charcoal fire and the heat was intense. Almost overcome by the smell of roasting meat, Kristy hurried out to the balcony.

'The sun is not too much?' Gopal asked: 'You are tired, Mrs Foster?'

'A little tired.'

Gopal was very concerned: 'You have walked too far but when we eat, you will feel better.'

Kristy realized she did not want to eat: she wanted to be back in her room at the Daisy. She no longer saw the day as a vacancy to be filled by any chance entertainment. She wanted to sleep. Sleep, it occurred to her, as the best pastime, the most desirable condition of life. Later, when she was too heavy to care, she would spend her days asleep. But now she had no chance to sleep. Gopal would not even let her stay in her chair but insisted that she come to the balcony rail and look at the river as it ran down through a hole in the city wall and rushed below them. He wanted her to appreciate the sight but in the hard light of midday, it looked to her shabby and over-exposed. Though the government did not permit the island rivers to be used as sewers or dumping places, here, away from official eyes, the water was full of household rubbish. Lifting her gaze from it, she looked up to the ridge and asked: 'Have you been to the other side of the island?'

'Oh, no, no, Mrs Foster. It is forbidden.'

'But why? No one seems able to tell us why.'

'I do not know why but there is, no doubt, a reason.'

'It is policy, as Musa says.'

Gopal laughed: 'Musa is a nice boy when you know him. In India we had the same problems so I feel happy to support and encourage such boys.'

'Is there no more to it than that?'

'Oh, no, no, no, no, no, Mrs Foster, no more than that. Except that I buy from their fathers. Many of the houses still have riches but the people want modern things. So they sell their old things to me.'

'At bargain prices, I suppose?'

They had returned to the table. Gopal rocked backwards and forwards in his chair, laughing till his eyes ran with tears: 'Oh, Mrs Foster, you are a very clever lady. It is true, I make bargains but, then, I must too find buyers. I take a risk, you see.'

'But you are employed by the government. Why do you need to keep a shop?'

'I had my shop before I entered government service. I am fond of the things I buy. I have my lodging above and my friends come, as you saw today. The shop is their meeting-place.'

'And the business gives you an excuse for associating with them?'

Gopal put a hand over Kristy's hand and, laughing, squeezed it. When he stopped laughing, she said: 'Tell me one thing: why did you and Lomax and that disgusting creature Gurgur go off by yourselves when we had the picnic?'

Gopal reflected on the question before replying: 'It is no secret. Lomax wants to develop that area, and Musa's family would be glad to sell the land, but they are all frustrated by the reactionary policies of the government. Lomax will not buy if he is not permitted to build. Are you surprised that the boy feels discontent?'

'I am on the side of the government in this, but I'm afraid when the island gets independence, development will be inevitable.'

'Yes, but when will this independence come? The people talk of it but do they want it? They are afraid, not knowing how it will be. The British, for their own ends, support black rule here but the blacks are lazy. They live only for the day and expect the fruits to fall into their mouths. The Arabs, too, they talk and dream. So,' Gopal threw out his hands in a gesture of hopelessness, 'what will happen here?'

'And the Indians?'

'The Indians work but they do not seek to rule.'

The proprietor came out with coffee and as Kristy glanced towards him, she noticed that Simon Hobhouse was at the table immediately inside the room. The sight of him gave her an irrational sense of shock. Feeling that Hobhouse did not like her, she had decided she did not like him. He must certainly have seen her with Gopal. Now, as he made a decided pretence of not seeing her, she seemed to feel disapproval come from him.

Gopal, following her gaze, also saw Hobhouse and assuming the tone of the born intriguer, he quietly asked: 'Do you know that man? Is he a friend of your husband? Your husband is aware, of course, that you came to visit me?'

'No. I forgot to mention it.'

'Oh, Mrs Foster, this is very bad!' Gopal, growing red, shifted about in alarm: 'Before this man can go to him and make trouble, I must go to your husband and explain, I think?'

'For goodness' sake! It is not necessary and he would be embarrassed. It is of no importance. He does not object to my having meals with my friends.'

Gopal was not reassured. He had noted her reaction to the sight of Simon Hobhouse and nothing would convince him that she had not suffered a shock of fear and guilt. Gazing anxiously at her, he leant forward to whisper: 'What would your husband do? He would not try to kill me?'

'Don't be ridiculous. He simply would not care. I am free to do what I like, within reason.'

Her very protestations seemed to unnerve Gopal who lost all his self-assertive loquacity and now only wanted to pay the bill and go.

Kristy was depressed, feeling the air infected by misunderstanding. In better times, she might have spoken to Simon, introduced Gopal and put everything right with a few words. Now she had not the spirit to break through Simon Hobhouse's ostentatious incuriosity: she simply did not feel well enough. She could not swallow the coffee, which was like bile in her throat, and the rush of water beneath the balcony sounded ominous. Like Gopal, she wanted to escape from the situation.

As they left, Gopal gave Hobhouse a rapid glance but Hobhouse, who had opened a book, saw nothing and no one.

Outside, Gopal said in a half-whisper: 'I think that man did not see you at all.'

Bored with the subject, Kristy said: 'I don't think he did.'

'You understand, Mrs Foster, personally I favour a social freedom but here the world is very small. Often I think it is too small for me. One day, perhaps, I shall open a shop in London and you,' he paused and laughed, 'you will introduce me to your important friends, eh?' He was suddenly diverted from this theme: 'Mrs Foster, you have left your lotus behind.'

'I'm sorry. Do you want to go back for it?'

Gopal did not want to go back but he sighed heavily two or three times as they took the steep lanes to the north-west of the city where, contained within the city walls, stood the Abubakr summer palace. The estate was hidden behind a very high wall that was incised with geometrical patterns. When Kristy stopped to admire the patterns, Gopal dismissed them as journeymen's work.

'All the richness is inside but we, I fear, will see only the ladies' reception court.'

They passed the great iron-bound gates of the palace and went on to a small gate where a grille was opened and an old suspicious eye looked out on them. The woman argued for several minutes before she could be persuaded to open the door. When she did open it, she looked blackly at them and strutted angrily ahead of them as they crossed the courtyard.

Gopal murmured: 'She is very strict. She thinks that by admitting such a one as myself, a mere Hindu, the ladies are too free.' He made some facetious remarks in Arabic to show Kristy that he did not take his treatment seriously, but the woman was sternly silent.

The whole courtyard was scented with jasmine and citrus blossom. The area, a very large area, was tiled in blue and white with here and there beds for flowers and the citrus trees that were hung with green limes. In the centre there was a small revolving platform intended, Gopal explained, for female musicians who came to perform here.

They were led towards a pavilion, the front of which was open to the courtyard but shaded by the overhang of the roof. Set in the pavilion floor there was a fountain and Gopal, taking advantage of the splashing water, whispered a warning: 'You understand, the sisters are beautiful?'

'That fact has been conveyed to me.'

The woman waved them to the divans that stood round the fountain and left by the door at the back of the pavilion.

The pavilion, like the music stand, was decorated in red and gold, its walls closely stencilled with strings of flowers small enough to escape the Prophet's proscription against living models. Gopal, as though overwhelmed by the imminence of the sisters, had lapsed into silence. He and Kristy sat listening to the pitter of the fountain and the occasional growl of a bee that found its way in, panicked, and then found its way out again. To Kristy it seemed they were kept waiting an unconscionable time.

She asked in a low voice: 'What do the sisters do all day?'

'Nothing.'

'I suppose they will soon be married?'

'Not they. They are too noble. Who would be worthy of them?'

A delicate rustling was heard at last. The door opened and the sisters entered. It was clear they saw their entrance as a condescension and an occasion but it was spoilt by Musa who, coming at their heels, threw himself down on a divan with an exaggerated air of boredom. He made no attempt to acknowledge the visitors but the sisters did all that courtesy required.

They smiled on Kristy, bowing slightly, and assured her that the house and everything in it was hers. Their manner of doing so was off-hand and when the greeting had been made, they sat down and carefully arranged their gauzy veils and robes as though preparing to pose for a photograph. When satisfied, they let their hands drop into their laps and, looking up, seemed to present their beauty for admiration.

And they were beautiful, Kristy agreed. They were the moon-faced beauties of Persian paintings but the face of the elder was becoming a little too full and showed the slight softening and fretting of a balloon that was slowly losing air.

The interval before they made their appearance had probably been spent on their faces: the pink of their cheeks was beautifully blended in, their eyes and lips were drawn with academic care, their long, centre-parted black hair shone like liquorice. As Gopal had promised, they were not veiled but each had on her shoulders a veil, transparent except for its gold embroidery, that could, at the first alarm, be pulled across the face. They wore green, the colour reserved for descendants of the Prophet, and their hands, lying idle before them, had the glowing whiteness of lilies on grass.

How sad that this beauty could not last! Uncertain how much English they knew, Kristy said to Gopal: 'Tell them that I think they are very beautiful.'

Repeating the message, Gopal spoke in English and the elder girl bowed her head in acknowledgement.

She said: 'Thank you,' as one who well knew that she was beautiful and both of the girls seemed pleased that the interview was going as it should. Then Gopal, in his ebullient way, said the unexpected:

'And Mrs Foster – she, too, is beautiful, don't you think?'

The sisters were startled but giving Kristy a glance, they politely agreed: 'Yes, she is beautiful.'

Gopal beamed his congratulations on Kristy, who said: 'I was asking Dr Gopal what you do all day.'

Musa, lying prone on his stomach, his chin on his arms, buried his face and sniggered. The sisters, shaken out of their composure, looked at each other as though baffled by the question. Kristy, realizing she would have to explain herself, said: 'I mean, do you play music or paint or do embroidery?'

Musa snuffled into his arms: 'A little of everything.'

The elder girl said, rather stiffly: 'We do many things. Yesterday, for instance, we made an excursion and visited our cousins.' She spoke rapidly to Gopal in Arabic and he told Kristy that the visit had been paid to the daughters of Yusef Pasha's brother who had a villa on the Abubakr estate. The ladies, of course, had been carried by haudaj.

'Do you never walk through the bazaars? For fun, I mean.'

The younger girl, speaking more slowly than her sister, asked: 'Why should it be fun? The bazaars are hot. They smell bad. There is too much noise.'

'Wouldn't it be an adventure?'

'An adventure?' the younger girl turned her puzzled glance on Gopal: 'What is this: "an adventure"?'

After he explained in Arabic, the elder girl told some story that caused him to raise his hands into the air in shocked astonishment. As he did so, his cuffs fell back and Kristy saw that he wore a gold chain tightly clasped round his arm, half-way between wrist and elbow. From the chain hung a small gold swastika, the insignia of the Jan Sangh.

When the story was ended, Gopal translated it for Kristy: 'A lady of high birth – but much spoiled, you understand, being the only child of her father – read of the freedom of ladies in Cairo and persuaded two of her friends to go with her, unveiled, into the bazaars. They suffered very much. The men jeered at them and encouraged the boys to throw stones at them.'

Kristy said: 'But this is monstrous! I hope they fought back.'

'The friends were too frightened and would not go again, but the girl, the leader one might call her, took her father's horse-whip and went out again. When the boys threw stones, she beat them.'

'How splendid!' Kristy laughed with delight at the girl's action but the sisters were displeased.

The elder said: 'It was scandalous. And no good came of it. The girl became ill with her nerves and, in the end, her father sent her to Beirut. She now attends the university.' The girls seemed to see attendance at the university as a well-deserved punishment for revolt.

'You feel you are happier as you are?' Kristy asked.

'We are happy,' the elder inclined her head in agreement. 'You must understand that Moslem ladies have privileges not known to English ladies. We are allowed to own our property and when we marry, we continue to own it. In England it is different, I think.'

Kristy laughed: 'No. In England it is the same. The old laws concerning married women's property were repealed a long time ago.'

'We have been told differently.'

'Then your informant was wrong.'

The sisters smiled their disbelief.

A safragi, led in by the old woman, brought coffee and sugared fruits for Kristy and Gopal. The Moslem ladies kept their eyes averted as the guests drank. When Gopal put down his cup, he

154

nodded to Kristy and she knew it was time to go. As she rose, the sisters made a slight demur but they rose with her and Musa at once swung himself off the divan. The audience was over. The girls said good-bye with regal nods and retired through the door at the back. Musa came with Kristy and Gopal to the gate then they all stood and waited till the old woman arrived to open it.

On the way back to the market square, Gopal said: 'I can tell you, Mrs Foster, it is not often they say so much to a visitor. You stirred them. You were, as they say in your newspapers, controversial. They will be discussing your ideas for months.'

'It depresses me to think they have so little to discuss.'

'Oh, why be depressed? As I said to you, ladies are fortunate. They have all they want. They are secure and treasured.'

'The treasured heart of an unreal world.'

'Ah, you are witty, Mrs Foster, and for myself, I agree you are right. This world is unreal. It is at a standstill. The Arabs here are behind the times and only the young, like Musa and Khalil, have advanced ideas.'

'Musa said he would kill his sister if she went off with Nimr. I did not find that idea very advanced.'

'But he would not wish to, you understand? His relatives would force him to do it. There you see the dilemma of these advanced young men.'

'Yes. I want to ask you, Dr Gopal, why do you wear the insignia of the Jan Sangh party? I noticed it when you raised your arms.'

'Oh, Mrs Foster, nothing is hidden from you.'

'I don't believe that any party, any political party that is, exists without a desire for power; yet you encourage Musa and his friends to see power here as an Arab right.'

'But the Jan Sangh is not political, I assure you. It seeks only to remind us of our ancient cultures.'

'Then why keep your swastika out of sight?'

'Oh, dear me, Mrs Foster, you look into my soul. I wear it out of sight to save dissensions. But I will not deceive you. It has come into my head at times that what is needed here is one who would hold a balance of power. Neither Arab nor African. An outsider, you may say. Why not an Indian? But if I assumed this responsibility, what would happen? They would be jealous because I am too clever and someone would kill me. Then what would we have? Chaos. Better, perhaps, for the British to stay. Their backs are broad. They can take the blame for everything and no one cares.'

Coming out into the open square, Gopal became uneasy, as though Simon Hobhouse or some other informant were likely to see him with Kristy. Yet he felt responsible for her and said he must walk with her to the plantations. His unease worried her, so she felt him like some tacky substance of which she could not rid herself. When they reached the south side of the market, she said firmly: 'Now I can go alone.'

He looked both worried and relieved by her determination and let her go. Having shaken him off, she hurried through the lanes, feeling the resilient lightness of her own company. Gopal had made her promise to visit the shop again but it was a promise she did not expect to keep. This, she thought, was the last outing of her freedom, her last venture before she was too dull and lethargic to go anywhere.

Her habit of freedom was such that she was astonished when, in the darkness of the lanes, she was seized from behind in a strong grip and a body was pressed against her. She felt the man's genitals through the thin material of her dress. A rapid assault. She had no time to apply Mrs Gunner's formula before the man was gone. She swung angrily round but only saw him for an instant, a shadow scuttling away between the walls. Her anger passed and she realized she was frightened. But why? No harm had been done. She had been held by a poor, frustrated wretch of the safragi class who had fled, more agitated than she was by his action. Yet she was shaken. She had seen herself as invulnerable and now it was plain she was not. She was no longer a self-contained unit that existed according to its own will. She had been invaded and now, inside her, there was another unit. This fact had so jolted her confidence that she felt anything might happen. It occurred to her that here, alone, in these dark and narrow lanes, she could be robbed or raped. She was not safe. She started to run and went on running till she reached the open, sunlit air on the other side of the city wall.

2

Returning that evening, Hugh found Kristy lying on the bed. When he switched on the light and pulled down the bamboo screens, she lifted her head and looked at him from smudged, wet, swollen eyes. She sat up, looking so tragic and despairing that he was alarmed.

'Are you ill?'

'I'm pregnant.'

He did not speak but went to the bathroom. Turning on the washbasin tap, he let it flow until the water ran cold. He was irritated, chiefly because Kristy, by nature self-reliant, had sunk into this helpless state. He held his hands under the tap until his resentment subsided then he went calmly into the room.

'Don't worry,' he said. 'It's not the end of the world. I'll try and get an advance on salary and a few days' leave. We can fly to Durban and get you fixed up.'

'It's no good. It's too late.' Speaking in a lifeless voice, she described her visit to Mrs Gunner: 'She says it's too late.'

'But you must have known weeks ago. Why did you leave it so long?'

'I thought it would come all right. Anyway, I didn't know what to do. I've no friends . . . no one I could speak to.'

'What about me? Why didn't you tell me?'

'You're the last person I'd go to for sympathy.'

'Sympathy? What's sympathy got to do with it? The situation calls for action. Unless . . .' he stopped and stared accusingly at her: 'You knew – but didn't want to be sure till it was too late. Consciously or unconsciously, you *knew* and did nothing because you wanted to keep it.'

'No.' She shook her head but he was not impressed.

157

'And now,' he said, 'you're all upset. It's an act, to disarm me.'

'No.' She drooped on the bed, looking, with the smudges under her eyes, like some frightened animal at bay. He realized she was frightened of him and he felt ashamed, recognizing the unnaturalness of his own behaviour. As he stood without moving, she asked:

'What are you thinking?'

The dinner-bell rang and, turning petulantly from her, he went to the drawer for a clean shirt, saying: 'I'm not thinking. You'd better wash your face.'

His tone roused her and she said: 'You're afraid to think. It's your bloody mother again. Did anyone else ever have a mother who deserted her child because a worthless husband had found another bird. Hadn't she any idea what she was doing to you?'

'Your remarks are obscene.' He was trembling so violently, he could not do up his shirt buttons. He let them go for the moment and picked up his hair-brush. Recovering, he said sharply: 'And how did you get the facts so neatly lined up? I told you nothing. I suppose you went to my father, or my ghastly step-mother: two people I haven't spoken to since I left home. I don't even know if they're alive or dead, yet you tracked them down and talked about me behind my back.'

'I've never met either of them.' She went into the bathroom and when she came out, he was ready to go down to dinner.

Now that the cooler season was established, the garden tent had been dismantled and meals were served in a room that had once been a coach-house. It was white-washed and had still the spare, raw look of an outbuilding.

Hugh, at table, was sufficiently himself to ask in a low voice: 'Well, where did you get that information about my mother?'

'From your school-friend, Meaker. If you remember, he introduced us.'

'And he talked about me?'

'Everyone talks about everyone. You know that.'

Having approached the subject as closely as he had ever done, Hugh retreated into silence. Watching his shut, pale face, Kristy knew that had she written and published the suicide novel, it would have been the end for them. Once she would not have thought this mattered but now? – could she afford a break-up? There was a story lost. She had always been impatient of considerations that hampered her work, and now she was hampered as she had never been hampered before. 'I'm hobbled,' she thought, 'I'm caught by the foot' and she could have wept before the whole bloody pension.

Towards the end of the meal, Hugh spoke in a coldly level voice: 'I suppose you know you'll have to go home? English infants don't thrive in this climate. I'll have to see if I can get my contract extended. I might get a semi-permanent post at a reduced salary.'

'You're certainly making heavy weather of all this. The film business will pick up again. Why shouldn't you go back to writing scripts?'

'Because, whatever happens, the good days are over. It would be too precarious. We'll need a regular salary. *And . . .*' he lost control and his tone became anguished. 'I don't want to go back. I *had* hoped, if we managed to save while here, that I would have a few months for creative writing. This is the end of that.'

'I'd no idea you had this in mind. If you feel you can write another novel, why not write it here and now. You've plenty of time.'

'I haven't plenty of time. And I've the nagging responsibility of another job. No one could write under these conditions, as you'll find out yourself when you're a mother. Motherhood's a pretty demanding job.'

'Why are you being so bloody minded?' Kristy's voice rose and Hugh became conscious of the listening silence about them: 'Anyone might think you'd nothing to do with this. Good God, you've always had my cunt when you wanted it.'

The listeners stirred. Hugh let out his breath and whispered: 'Be quiet.'

'Oh, to hell with this lot.'

Sullenly, in a state of mutual hatred, the Fosters went into the salon, and saw Simon Hobhouse sitting near the bar. He had been waiting for Hugh and gave a delighted laugh at the sight of him. Hugh expressed equal delight. Stretching out his hands in welcome, he hurried away from Kristy and joined Simon. Holding to each other, the pair laughed with pleasure. To Kristy they appeared jubilant. It was like a meeting of lovers.

She remained at the back of the room where she and Hugh usually sat, wondering if Gopal had been right and Hobhouse had indeed come to inform on her. Watching them as they sat talking together, she saw that, whatever they were saying, she had no part in it. They were rejoicing in each other, a male co-operative designed to exclude her and all other females.

She knew that exclusion. She had experienced it more than once during her married life. Hugh had what she called 'a trick' of picking up men who, for a while, became heroes to him, and using them as a shield against her. She suddenly felt a bitter anger that she had been foolish enough to marry against her own instinct. She had been told the suicide story. Meaker had warned her that Hugh was not the mild, kindly, uncomplicated man that he seemed. Beneath that gentle manner, those golden benign looks, he was, in fact, one of the deranged.

Hugh had told her she would have to return to England, so why not have the child there? – and keep it as her own? With the illuminating joy of discovery, she saw the child as a creature belonging only to her: her unique responsibility.

Simon, reaching out to catch Hugh's hands, said: 'So there you are!' as though a search had been concluded. When they sat down, he was grinning at what he had come to relate.

'I got back yesterday,' he said, 'and you'll scarcely believe what I found awaiting me: a communication. From whom do you think? No less a person than your august boss, Sir George Easterbrook. Let me read it to you.' Simon opened a brief-case that was beside him in the chair, and took out an official letter. Gleefully, he handed it to Hugh. Reading it, Hugh was less than gleeful. It was a request that Dr Hobhouse's pass to the Forest Area be returned for possible renewal.

'Possible renewal!' Simon gulped his laughter at the thought of it: 'Once your chaps get their hands on it, I'll never see it again.'

'But if it's not renewed, it will be invalid.'

'That doesn't matter. Most of the police have only the vaguest idea what they're looking at. They have a smattering of English and can recognize an official stamp, but they couldn't check the date on a pass. And no one's greatly concerned to catch me: I'm not important enough. To tell you the truth, when the Land-Rover's not loaded up, I can go cross-country; but, taking my camping stuff over, I thought it wiser to go by road. The thing could overturn on rough grass. But you haven't seen all.' Simon returned to the brief-case and brought out a written note. Hugh recognized Pedley's handwriting. 'This,' Simon said, 'was slipped into the envelope, probably unknown to Easterbrook. Still, I'll take it as official.'

Pedley's note read: 'You were a typical rat, Hobhouse, taking advantage of a new employee. I won't talk to you about playing the game, you wouldn't know what I meant. But if I see you around, I'll tell you exactly what I think of you.'

'Here is my reply.'

Simon, rejoicing in his own composition, watched Hugh as he read: 'Dear Sir George, It has long been my belief that the official mind is puerile, limited and vulgar. This belief has been confirmed by your assistant, Pedley, who states that I took advantage of a new employee. The officials on Al-Bustan are known to be the throw-outs of the Diplomatic Service. The fact that you, yourself, regarded a knighthood as fitting reward for fifteen years wasted in Jumblijah (better known as the 'Arsehole of Asia'), tells me all I need to know of your moral values . . .'

Leaning over Hugh, Simon ran a finger under this last sentence: 'Particularly rich, don't you think?'

'You haven't sent it, I hope?'

'Certainly I've sent it. I dropped it into the office on my way down. Old George's probably brooding on it now. I must say, I think he won't much like it.'

Making an effort to steady himself, Hugh read the letter through again and found it more alarming than he had at first. Why had this happened now, when freedom of action had been filched from him?

'Don't you think it's rather harsh? Couldn't you ring him tomorrow and say you meant it as a joke? The trouble is, my wife's just told me she's going to have a baby. I'll have to find some sort of permanent job and I was meaning to approach Sir George and . . .'

Simon threw back his head to laugh: 'You can't be serious. No intelligent person could settle into this fossilized service. These people are relics. They're like those Japanese soldiers they found in the jungle, still fighting the war. They still think the empire exists. They still believe in the inalienable superiority of the British race. Do you want to become one of them? For, you would. In a few years you'd be as solidly stuck in here as a currant in a suet pudding. No, my dear fellow, don't consider it. It's bad enough living here as a private person. Nothing would induce me to stay if I were not doing my bit of research.'

'On the Pteridophyta?'

'Hah!' Simon laughed again: 'And not a bad subject, either. Ferns are among the oldest life-forms on this planet. And, what's more, some of them could harbour another form, as ancient but much more deadly.' He emptied his glass and refused Hugh's offer of another drink. Surveying the people about him with tolerant contempt, he said: 'Talking of life-forms: we have them here in brutish variety. There's that old fool, Simpson. What does he look like? A monstrous flea. Puce is the word.' Simon sat upright, animated by this new topic: 'The flea! Yes, indeed! We could be due for another killer as all-pervasive as the plague.'

'Where could it come from? Outer space?'

'Who knows. It could be hibernating in some unexplored corner of the earth, some fragment of primitive forest, and carried by a creature so small, no one has noticed it.'

'A new virus?'

'Not necessarily a virus, but probably: a disease as contagious as smallpox, as virulent as plague, coming newly into a world without inherited immunity and no present knowledge. It would take time to isolate. Before being isolated, it could bring human numbers down at a very satisfactory speed.'

Disturbed by the hard sapphire of Simon's eye, the grin inside the black beard, Hugh said fretfully: 'You've wrecked my chances with Sir George. The least you can do, is tell me what you're talking about.'

'Perhaps I will. But another time. I promise: when and if I have something to tell you, you'll be the first to hear of it.'

*

Mrs Axelrod and Mrs Prince, on their sofa, with their backs to Kristy, were keeping an eye on Simon Hobhouse. Mrs Axelrod said: 'What do you think he's doing here? He's a doctor, you know. I wouldn't be surprised . . .' Before saying more, she took the precaution of glancing behind her. The sight of Kristy brought her to so abrupt a stop, Kristy felt a sense of triumph. Head high, she walked round the sofa to the staircase and took herself to bed.

'How about strolling up the hill with me?' Simon said. He and Hugh were about to get to their feet when Ambrose came towards them.

Simon, ironically pleasant, said: 'Why, Ambrose, happy to see you. You've been avoiding me.'

Ambrose lifted his hand and struck Simon across the face. The blow sounded through the room and the guests were startled. Some of the men stood up to see what had occurred.

Putting his hand to his cheek, Simon said: 'Really, Ambrose! That was a bit rough.'

'Why did you do that?' Hugh asked but it was obvious that Ambrose, standing in front of them, rocking slightly on his heels, did not know why he had done it. His eyes were glazed as though he had just wakened from sleep while remarks like 'Quite un-called-for' and 'Disgusting behaviour' were being directed at him by Ogden and others.

The telephone rang in the office and he hurried to it, escaping his self-made predicament. Almost at once, he put the receiver down and called Hassan from the bar: 'To the Harbour. Get a taxi. *Halan. Asra.*'

Hassan took to his heels. Ambrose, standing just inside the salon, looked like a sleepwalker that had lost sense of direction. The guests, diverted by his strange appearance, watched him while Simon, getting no sympathy now, smiled ruefully, and rubbed his cheek.

There was a long, silent pause before Hassan came back, breathless with anxiety, shouting: 'Taxi, *sayyid*, taxi,' and Ambrose, moving his arms as though against a hostile crowd, trotted out through the front door.

3

Mrs Gunner was dead before Ambrose reached the hospital. The matron, called from her bed, received him with the eager interest that she bestowed on other people's misfortunes. His mother, she said, had had a second heart attack. She had rung her bell but was unconscious before the nurse could reach her.

There were formalities that had to be got through with all possible speed. Moving close to Ambrose, the matron murmured: 'The humidity, you know. Much worse than the heat.' He stepped back from her, catching in her breath intimations of a more imminent decay.

Dr Dixon had been called to sign the death certificate. The funeral must follow without delay.

Ambrose, taken up to the half-lit corridor of the women's floor, was shown into his mother's room. The matron, making the most of the importance conferred on her by such events, hung about until Ambrose indicated that he would like to be alone.

Mrs Gunner lay under a sheet. When Ambrose uncovered her face, he saw she was smiling her old, mischievous smile. A coffin had already arrived from government stores. It stood upright, opposite Ambrose: a flimsy box without fittings, small like a child's coffin.

Hearing the orderlies whispering and shuffling outside the door, he tried to think of some suitable word of farewell. Constricted by the need for haste, he muttered crossly: 'You mean old bitch, I loved you.' He bent and kissed her brow, feeling it beneath his lips as cold and hard as a waxen apple. He thought he could have bitten into it and appalled and revolted by such an idea, he knew it would haunt him for weeks to come.

He opened the door and found four down-at-heel Arabs

waiting, two old women to lay out the body and two men to lift it. They looked at him, expectant, their eyes bright with sympathy, and as he left the room, they entered and closed the door.

Dr Dixon was sitting at the table in the corridor, the death certificate in front of him. His heavy old face, inflamed by long devotion to the bottle, had settled into folds of grief. When he lifted his eyes, Ambrose saw they were full of tears.

'Knew her for thirty years or more,' said Dixon. 'I'll miss her. We'll all miss her. She was a gallant girl.' The matron, at his elbow, murmured agreement.

Ambrose was touched but, at the same time, with preternatural clarity saw that the matron's face-powder, hastily thrown on for the doctor's visit, had drifted like snow in the runnels on each side of her nose.

Her voice, more than usually lady-like, snivelled at him: 'Sit down, please, Mr Gunner. Things won't take long.'

The doctor and matron went downstairs and Ambrose was left in the meaningless width of the corridor. The building was silent, held in the stillness of sleep. Ambrose, putting out antennae of hearing, listened for any sound that might come from his mother's room. He heard nothing. The doors to the balcony stood open and when he went out, he was met by the scent of the night-blooming cereus in the Residency garden. He sat on the day bed, that had been stripped of its cushions, and looked over the reaches of darkness, breathing in a sweetness too luscious for common life. His surroundings enhanced the strangeness of his situation.

He remembered he had a hip-flask on him. With some pre-science of this very night, he had filled it that morning with his mother's best brandy. He put the flask to his lips, then gazed mournfully over the scene before him.

The misted sky gave no light and there was no light in the Residency, but the great garden sparked with the movement of fire-flies. Beyond the lawn edge, there was refulgence: the Chief Secretary was entertaining. The sea, too, had a gloss, like the sheen on satin, for it was the season when phosphorescent animalcules drifted about in shoals.

The scene distracted him from his present state. He closed his eyes, took another swig of brandy, and sought in himself some adequate emotion: sorrow, regret, a sense of loss. All he could feel was a desolate consciousness of his own loneliness in the world.

What would become of him now? His mother had, often enough, let him know he would get none of her money. He had waited for months on Lomax without result. But Lomax and his mother were only the last of those who had failed him. Looking back over his wives, lovers and friends, he nailed each name with a word: tart, bitch, skivvy, serf, scrounger, creep, Judas, twister, pervert, vulgarian, ponce. What a crew! And yet, if he could return to them, he would. Al-Bustan might be paradise but the Fulham Road was home.

He wondered if, perhaps, she had left him something after all. Some little thing: just enough to fly him back to England with a bit over so he could settle back into the routine of London life! A thousand would do it.

Bemused by brandy, he could not understand why he had had to stay here so long, then it came back to him. He was what the law did not allow; a double bankrupt. But that was not the only hindrance to his return. If he reappeared in his old haunts, he would be let in for such a round of explanations, apologies, re-payments of loans and settlement of debts, he would be beggared in a week. And money was only the half of it. His friends had turned against him. He brooded on his own tragedy. He had been thrown out of the autarkical literary half-world to which he, a man of genuine talents, had given distinction. There was in-gratitude for you. All because he had sometimes knocked down the wrong person.

Swallowing the brandy, suffering again the injustice done to him, his indignation was roused. He remembered those last days when, oversensitive to criticism, too honest of speech, he refused to be rejected by a bunch of sharks, duns, bums, catchpolls. . . . (He ran out of words.) If he were not invited to a party, he went uninvited. There had come a time when not only old friends but mere outsiders – inglorious ingrates, groundlings, mental paupers, intellectual scavengers – had had the effrontery to turn him out of some wretched bun-fight. In the end, he had even been ejected from a party at Putney. *Putney!*

If he were forced out of the Daisy now, where on earth would he go? He had once thought of entering a monastery in some warm, wine-drinking country. He thought of it now. He had seen Franciscans begging around the cafés in Florence and thought they had an easy time of it. Comforted by this solution of his plight, he finished the brandy.

When a nurse came for him, he went down to the hall and demanded to see the matron. She appeared, all sympathy, and found him in a state of lofty belligerency.

He said: 'I must get in touch, *at once*, with Father Matthew at the Mission. My mother was of the True Faith and he must be informed of her demise.'

The matron, a church-goer, stared at him in astonishment: 'You must be mistaken, Mr Gunner. Your mother was a regular communicant at St George's.'

'She was merely being tactful. We Gunners are an old Catholic family. I must ask you to let me use the telephone. It is essential I contact Father Matthew.'

'It's late. It's after midnight.' Displeased, the matron put him into the porter's lodge and left him alone to search through the greasy telephone directory.

The Mission telephone rang a long time before a high, frightened female voice answered him. He shouted: 'Bring Father Matthew to the phone. It's a matter of great urgency.'

'That not possible. Father Matthew fast asleep. He got early mass in morning.'

'Wake him at once. His help is needed. Tell him it's a soul in torment.'

There was a protracted silence then the woman – 'Bloody Christian Arab,' Ambrose said in an audible murmur – replied 'All right. I go.' He heard her shuffling away. After another interval Father Matthew, as nervous as his housekeeper, was brought to the telephone.

'You're not one of my flock, are you?' he asked.

Exasperated by these quibbling delays, Ambrose said: 'No, but I've decided to embrace Catholicism. I wish to make a full confession and a firm purpose of amendment.'

'Oh!' Father Matthew seemed very relieved: 'There's no hurry for that. Come up tomorrow morning and we'll have a chat about it.'

'You are to come here now. I demand it. There was a time when we Gunners had our private chaplain who could be called on at any hour of the day or night.'

Father Matthew made no comment. Ambrose shouted: 'Are you listening, you old hypocrite?' His question was met by silence. He threw back the receiver and dialled the Mission again. He got the engaged signal.

The Reverend Pierce entered the hospital door, come to claim his own.

The matron, looking in on Ambrose, said sternly: 'Mr Gunner, they're waiting to screw the lid down.'

The coffin was on a table in the hall. Ambrose gave up the Mission and went to see the last of his mother. She was dressed in the sequinned trousers and jerkin which she had been wearing when she was brought into the hospital. Her little, brown withered hands were crossed on her breast, her little red shoes pointed upwards. The smile had gone somewhat awry. Ambrose, sobered, noted the change in her and knew there was no time to lose.

Only two orderlies were needed to carry the coffin to the grave-yard. The porter, holding a paraffin flare, led the procession and Ambrose and the Reverend Pierce walked behind, the matron and two nurses bringing up the rear. Dr Dixon, despite his tears, had excused himself and gone home to bed.

Ambrose did not like Pierce, chiefly because the clergyman carried about him the reek of a foul tobacco pipe and felt offended that he had to tolerate the company of this man on so solemn an occasion.

As soon as the procession entered the damp, leaf-crowded atmosphere of the cemetery, it was assailed by insects of every sort. Driven mad by the brilliant, streaming flambeau, they dived through the flame and, sizzling, struck the light-reflecting faces of the mourners then, half-incinerated, fell to the ground. As the procession went slowly through a stench of burnt insects, Ambrose thought it as well that Kristy was not here to suffer with them. Nocturnal animals, alarmed by the invasion, screeched, chattered and hooted among the trees. They had some difficulty getting the coffin round the sausage tree which had grown enormously since Ambrose had seen it first thirty years ago. All the way, the girls who had nursed Mrs Gunner, an Arab and a negress, sobbed and wailed, putting Ambrose to shame.

The light touched ancient gravestones throttled by weeds. There were few new graves. These days people were not snuffed out as they used to be. When threatened by some mortal condition, they usually had time to fly home for treatment.

Half-way down the path, there was a roundpoint with an obelisk commemorating the officers and men of the brigantine *Hester Gracey* that, in 1765, had put into Al-Bustan harbour flying the yellow jack. No one would go near the ship but when it was assumed that all on board were dead, the harbour officials, mouths and nostrils covered, rowed out and fired it.

On reaching the obelisk, the Reverend Pierce began the burial service. At the end of the path, a dozen or so acetylene lamps hung on the walls and the grave-diggers, who must have gone out at once on news of Mrs Gunner's death, stood in a group awaiting the dead. They had not only dug the grave, but had cleared away the maidenhair and thorn-apple so the mourners would have space to stand. When they had helped the orderlies to lower the coffin, they drew back into the shadows, courteously inconspicuous, to watch the proceedings.

Listening to Pierce's monotonous mumble, Ambrose thought: 'He believes none of it.' His father's stone – an angel pointing the way to heaven – stood near by and he remembered that Mrs Hampton, whose own husband lay under a plain slab, was said to have made fun of it. It had been his mother's choice and if he added her name to it, it would save the cost of another.

Sniffing the dawn, the Reverend Pierce speeded things up. Having said: '. . . in sure and certain hope of the Resurrection to eternal life', he gabbled through the Collect. He explained to Ambrose that he would have to hasten away because he was prone to stomach chills.

Ambrose said: 'I would have preferred Father Matthew to conduct the burial.'

'But your mother was one of my congregation.'

'Her heart was elsewhere.'

Wounded, the Reverend Pierce went off, taking the women with him, and Ambrose, left alone, saw the sky break and dawn roll out in furbelows of violet and wine red. The graveyard that had been dark, quickly became over-light, the tombs and trees and weeds standing out with shocking clarity.

The grave-diggers, downcast like men called on to perform a distasteful act, waited for Ambrose to follow the others. He decided to stay. Motioning them to continue their work, he watched as the earth fell on the paltry coffin and was troubled. Surely they could have found her something better!

Someone had told him that the cemetery had been put up here because the site was away from the river and the land-crabs. But land-crabs were not the only predators on human flesh. As the grave filled, Ambrose saw an army of red ants marching out of the weeds and moving purposefully towards the broken earth. The leaders disappeared into the grave and the others followed in formation. Ambrose, enraged, made to stamp on the column but as he moved, he saw another army of ants advancing from the other side, then a third army and a fourth. The clearing was a-shimmer with ants. Uncountable numbers of them were pouring into the grave.

Standing helpless against them, Ambrose watched the certainty with which they made their way underground. The grave-diggers, who were putting out their lamps and knocking the earth off their spades, noticed him with concern. Smiling apologetically, one of them, an old man, said:

'*Hadhihi iradatu'llah.*'

Ambrose nodded. Yes, it was the will of Allah. He felt in his pockets and found a few rupees which he distributed among the men who bowed and touched their brows and breasts. And that, he thought, was the end of that. In the face of penury, he felt a perverse satisfaction in having given away all he had. His satisfaction failed him when he saw his taxi under the eucalyptus trees. He had told the driver to wait for him and the driver had waited. He tried to slip by unseen but the man was on the alert.

There was only one thing for Ambrose to do. He would drive down to the Praslin and make his peace with Lomax.

4

For a week the Daisy had been in a state of delayed revolt. The splendid kaftans still hung in the closet but Akbar himself could not be found. The police had been asked to search for him, assure him he had done no wrong and would be welcomed back at the pension whenever he chose to return. There were about thirty pure-bred Nubians on the island, all much alike and each, when questioned, swore he was not Akbar. One of them, cornered in the Medina, said: 'Me no Akbar, me Akbar's brother Amin' and he promised to send Akbar back to the Daisy. But Amin, if he were Amin and not Akbar, did not produce Akbar and the guests continued to suffer Hassan's muddle-headed rule.

No one knew of Mrs Gunner's death till the church-goers saw the matron in church. The matron, giving out the sad news, added: 'You've no idea how strange Mr Gunner was,' and they listened, amazed by the story.

In the dining-room Mrs Axelrod, too excited to take off her church-going hat and nylon gloves, waited till everyone was seated before springing on to a chair and shouting: 'She's gone and that's the last straw. We've got to take action. We must have decent food and service. I vote,' she held up her arms, hands hanging as though broken at the wrist, and jumped up and down, 'I vote we send a round-robin. We'll tell Gunner we'll not pay our bills till things improve.'

Ogden broke in gravely: 'Mr Gunner has just lost his mother. I agree, we've been patient but we must be a little more patient. We must give him time to get over his loss.'

Everyone looked at Ambrose's vacant chair and Simpson asked: 'Where's he got to, anyway?'

'I expect,' Ogden said, 'he's shut himself in his mother's room to mourn. Let us respect his grief.'

Not much impressed by Ogden's plea, Mrs Axelrod said fiercely: 'O.K. We'll give him twenty-four hours to get over it, but we've got to have a discussion. It's service or else.'

She would have gone on but Axelrod, a stout, genial man younger than his wife, seized her from behind and lifted her off the chair, thus diverting her rage on to himself.

After luncheon – a deplorable meal of salt-fish with breadfruit sauce – there was a drift to the salon where the men sat silently, fearful of disturbing a mourning Ambrose; and the women, keeping well away from the door to Mrs Gunner's room, awaited Mrs Axelrod's directive. When she appeared, she led them into the Lettuce Room and closed the door. She could be seen talking vigorously inside.

The Fosters, out of all this, were preoccupied with their own affairs. Hugh, thinking Kristy unnaturally resigned to her condition, had telephoned Dr Mueller and, as he pressed the urgency of the matter, had been given an appointment for that very afternoon.

They set out at three o'clock. When they reached the square, they went left down a lane that overhung the cliff-face. The lane was planted with shade trees but the foliage seemed rather to keep in than exclude the afternoon heat that hung like a fog in the air. Though this expensive enclave was a residential stronghold of rich Moslems, Hindus and Jews like Dr Mueller, it seemed held in Sunday rest. No one sat in the flower gardens. There was quiet except for moments of flurry and panic, when the Fosters startled some brilliant bird.

Though the lane had levelled out, Hugh noticed that Kristy walked in a plodding way, like someone much heavier and older, and suspecting she was deliberately adopting the rôle of gravid female, he could scarcely hold in his exasperation. Her silence, too, seemed to him no ordinary silence but a broody lack of will to speak. When they reached Mueller's house, she paused beside the low front wall that held boxes of Cape primroses, claret, rose and rose-violet, and said: 'Yesterday, Mrs Gunner advised me to come and see Dr Mueller. Well, here I am and she is dead and buried.'

'It could happen to any of us,' Hugh impatiently said and taking her by the arm, he led her into Dr Mueller's compact, white house.

For the sake of his Moslem patients, Dr Mueller kept the curtains drawn in his waiting-room but when he saw Kristy, he laughed and said: 'No need for these precautions, eh?' He pulled the curtains and they opened to reveal the great vista of the Indian Ocean, almost colourless in the blazing afternoon, with the ships at anchor in the harbour, all straining towards the south-west.

Dr Mueller held out his arms towards Hugh and Kristy as though he would enfold them in his good-humoured vitality: 'Now, what's the problem?'

His manner reminded Kristy of Dr Gopal and though she had no particular trust in Gopal, she took to Mueller because he seemed already familiar. He was a thin, small man with a large head, large nose and thick, reddish, curling hair. He led her off to the surgery, patting her shoulder to encourage her. Used to the formality of English medical men, she was entertained by Mueller and felt at ease during the intimate, uncomfortable examination necessary to confirm pregnancy.

When it was over, he patted her abdomen and laughed: 'He is very happy in there, I think. And you are happy? That's good. You feel well? For you, I think, pregnancy is the ideal condition. If you were always pregnant, you would have no worries at all.' He laughed joyously at his idea of a permanent state of pregnancy and was still laughing when he returned her to the room where Hugh waited. Hugh moved forward, eager to hear that it was all a mistake. Instead, Mueller congratulated him, saying: 'You will become the father of a fine child.' Hugh, refusing to listen, interrupted to ask if the pregnancy could not be terminated.

'Do not think of it,' said Dr Mueller.

Hugh insisted: 'Supposing I flew my wife to Durban or Cape Town? There must be clinics where this could be put right, no matter how long it's been going on.'

Mueller patted Hugh as he had patted Kristy: 'Come now, Mr Foster, this will not do. You would not submit your wife to a dangerous operation? That would be cruel. And she would suffer in other ways. She would suffer mentally for such a deprivation.

But I do not think you are serious. Consider, rather, the joy of bringing up a family. Your wife is well and happy. Look at her! Would you take her child from her? No, I am sure you would not.' He put out his hand to Kristy and led her to the front door, saying to Hugh: 'She has fine health. She will do very well, I think.'

Outside again, committed to parenthood, Hugh had a sulky sense that he had been fooled. Kristy, looking down on the harbour, saw that during her spell in the surgery, the tide had changed and all the boats now strained towards the north-east. When she mentioned this to Hugh, he refused to look or reply but at the main road, he said: 'You'd better go back and rest. I want to walk to the Medina.'

'I'll come with you.'

He kept ahead of her all the way to the plantations. A delicate veil of smoke still hung over the sugar canes but the workers were elsewhere. The birds, too, had left the mango tree or were hidden in its foliage. Only the tree creeper was still clinging to the bark and moving upwards, catching food for its insatiable young. Kristy stopped to watch it and said in a tender voice: 'She's wonderful.'

'How do you know it's a female?'

'What else could it be?'

He realized she had come here only to look at the tree creeper. As she stood, hypnotized by the bird's movements, swaying a little, her smile ecstatic and sleepy, he pushed her crossly and said: 'Oh, come on.'

'Is there any hurry?'

He walked away from her and she came plodding after him. Remembering how Mueller had said: 'Your wife is well and happy', he was resentful, feeling she had lost one creative dimension only to find another. He knew his resentment was unjustified. It could be explained by nothing but envy, the cardinal sin he most disliked.

When she caught up with him, he said crossly: 'If you'd stayed in London, we wouldn't be in this fix. You could have written your book. *And* I wouldn't be stuck . . .' Stuck, it was in his mind, in the position of breadwinner, wasting his life so she could add to hers.

She said nothing but followed him through the lanes to the market square. He said: 'I'm going to see Simon Hobhouse.'

'I guessed that.'

'You don't want to come, do you?'

'Why not? I'd like to see how he lives.'

Leading the way up Simon's stairs, Hugh was discomposed, wondering how Simon would react when he saw Kristy. Till now, he had behaved as though she did not exist but he could scarcely keep that up when he came face to face with her in a small room.

Hugh need not have worried for Simon was too preoccupied to notice either of them. A naked youth lay on the bed, the lower half of his body covered with a towel. Hugh stopped, shocked and embarrassed until he realized he had walked in on a doctor–patient session. Simon was intent on his subject.

Kristy, unsure of her welcome, remained in the doorway while Hugh moved forward to say: 'Hello.' Simon, jerking round, greeted him as friend and comrade and called him over to the bed.

The boy, if he were a boy and not an old man, strained his eyes in Hugh's direction but remained otherwise motionless as though fearful of disaccommodating the doctor. He was a thin, small creature with one shoulder higher than the other. His face was sallow and flat, held in an expression of habitual suffering to which was now added the strain of a self-respecting person who is exposed before strangers. His clothes – the cheap dark Western suit which was the Sunday wear of the Christian Arab – hung on a chair. His shoes, shabby, the laces missing, stood beneath it.

Hugh murmured: 'Perhaps we should go?'

'Don't go. I have a very interesting case here. Rare, too. The mission has had no experience of it but I struck another in Sumatra once. Every time I come back, I take a look at him to see how the disease is progressing. Come closer.'

Hugh edged unwillingly towards the bed while Kristy was careful to remain beyond range of the boy's sight. She saw his eyelids flutter nervously as Simon threw back the towel and placed a hand on the boy's abdomen. Hugh, a worried frown on his face, was doing his best to show interest in what he neither liked nor understood. Simon, speaking as to a fellow practitioner, said:

175

'Polycystic disease. Kidneys as well as liver.' Simon removed his hand and motioned Hugh to palpate the abdomen himself: 'If you press there and there, you can detect the organic change.'

Not having the courage to refuse, Hugh did as he was told. As he put his hand on the boy's flesh, Kristy could see, even from the back of his head, his agony of distaste.

'I give him another couple of years,' Simon casually said.

Kristy, who pitied the poor doomed creature on the bed, was angry that this prognosis should be declared so openly. Then she realized the boy knew no English. He saw both men as doctors, savants, people apart, conversing, as they might in the Middle Ages, in a learned language he could not hope to understand.

Simon moved over to the window and Hugh followed him. As Simon discussed the case, Kristy, watching, saw that Hugh, giving his attention to Simon's face, movements, the solemnity of his voice, did not understand a word of it. Kristy, who wanted to know more about the boy, felt again the assertion of a relationship that excluded her. If Simon had noticed her, he did not want her to be there. He ignored her, as he always did. The men wanted to be alone to pursue their homogeneous understanding.

Very well, if they did not want her, she would go. She turned to go down the stairs and neither called after her. When she reached the sûk she looked up at the open window of Simon's room but no one was looking out to see where she had gone.

Not knowing what to do with herself, she wandered back to the market. She knew Hugh would expect to find her waiting somewhere near by, but she did not intend to wait. She had decided to return to the Daisy when she noticed Musa coming out of Gopal's shop. He hurried towards her, smiling meaningfully: 'How are you, Mrs Foster? Perhaps you are on your way to visit our friend, Dr Gopal? Alas, he is not here. He does not go very often to his office but it seems he has gone today.'

'I had no intention of visiting Dr Gopal. I advise you not to let your imagination run away with you.'

Musa's smile widened: 'Are you trying to shock me? I am not easily shocked. I know something about English freedom. I have other English friends.'

'So you mix in government circles?'

Musa burst out laughing: 'Government circles? Do you think I would have anything to do with such people? But you are a government lady, so you think the officials are the only English people here. You should come and meet my friends, Mrs Foster.'

'I'd be glad to.'

'Then let us go. I wonder what you will think of them!'

There was malice in Musa's smile and his tone suggested to her that he was teasing her or intended to play some trick on her. Going with him for lack of anything better to do, she went uneasily, noting how his manner had changed. In the company of the other young men, he had been aloof or angry but now there was something flirtatiously forward in his manner. She felt him giving her speculative, sidelong glances and when they entered the narrow sûks, he kept beside her and several times managed to touch her hand with his own. She was not much flattered, knowing that in a restrictive society, young men were easily overthrown. As well as that, Ambrose had told her that the example of the Praslin inmates had led the Arabs to suppose that every Caucasian, female or male, was available at a price. Still, Musa's looks attracted her. At another time, she might have responded to him but now she did not feel free to respond. There was another claim on her. She kept him at a distance by making fun of him:

'How is it you and the others are influenced by Gopal? What have you got in common?'

'He is our friend.'

'And fellow conspirator?'

'You are laughing, of course?' Musa's sidelong glance turned on her. His eyes were hard and she saw that for all his inculcated courtesy, he was a wild creature: 'Do you think I intend to live like my father; spending the day in idleness, grateful for the patronage of that old man in the Residency? My grandfather died of ennui. My father is dying of ennui. But I shall not die that way. You think we are powerless. You think we can do nothing against you: but if you stay here, you may be surprised.'

'Yes, you could stir up trouble if you wanted to. But you're up against more than the British. The blacks say this is an African island and there's Gopal. I suspect he has ambitions of his own. If it came to a struggle, you might wish you had the British back again.'

'That remains to be seen.' Musa hung his head, his playfulness gone: 'The other day we spoke of the right of conquest, but there is another right: the right of ownership. The British government pretends to respect it. They did not seize our winter palace and say: "Now it is ours" – no. They gave us a lease and each year a little money and said: "It is still yours, but the Governor will live there for as long as he chooses." In that way, they are within the law. But there is more to it than that. Most of the land here belongs to my family, to the Abubakr, but we have no right to develop it. The government does not take it from us. Instead, they say politely: "We regret we cannot let you build an hotel." "We cannot let you build high-rise blocks." "We cannot let you sell to a property firm", and so on.'

'You want to sell to Lomax? Do you trust him?'

'I trust no one.'

They had reached the western gate that looked out on the car park and the orchards, the distant grassland and the white fortress of the police-post that straddled the road to the pass.

On one side of the gateway, set in the thickness of the wall, was a small café. Its space, lit by holes in the brickwork, held half a dozen tables where Arabs sat before their coffee cups and played tric-trac. They were a grimy lot and one of them, more grimy than the rest, was, Musa said, the owner of the petrol pump. They all lolled about, as indolent in the semi-darkness as they would be in the heat of midday. Recognizing Musa, they stirred slightly and touched their brows and breasts in greeting. They eyed Kristy and as Musa led her into the darkness beyond the café, she began to doubt the wisdom of going farther. She caught the peculiar smell that sometimes came through the kitchen door at the Daisy, and said: 'I ought to be going back.'

'Don't be afraid. No one will hurt you.' Musa, climbing a stair formed in the broken brickwork, put a hand down and helped her up. They came out on to the top of the city wall. Before them there was a tower, built as a strong-point but now as ramshackle as the wall itself.

'This is the casbah,' Musa said.

'Surely your friends don't live here?'

'Why not, if they have nowhere else to live?'

The sun, beginning its decline, sent a slanting light over the orchards and Kristy knew she should start back while it was still light. She paused then, having come so far, she thought she might as well see what was to be seen. Musa had passed through a doorway into the tower and was descending steps to a floor below. When Kristy followed, she was repelled by the atmosphere inside. Outdoors, the wind blowing off the orchard had been as fresh as a sea-wind. Inside, they were met by a sickening, goat-like smell that became heavier as they descended. The lower room was large and derelict. It was so dark that Kristy stumbled over someone before she realized that people were lying on the floor. There was no movement among them. They were heaped together like bodies collected after a massacre.

Musa shouted: 'Wake up, my English friends.'

One of them, a young red-bearded man, let his head loll round and looked at Musa through half-closed eyes. He mumbled: 'You brought anything?'

'Yes, a visitor. An English lady.'

The bearded man rolled his head away and said: 'Drop dead.'

'There may be more life in the next room.' Laughing with a boisterous unease, Musa led Kristy through a hole in the wall into a second room that had more light because part of its outer wall had fallen in. Here someone had tried to make a living-room with a table and a couple of greasy chairs that had probably come from the café. Two creatures – Kristy took them to be dogs – were scuffling about under the table. Though there was light and air, the atmosphere was heavy with an acrid, inhuman smell that came, she realized, from the dead birds that lay about on the floor.

'This,' Musa said, 'is where the pigeons come to die. And under here, we have Billie and Laura.'

Billie and Laura were not dogs after all: they were children.

Kristy asked: 'Whose are they? What are they doing here?'

'The parents brought them here, then went off and left them.'

They were playing with what looked like a basket of rags until the rags began to whimper. Musa said: 'The baby was born here.'

'Here? In this room?'

'Yes. They settled in for a few weeks, then, one day, they'd disappeared. It was the day the boat left. They'd gone.'

'Leaving the children! But who looks after the children?'

'They look after themselves. Billie is very good with the baby, aren't you, Billie?'

The boy nodded complacently and pulling the basket into Kristy's view, stared up at her as though expecting her approbation. The baby's skin was a greyish white but there was an unnatural tinge of pink about its eyelids and nostrils. Its eyes were bleared and milky, like the eyes of a very old person, and its mouth moved round and round, giving out a high whine of misery. Coming from under the table, the boy began to lift the child from the basket. He may have been eight or nine years of age but he was very small and Kristy was moved to help him.

He said: 'No, I can do it.' With the baby in his arms, he walked round the room, looking in his kaftan, that trailed about him like a dirty night-shirt, a parody of comic fatherhood. But he was more than that. As he went, he rocked the child to comfort it then, having stopped its cry, he put it on the table and took a feeding-bottle from the basket. Pressing the teat between the child's lips, he talked gently, coaxing it to drink. The whimper started again, the milk spluttered over the table and the girl under the table said scornfully: 'What she wants is her nappy changed.'

'You hold her, then', the boy said. 'I'll get some paper.'

The girl came out and took hold of the baby while the boy, picking up a jug, went through a door and down some steps.

'How on earth do they survive?' Kristy asked.

'They don't do badly. They go to the Mission School and Father Matthew lets them eat there. They arouse pity. People give them money and my English friends send them out begging. They get half of what they pick up. And they're practised thieves. They lift stuff from the market stalls. One way and another, they get all they need.'

Billie, returning with a jug of water and a roll of toilet paper, began to clean the baby. While this was going on, a young woman sidled in from the first room and smiled on Kristy. Musa said:

'This is Agnes. She's rather sweet.'

Agnes, hearing her name, came towards them, moving as though time had a different, slacker pace for her, and, as she came, she waved slowly towards the chairs and whispered: 'Sit down. *Do* sit down.' In her dream state, it seemed, she had reverted to the manners of a conventional upbringing.

'I suppose she helps with the children?'

Musa laughed: 'How could she?'

Laura, her arms on the table, her head on her hand, was gazing at Kristy. She would have been, in normal circumstances, a pretty blonde child. Now, for some reason, her long, neglected hair was falling out in patches so, together with her extreme thinness and dirt, she had a sick appearance. Having caught Kristy's attention, she began to giggle and, bending down, she picked up a dead pigeon which she swung backwards and forwards over the baby's face. Kristy moved to stop this play but before she could do anything, Billie had given his sister a blow that sent her back under the table.

Laura began to bawl: 'God'll sock you for that.'

'No, he won't. You're the one he's after. He made your hair fall out.'

The girl snuffled a while then asked: 'Why is God such a ratty old bastard?'

'Because he doesn't exist, silly.'

'They're rather confused,' Kristy said.

'The Mission teaches them one thing and here they learn something different. And Laura's faith has been shaken. She told the pigeons to rise and walk and they didn't.'

'I feel I should do something to help them, but what?'

'Don't worry. They don't want your help. They've discovered how to live on their own. They're like little wild cats: they don't want to be tamed. And they can stay here as long as they like. This property belongs to my family and these people are my guests.'

Kristy turned away: 'I must go.' As they descended a stair to the ground, she said: 'The truth is, you encourage them to live like this.'

'They don't need encouragement. Would you rather I turned them into the street? That I cannot do. We Arabs have traditions of hospitality.'

'You didn't bring me here to show off your hospitality. You wanted me to see them. You think they justify your contempt for us.'

'What do you think?'

'I think they're afraid. They see the world being destroyed about them. They feel helpless and want to get away. The destroyers are too many and too powerful. You are one of them.'

'Me?' Musa laughed, disconcerted: 'Because I want my family to profit by what it owns? Surely that's a natural ambition?'

'Yes, I'm afraid it is.'

At the bottom of the stair, Musa said quietly: 'Your people destroyed a way of life for us. When my father revolted, you deposed him. You were once a great race but now, I can pity you.'

'Your pity excites your pride. And what do you mean to do?'

Musa laughed again: 'Why should I do anything?'

They entered a ground-floor room that had been a stables but was equipped now as a mechanic's yard. Two stripped-down car engines stood in the middle of the floor. A heavy double door led to the road outside. Two men were working here. Unlike the crowd upstairs, they were awake and knew what they were doing. And what were they doing? Kristy wondered.

One of them was putting a greyish material, like dough, into a barrel. He jerked his head round as they entered. Seeing Kristy, he slapped a lid on to the barrel and stood grinning self-consciously. There were other barrels standing around. The other man was at a work-bench, tinkering with a piece of metal. A pungent smell of almonds, as from a quick-drying agent, filled the air.

Musa introduced the men as Ahmed and Mohammed. 'My assistants. We are all interested in mechanics. I like to recondition old car engines and if I can, I improve them. It is my hobby. We do it, as you would say, for fun.'

Kristy laughed: 'You are an amateur artisan, like Peter the Great.'

'Exactly.' Musa undid several bolts on the double doors and pushed them open. Outside, the orchards scented the air. He said: 'It is more pleasant to return this way.'

He smiled, knowing the sight of the young people in the upper rooms had shaken her. To show her composure, she breathed in the sweetness and said: 'Delicious. Is that orange blossom?'

'There is an orange grove near by. You have no fears walking back alone? Perhaps I should come with you?'

'No, I have no fears.'

'You are, as Dr Gopal says, advanced.'

'I am less sure of that than I used to be.'

Going off down the macadam road with its weeds and pot-holes, she compared herself with Musa's English friends and knew that so far as they were concerned, she was as limited by convention as the other women at the Daisy. They had settled into the Casbah like a pack of rabbits and that was freedom if you did not mind the ruins falling on you. Yet, lying there, piled together, unconscious most of the time, they were the prisoners of their own habit. They were as trapped as she was. And she, caught up in the machinery of reproduction, found herself, for the first time in her life, content.

She imagined, as she walked, that Musa was watching after her but when, at the corner, she turned to wave to him, he was not there. It was the moment of evening when the peaks appeared. She paused and watched for them. The sky was empty. Then in an instant they were there; the stone revenants that dominated the island.

Whenever she saw them, she felt a frisson of wonder. They seemed to materialize like supernatural objects. She had heard them called the Guardians but did not know what they were supposed to guard. It might be the island but that, she suspected, was a lost cause. Perhaps they protected the one wild area that remained, the dark area of the rain forest. She could imagine, if one tried to invade it, they would close to keep it inviolable. She lifted her hand to them then began to run. Though she had told Musa she had no fears, she did not want to cross the plantation at night.

She reached the Daisy in darkness. Coming in out of the spacious evening, she had a sense of mental contraction and need to adapt herself to a smaller environment.

Hugh, who was sitting near the door, said angrily: 'Where did you get to? I looked everywhere for you. It's not safe for you to wander about the Medina alone.'

'If you think that, you should take better care of me.'

'You look as though you've been up to something.'

'Perhaps I have. I saw that you and Hobhouse were in a state of emotional rapport so I took myself off and met a friend. What did you and Hobhouse do?'

Hugh frowned and, looking away from her, pretended to be absorbed in the dissatisfaction about him. The bar should have opened up fifteen minutes before and the inmates of the pension, conditioned to alcohol at this hour, were restless with irritation. Hassan, now the appointed barman, was on the telephone, earnestly listening to someone who had been talking far too long. His second-in-command, an elderly African called Negumi, stood propped against the bar grille with half-shut eyes. Ogden called to him and pointed to his wrist-watch but Negumi shrugged as though time were a baffling Western concept in which he could not involve himself.

Under the impression that Ambrose was mourning away inside Mrs Gunner's room, Mrs Axelrod went to the door and looked at it. She said: 'I've half a mind to give it a damned good rap.'

Ogden, to stop her, called on a note of stern command: 'Negumi, open that bar.'

Negumi spread his hands to show he did not have the key. Hassan, trembling at this threat to his office, gestured to reassure Ogden while keeping the receiver to his ear.

Simpson said: 'Who's on the line, Hassan?'

'Ya sayyidi,' Hassan answered miserably: ' *Ya sayyidi* want special dinner.'

'What?' Released from all restraint, Mrs Axelrod let her voice rise to a screech: 'So Gunner's not here at all!' She marched on Hassan in a menacing way, demanding: 'Give me that key.'

Hassan pleaded: 'A little minute, *sayyida*. Only a little minute.' He crouched away from her as she gripped his left wrist and prising open his bony, yellow fingers, found the key and waved it triumphantly in the air. Near weeping, he cried into the telephone: 'Good-bye, please, *sayyid*. *Sayyid*, please say "good-bye".'

'Good-bye' must have been said for Hassan was free at last to put down the receiver and stand, dejected, as Ogden and Simpson pushed up the bar grille and ordered Negumi to go behind and serve the drinks.

'Bloody people,' Kristy said fiercely. 'They rage about the young, but look at them: avid for their own fix.'

The inmates, excited by having got what they wanted, were having fun at Negumi's expense, shouting orders – comic orders, for the most part – to 'pot-boy, tapster, skinker or wine-waiter' while Negumi grinned widely, delighted at having achieved prominence.

Kristy said: 'They've already forgotten Mrs Gunner.'

'It's the usual reaction. She's gone but the rest have to carry on.'

Hassan, unable to regain his invaded territory, went to the kitchen to order Ambrose's special dinner. At seven o'clock, a taxi drew up and the front door was thrown open to admit Ambrose with Gurgur behind him. To Kristy, who loathed Gurgur, it seemed that Ambrose had brought in a real gurgur: a filthy and obscene carrion bird.

Crossing the salon with an unsteady sway, Ambrose announced: 'Mrs G.'s dead. Long Live Mr G. The old girl left me everything she had.'

He seemed to expect condolences and congratulations but he got neither. He surveyed the guests with a tipsy smile and they stared back in cold disapproval of his riotous air. His face was red and his whole large person seemed to be extruding liquid. He brought in with him a smell of garlic and good eating, and a heavy, plummy scent of wine.

Mrs Axelrod said: 'I can see you've been celebrating.'

Ambrose tilted up his chin in noble disgust at this suggestion and, stumbling and brushing against the tables, he led Gurgur to the Lettuce Room. As he went he shouted towards the bar: 'Whisky. Two glasses and a bottle.'

Ambrose's dinner-table was a centre of attention. Mrs Axelrod went straight to it and called the other women to her. They walked round it as though it were a bier. It was not one table but four placed together and, no tablecloth being large enough, it was covered by a bed-sheet. On it, Hassan had placed every piece of plated tableware the kitchen could provide. They were all so

185

garlanded with flowers and greenery, it was not easy to see what was what but Mrs Axelrod, poking about, discovered six silver egg-cups and a toast-rack among the furnishings. Greatly elevated by her triumph over the bar key, she paraded and gesticulated so wildly that Kristy said:

'That woman'll end up in the bin.'

Mrs Axelrod was still by the table, standing with hands clasped, head on one side, when Ambrose and Gurgur arrived.

'Tell me,' she smiled at Ambrose, 'when *is* the wedding?'

Ambrose ignored her but he looked flustered. He called to Hassan, who stood by expecting praise, and ordered him to remove some of the objects so there would be room for the plates. Order was brought to the table but nothing could disguise the poverty of the food.

Simpson shouted to Ogden: 'If Mrs Gunner could taste this meat, she'd turn in her . . .' He gulped to a stop and Ambrose rebuked him with a look.

At breakfast next day, Mrs Axelrod announced that Ambrose's day of grace was over. 'Either he pulls his socks up, or we will withhold cash.' The guests watched for Ambrose's arrival in the dining-room, but he did not appear. His table, over-loaded the previous night, was now bare. The men had to leave so the women were to present the ultimatum alone. They went to the salon to await Ambrose and Kristy followed to see what would happen. Nothing happened. Growing impatient, Mrs Axelrod hammered on the door of Mrs Gunner's room and, getting no reply, opened it. There was no one inside. She then went to the office, looked in and said in a low threatening voice: 'The bird has flown.'

Hassan, who was cleaning the bar, tried to hide himself but could not. 'Where has Mr Gunner gone?' asked Mrs Axelrod.

Almost too distressed to speak, Hassan said: 'Ya Sayyidi say he eat every day at Praslin. *Ya sayyidi* say he no like Daisy food.'

For a moment Mrs Axelrod seemed at a loss then, with more than her usual fierceness, she said: 'Wait till I get my hands on *ya sayyidi*.'

Ambrose remained out of sight and Hassan muddled on. A week after Mrs Gunner's death, Simpson asked his safragi for a siphon of soda. The request was referred to Hassan behind the bar. Hassan mumbled: 'No siphon now. All gone,' and, turning his back on the room, hoped he need hear no more about it. Ogden took the matter up in his authoritative way.

'There must be siphons in the store. Send a safragi to get one.'

Hassan turned his worn, unhappy face: 'Not any more. Siphon all gone. Tomorrow more things gone. Soon no whisky, no gin, no rum. Soon all booze gone.'

Ogden laughed irritably: 'Then go to Aly's and order more, you silly fellow.'

Looking down, Hassan hung his head and wrung his hands. Questioned with fatherly patience, by Ogden, he said: 'Aly say no more booze from Aly. First pay the bills.' After which, it all came out. The kitchen was bare of necessities. Tomorrow or the next day, the guests would not even have food. Aly's monthly account had been due for payment on the day Mrs Gunner went to hospital. Ambrose had promised to pay when she returned but she did not return. Aly was very strict about overdue bills. Had the creditor been an Arab or an African, things might have run on indefinitely but it was Aly's policy to allow only one month's credit. The Daisy was well into a second month. Matters were made worse by the fact that the island gossips had put it about that Ambrose was squandering money at the Praslin. That very morning, when Hassan went down to beg for the next day's supplies, Aly had chased him from the shop.

Hassan told all this unwillingly, his face creased with sorrow, knowing he was betraying the man who had promoted him to greatness.

Ogden said: 'We must corner Gunner. We must sit up and wait for him.'

The men decided they would sit up alone. Ogden told Mrs Axelrod that he could deal more easily with Ambrose if 'the ladies retired'. Mrs Axelrod, still excited by her own powers of leadership, was hard to persuade but eventually she and the other women did retire. Kristy, nowadays half-asleep at ten o'clock, went happily to bed but Hugh, though not in the circle of protest, remained in the salon with some idea of supporting Ambrose should Ambrose need support.

Hassan, ordered to keep the bar open, was wretchedly on edge.

When, in the early hours, Ambrose arrived back in a taxi, Hassan gazed pityingly at him and moved his head as though to say: 'Don't blame me, sayyid. Don't blame me.'

Ambrose, standing just inside the front door, saw himself ambushed. He had lost weight and was wearing a silk shirt and a new suit of cream tussore. He looked fresh and youthful, but he was in trouble. Turning quickly from side to side, he seemed to be seeking a way of escape.

Ogden said: 'We've been waiting to speak to you, Gunner. You must be aware that here, at the Daisy, things have been going from bad to worse.'

Tackled, Ambrose at once passed the ball. He swung round and going towards the bar spoke to Hassan in a stern and lofty manner: 'What is this I hear, Hassan? You've been letting things slide?'

Hassan, bending down in anguish, whispered: 'Aly . . .'

'Oh, it's Aly, is it? First thing tomorrow morning, go down and tell him if the food isn't better, we'll close our account.'

Hassan raised his head to wail: 'Never be better without you pay bill. No whisky, no gin, no washing-up liquid. All gone. Tomorrow no food. I work, work. The other ones do no work. They say "Why we work? *Ya sayyidi* pay no money." For Akbar, they work. For me, they laugh. I do bedrooms, salon, dining-room, bar . . . I do all for you, *sayyid*, and what do you say me? Tomorrow, next day, when boat comes, I go to Egypt to my village.'

Much moved, Ambrose put a hand on Hassan's shoulder and looked reproachfully at the men around him: 'Hassan does his best. What more can anyone ask?'

'A great deal more,' Ogden told him. 'You owe Aly for two months' supplies and he refuses to serve the Daisy till he's paid. We keep our part of the bargain. We pay our monthly accounts and in return we get wretched food and deplorable service while you spend your days at the Praslin. We have waited for you in order to say that if things don't improve, and quickly, we'll withhold our payments till they *do* improve.'

The others said: 'That's right.'

During this address, Ambrose had gradually stiffened and when he spoke, he did so with extreme hauteur: 'You will have no further cause for complaint. The pension is closing down.'

A shock of dismay passed over the guests and Simpson shouted: 'You can't do that. We've nowhere to go.'

Ambrose relaxed. Raising his brows, he smiled gently: 'I must have misunderstood you. I thought you were dissatisfied and so, to please you, I decided to close the place down. However, I have no wish to disaccommodate you. My mother loved the Daisy and devoted herself to your comfort. I, myself, have had no experience of running a place like this. In view of this, I think you might have had more patience with me. I have had a worrying time, settling my mother's affairs. However, I will go down to Aly's tomorrow and sort things out. I am also arranging for a manager to take over here and I can assure you things will improve.'

Murmurs of gratitude and sympathy came from among the men. Ambrose nodded, acknowledging their response and dismissing them. With nothing more to be said, they rose and took themselves up the stairs. Hugh remained seated and when he and Ambrose were alone, Ambrose said: 'I'm getting out of this dump. Drop into the Lettuce Room tomorrow evening, before supper, and we'll have a parting drink.'

The Fosters were saddened by the loss of Ambrose from the Daisy but he welcomed them with so much pleasure in his position of host – a position too long denied him by poverty – that they had to see the occasion as one for gaiety.

Four bottles and four glasses stood on the Lettuce Room table.

'Mrs G.'s iron rations,' Ambrose said. 'I found them hidden in her wardrobe. What will you have? – whisky, gin, vodka, rum?' He poured Kristy's gin with a lavish hand and she did her best to drink it.

All around them the infant lettuces stood up fresh and green, carefully tended by Hassan. The room was kept at a pleasant temperature and through the glass the stars shone like the eyes of giant cats.

Ambrose sighed: 'Mrs G. wouldn't allow me in here. She thought it was a bad thing for the guests to see the family lounging about. She hardly came in herself, for the same reason. The old thing knew how to run a business and, I must say, she didn't do badly out of it.' There was a new splendour about Ambrose and his voice took on the exalted coo peculiar to him when he spoke of matters that gave him satisfaction: 'Dr Dixon is her executor and he's been more than kind. He tracked me down to the Praslin in order to let me know, *on the very day of the funeral*, that I was the sole heir. I was astonished. She always said she'd leave me nothing. Dixon went to see the Chief Secretary, who acts as legal representative here, and got me letters of administration. Yesterday I heard from her London solicitors who said that when everything's cleared up, I'll get a very tidy sum.' Leaning towards the Fosters, he indicated with a gesture that that was not all: '*And* . . .' Glancing at the door to see that none of the guests were lurking there, he lowered his voice to a whisper of immaculate clarity: 'I have reason to hope that Lomax is about to come across.'

'You mean, he'll finance the treasure hunt?'

Ambrose nodded, smirking: 'We're on much more of a footing now. Surprising how that has affected him. But we'll speak of it another time.'

Aglow with the munificent affability of success, Ambrose looked like the old photograph in which he resembled a young bull, a bull that should be wreathed in flowers. At last, after all his ploys, projects and failures, life had rewarded him. Serene, he made small gracious gestures. He patted Kristy's knee and his sweet voice became more sweet: 'Think of it! A ship laden with pure gold! In these days it should be worth its weight in – what, I wonder?'

'Blues and tenners?' Kristy suggested.

'My God, yes. You're just about right.'

He had, of course, another project. He had decided to marry again. The Fosters were eager to know who would be the bride but, alas, he had not yet met her. He put out his hand to Kristy: 'I would like someone like Kristy here. Older, of course, but small, dark, subtle, intelligent. I have never had a wife like that before.'

Kristy was facing the back wall of the Lettuce Room. This, like Mrs Gunner's bedroom window, looked on to the small service courtyard. She could see directly into the kitchen where there was a great deal of merriment. The cook, a fat, dark-skinned half-breed, was seated among the debris on the kitchen table, one leg bent under him, the knee forming a prop for his other foot. The foot, sticking up in the air, was evidently the cause of all the fun. Bending over it and using one of the dining-room forks, the cook was digging something out of his sole and making the most of the operation. His dark, glistering face grimaced in simulated agony while the safragis and sweepers bent about in an ecstasy of appreciation, slapping themselves and slapping each other. He extracted a worm-like object which he held up for all to see. The worm – it certainly looked like a worm – seemed to wriggle on the fork and the cook, giving a laugh that reached the Lettuce Room, flung it backwards over his shoulder, in the direction of the pots on the stove.

Ambrose, who had his back to this episode, said happily: 'And I shall have work to do. I'm planning a modern Mayhew: a comprehensive study of the London underworld. Crime, sex, perversion, violence, the lot. A money-spinner.'

'Has this been commissioned?' Hugh asked.

'Commissioned? No. Thank God I am no longer dependent on the good will of publishers. I do what I like. When it is finished, I shall order my agent to put the manuscript up to auction. The highest bidder will get it.'

Hassan came to say that Lomax's car was waiting at the door. Taking very few of his old possessions, Ambrose departed to live at the Praslin. As he had promised, he settled with Aly and the food improved. The bar was restocked, but, for the time being, Hassan remained as nominal head safragi.

5

Kristy realized that a new interest possessed the women at the Daisy, though they discussed it so cautiously she had no idea what it was. And she did not care. She was feeling her increasing weight and the humid heat was a burden to her. She was in a state of mental lethargy and physical well-being. Looking at herself in the glass, she smiled to see how she had changed. Ambrose had described her as 'small, dark, subtle, intelligent'. He was remembering her as she had been when he first saw her. She had been pale, over-thin and had looked delicate. Now her face had filled out and her complexion was brilliantly pink and cream. Her breasts, that had been too small, began to strain against her cotton shirts. Big, round, pink-cheeked, she looked a totally different person. She was turning into a mother. Mentally, too, she was melting into motherhood. Her emotions were becoming very tender. Remembering how she had found her mother weeping at the police-station, she now understood why she had wept. They had fought day in, day out: they had disagreed on every subject. At times Kristy had felt pure hatred for her mother and imagined herself hated in return. Yet they were one flesh. However outrageously Kristy behaved, she remained what she had been and always would be: part of her mother. She thought: 'I'll write and tell her that I understand' but from sheer lack of energy, she did not write.

She went once a week to see Mueller. At first Hugh had felt it was his duty to go with her but he was soon discouraged for the relationship between patient and gynaecologist was so warm, so intimate, he felt an extraneous third party. After three visits, he went no more.

On Mueller's advice, Kristy walked, each morning, for two or three miles. She would plod up to the plantations or go along the quay to the shore road and watch the flying-fish. Having done this, she could spend the rest of the day idle and thinking of meal-times. Previously a non-eater, she now ate ravenously. When she lay about in the salon or in her own room, she was poignantly conscious of the creature developing within her. She had decided not to return home until it was born. She would not risk the long, exhausting journey. But she still thought of it as her very own, inseparable from her however separated in space, and independent and unco-operative, it might one day become. It seemed to her – a fact she faced sometimes with joy, sometimes with irritation and a sense of revolt – that she would never be free again.

She had nothing to wear but an Arab skirt, bought in the harbour market, and a blouse to hide the gap at the waist-line. She could tell from glances in the salon that the progress of her pregnancy was being noted. It was noted most frequently by Mr Simpson who, whenever he caught her eye, parted his lips as though on the point of speech.

Mrs Axelrod occasionally slid her eye in Kristy's direction but looked the other way if Kristy met her glance. She had a new activity that increased her importance among her following. She was making, with an unusually large crochet-hook and some fine string, a circular table-cloth which she frequently spread out for the admiration of the others. It rapidly took on size so it was soon too big to display on the salon coffee-tables and had to be unrolled on the floor. Watching her as she crawled round it, flattening its uneven surface with the heel of her hand, Kristy thought: 'Poor old thing, what has she got in life?' Mrs Axelrod, unlike most of the other women who had children in England, was childless. When the talk was about schools, examinations or careers, she no longer ruled the conversation though, when possible, she gave advice as one who was likely to know more than the next woman. Still, she needed no one's pity. She observed her work with self-congratulating complacency and spoke of it in the same way. She was frequently asked how much bigger she planned to make it. Each time she considered the question anew, saying: 'I expect they'll have a sizeable place. They'll entertain in style. Big dinner parties: that sort of thing.'

Kristy, drowsily listening in the background, had a vision of a fine manor house, a dining-room and a highly polished hunting-table overlaid with Mrs Axelrod's lumpy string table-cloth. If the vision did not appeal to Kristy, it roused in the others envy and annoyance. As the work grew ring on ring, like the growth rings of a tree, even Mrs Prince sounded acrimonious. The work was clearly intended to mark some great occasion but, whatever the occasion was, the women felt that Mrs Axelrod was overdoing it. Or perhaps they were guilty because they themselves were not doing enough.

Eventually, from one remark and another, Kristy learnt that the crochet-work was a wedding present. The Governor's daughter was to marry Cyril Millman, the aide-de-camp. Oh, fortunate Miss Urquhart, Kristy thought, and was glad for the girl whom Mrs Axelrod had long written off as 'no longer young, poor thing' and for Millman whom Mrs Axelrod had once described as 'one of those sort of bachelors, you know what I mean?' It seemed that she intended now to compensate them for her earlier opinions.

Hugh did not hear of the wedding until Pedley said: 'Best bib and tucker tomorrow, eh?' Seeing Hugh's puzzlement, he said: 'The wedding. The wedding.' When he heard that the Fosters had not been invited, he was deeply shocked. Hugh said he did not care whether he was invited or not but his not caring had nothing to do with it. The Fosters had a *right* to be invited. Pedley felt this flouting of protocol was a slur on his department.

Though he had spoken truly when he said he did not care, Hugh, alone in the office building next day, felt forlorn and aimless. The junior staff had been given a holiday and the place was as empty as when he first entered it. After monitoring a morning programme, Hugh went up to the ministerial floor, hoping to meet Diddar, Murodi or Dr Gopal, but he met no one. The ministers had also gone to the reception. At one end of the corridor there was a window that looked towards the Residency wall. Hugh went to it and found he could see part of the palace and the famous garden. An Arab contractor had erected tents: the traditional Arab wedding tents that were appliquéd all over with linen cut-outs in umber, blue and Venetian red. In the distance he could see people moving on a corner of the terrace. He could hear the music of the police band.

The reception, formal, dull, held at the most uncomfortable hour of the day, was the sort of entertainment he liked least: yet he was oppressed by the fact that he and Kristy had not been invited, feeling their exclusion came of a quagmire of misunderstanding. He remembered how charming Cyril Millman had been to them and wondered why he had not required their inclusion. Hugh felt they had been treated unjustly. He felt that a sinister force working away on the dark side of his life, had come between him and his true self.

Something separated him from the world – but what? He had a habit of blaming Kristy for his troubles but he knew Kristy was only partly to blame. Many successful men had worse wives. He knew one whose wife was an alcoholic and there had been gossip about another married to a nymphomaniac. In both cases, because the man was liked, the wife was seen not as a fault but a misfortune that had to be shared.

Supposing he had, in spite of everything, continued his writing and attained some success! Would they have treated him like this? The question was futile, of course. As a writer, he would have been his own man. He would not be in their power.

Walking down the hill in the midday heat, he felt the silence. His feet made no sound on the sandy road. The villas were empty. No bicycles passed. The whole island, it seemed, had gone to the Residency. Only he and Kristy had been left out. They had the dining-room to themselves.

'I could hear the music at the reception,' Hugh said casually.

'Thank goodness we did not have to dress up and go. Or buy a bloody present.'

'You could have written it up. "Subject for a short story".'

'I could do that without the bother of going there. I can imagine every bit of it. A steaming bore.'

Hugh mentioned the reception again over coffee but Kristy refused to talk about it. She knew he had been hurt by their exclusion and was brooding on the reason for it. He was prone to anxiety and she could see that in this place anxiety could become a parasite of the mind, continually seeking injury, insult, injustice or malice on which to feed. She would not encourage it.

He, for his part, was irritated by her indifference. She, of course, had a more important matter to distract her. Whatever happened, she could remain apart, content and preoccupied by motherhood. He realized that her previous outspokenness and independence had been necessary to him. He had needed to blame her. He had needed to grind his teeth on her. Earlier than necessary, he went back to the office and heard the music again.

Just before sunset, the helicopter passed over the Daisy, taking the bride and bridegroom to Réunion to board the Paris plane. Kristy, sprawled in the salon, knew the reception was over. Simpson was the first one back. Seeing her in her washed-out maternity garments, sandals on bare feet, he was so astonished that he stopped to stare with eyes wide open, shrimpish bristles twitching. Having stopped he came, at last, to the point of speech:

'You not been to the wedding?'

'No. We weren't asked.'

'Weren't asked? But you should've been asked. You'd a right to be asked.' He would have said more had the Axelrods not come in behind him and he hurried up the stairs. But that was not the end of it. After supper, Kristy, hearing a hiss, turned to find Simpson looking at her through the bead curtain. He beckoned her to come into the garden. Hugh was reading. Without speaking, she rose and went out into the warm, night-scented garden where the only light was the light of the stars.

'Want to show you something,' Simpson whispered. He led her across the lawn, moving like a waggish dog, and stopped beside a small citrus tree: 'You stand just there,' he said and put his hand into his pocket.

She thought: 'Oh, God!' but all he produced was a box of matches.

'Now, watch!' He lit a match and played it gently about the leaves. There was a plop, like the plop of an igniting gas-jet, and the whole tree was surrounded by flame. Nothing seemed to be burning. The foliage was unharmed. It was simply haloed by the wavering blue-white flame that appeared to feed on air.

She caught her breath and asked: 'How did you do it?'

'Not me. I didn't do it. It's nature. Nature did it.' He explained that at certain seasons the heat drew a volatile oil from the leaves so they became flammable.

They stood side by side, rapt, watching while the flame licked over the tree, consuming the oil.

'A burning bush,' Kristy murmured.

'That's right. Like a Christmas pud, isn't it?' Simpson was delighted by her pleasure in the glowing tree. Then, suddenly, the flame was gone and he gave an 'Oh!' of disappointment. 'That's it, then,' he said.

Strolling back with her to the salon, he said: 'You're very happy, you two young people; beginning a family, beginning life.'

Kristy wondered what age he imagined they were.

'Wish I could start again,' he said.

'You've been married, I suppose?'

'Oh, yes. The wife went home long ago; never came back. Wanted to be with the children. I was in India then. She didn't like India. Funny, I liked it, though it wasn't a good time. You'd've thought to listen to them that there was nothing worse than living under British rule. Now what are they doing? All crossing the *pani* to get back under British rule. I say, I'm sorry you weren't asked to the tamasha. Not nice, that; leaving people out. Not a nice thing to do.'

'I didn't expect to be invited. We don't belong. You know that. Except for Ogden, you're the only government person who's even spoken to us since we came to the Daisy.'

'You don't say!' Simpson was genuinely surprised but on reflection, added: 'You know, they thought you looked down on them. You thought we were a lot of old fogies first time you saw us.'

'No. We'd come to a strange place. We were confused.'

Simpson laughed: 'So were we. We'd never seen smart young people like you. You made us realize how the world has changed. We were young at a bad time. We thought things'd get better as we got older, but they've got worse. Our children despise us. Don't want to talk to us. It's no fun getting old, like a worn-out car. You think you've learnt the game, then you find all the young ones are playing a different game.'

197

'Not so different, really. The trouble is, life seems so temporary now. There is to be no future for us.'

Simpson stared at her in astonishment: 'Why do you say that?'

'Surely you know the world is being used up. Even England is becoming an over-populated, polluted slum.'

'You don't say!'

He took a step away from her and looked as though he thought her a little mad. She went in through the bead curtain feeling that at his age, he might as well retain his innocence.

6

Hassan, serving the breakfast coffee, bent over the table and whispered: 'Manager come.'

'Today?' Hugh asked.

'Today, come.'

Hassan told everyone the same news and it was taken as a cause for congratulation among the guests. Hassan, however, seemed more frightened than pleased and as he whispered the news around, he seemed to be appealing against the new management. What changes would it bring? The first was apparent that evening at dinner-time when the diners entered the room to see Akbar standing at his old place, beside the serving-table. He had grown heavier during his absence and he was wearing a new kaftan of dark blue silk with a gold cording at the neck. When the guests welcomed him, he gave each a nod of solemn dignity. His return had confirmed in him his sense of personal consequence. He did not smile. He controlled the servants with the utmost gravity, lifting a finger here, an eyebrow there, and they scuttled about, eager to obey him. Hassan, demoted to second-in-command, observed his power with reverence.

Akbar, now, did not even draw corks from bottles. All his old duties had been delegated to Hassan who worked harder than ever. Then Kristy's lemur came in through the window. The creature had found her out when the dining-room moved indoors so even Hugh had to admit it was her lemur and let her call it her friend and companion, her totem, her pet, her *alter ego*. Akbar knew nothing of these relationships. As the lemur leapt on to the Fosters' table, he strode across the room, clapping his hands. The lemur sped off in alarm and leapt out of the window. Akbar closed the window.

Kristy cried out: 'Why did you do that?'

'Manager say no animals in dining-room.'

As Kristy looked in helpless misery at Hugh, he realized how defenceless she had become. He did not want the lemur on the table but seeing her near tears, he said: 'Don't cry. I'll speak to the manager. I'm sure he'll understand.'

Hugh asked Hassan where the new manager was and Hassan, too nervous to speak, jerked his hands right and left to indicate that the manager was here, there, everywhere, an all-pervading, terrifying force. In spite of that, he was nowhere to be found. Nearly a week passed before anyone saw him but there were more changes. Workmen arrived and boarded over the glass door to the Lettuce Room. A new door was constructed at the garden end of the room and marked 'Private'.

'What's happening to the lettuces?' Mrs Axelrod asked.

Hassan sighed deeply: 'Lettuces no more.'

For a few days anyone in the garden could look through the glass and see the lettuces wilting and dying, then the workmen tore out the shelves and carted them away. The lettuce boxes went with them. After that the bamboo blinds were pulled down and there was no knowing what went on inside.

Like children bored by misrule, the servants had meekly returned to their routine, having learnt that without Akbar, their world was chaos. The food was more plentiful than it had been in Mrs Gunner's day but it was coarse and uninteresting. Ogden complained that the meat – dark and tough, coated with breadcrumbs to hide its colour – was the same for every meal. He said to Akbar: 'What's Aly thinking about, sending this stuff every day?'

The guests then learnt that the manager had taken the Daisy account from Aly and now bought direct from a Syrian wholesaler whose depot was at the Dobo. Ogden thought the meat was goat, probably frozen. It was served with large plates of chipped sweet potatoes but no green vegetables. Ogden asked: 'And why don't we get vegetables these days?'

'Manager say vegetables too much money and bad, bad,' said Akbar: 'Make belly bad. Too much wind.'

'Rubbish. Go and get the manager.'

Akbar did not move.

Ogden, speaking sternly and distinctly, said: 'I told you to go and get the manager.'

Akbar stared insolently at him then, from habit, turned and made a dilatory journey to the kitchen. He was back in a minute or two and, taking his place by the serving-table, said nothing. After a long interval, Ogden said: 'You told the manager I wish to speak to him.'

'Me told 'um.'

'Then where is he?'

Akbar, his eyes protruding, said with barely a movement of his heavy lips: 'What you think? You think Akbar keep the manager up him arse?'

Mrs Ogden, who had been trembling throughout the exchange, now gave a gasp of horror. Ogden clenched his fist and raised it as though to fell Akbar to the ground. 'You speak like that again before ladies and I'll . . . I'll . . .'

Akbar, twice Ogden's weight and half his age, advanced on Ogden and gazed contemptuously down on him: 'What you do, *sayyid*? Yo' tell Akbar what yo' do.' Getting no reply, Akbar swept round and went back to his post.

Ogden, who seemed bemused as though he had received a blow, sank back in his chair while Mrs Ogden, bouncing from side to side, cried out: 'How can you let him treat my husband like this?'

Axelrod answered in a reasonable tone: 'What can we do? We can't band together and attack a coloured servant. Think what the F.O. would say!'

'Besides,' Mrs Prince spoke amiably, 'we can't have Akbar going off again. You know what this place is like without him! I think it's better to take no notice.'

There was a general murmur that suggested Mrs Prince had spoken wisely. It also seemed to suggest that Ogden had been in the wrong. Akbar was too valuable to be provoked in that way. Only Mrs Axelrod remained silent, looking down as though she would dissociate herself from the whole incident: while Akbar seemed unaware that the comments concerned him.

That evening a man with a face like a vulture came into the salon and gave a batch of envelopes to Negumi. The new manager, seen for the first time, was Gurgur.

The envelopes were handed round and found to contain the monthly accounts. They gave rise to considerably more indignation than had the fracas between Ogden and Akbar. The monthly rate, payable in advance, had risen by twenty-five per cent. A note was pinned to Hugh's account: Mr Foster was required to see Mr Gurgur in the office next morning at ten a.m.

'For God's sake,' said Hugh, 'why did you have a quarrel with him? If he chucks us out, where do we go?'

'He's only a manager. Ambrose wouldn't let him chuck us out.'

But where was Ambrose? The Fosters had heard nothing from him since he went to the Praslin.

Though he knew that Kristy would be the worst possible emissary in this case, Hugh said: 'Well, I'll be in the office at ten. You'll have to see Gurgur.' Kristy suggested that he change the time of the appointment but Hugh refused. She had brought trouble down on them and she could deal with it.

When Kristy went to the office next morning, Gurgur took his time before acknowledging her presence. At last he asked: 'What can I do for you?'

The office had been cleared of Ambrose's possessions but still had the stale atmosphere of an unaired sleeping-place. It was an atmosphere that was, she felt, suited to Gurgur's self and she could scarcely speak for dislike of the man.

'You wanted to see us.'

'The note was for Mr Foster. My business is with him.'

Gurgur's tone was offensive, deliberately so. He made it plain that he saw her as an inferior and irresponsible partner in the marriage. She answered, mildly enough: 'My husband is at work at this time.'

Gurgur had a ledger in front of him full, Kristy noted with surprise, of Ambrose's small, delicate handwriting. Gurgur picked up a pen and began to write. Ignored, Kristy felt she had had enough.

She said: 'Very well. I'll ring up Mr Gunner.'

The threat caused a lift of Gurgur's narrow, vulpine head. He gave her an oblique glance of dislike: 'I am arranging for you to change your room.'

'Why?'

'It is too big for two people. It is a room for three people.'

'Three people? Three people can't live in one room. It's un-heard of.'

His face seemed to shrink in on itself and she knew she had said the wrong thing. To him three people in one room was not unheard of and he supposed she meant to reflect on his standards. She added weakly: 'And there is no other room.'

'Yes, I can provide another room.' Gurgur pointed through the open office door towards the door of Mrs Gunner's room: 'There is a vacant room for you.'

'Mrs Gunner's room? But that's much too small for two people.'

'On the contrary. It is a good room and has a large bed and a large wardrobe.' His eyes, more yellow than brown, were fixed severely on her: 'This is a small island, Mrs Foster, and there are many people. A whole family – a man, a wife, eight, ten, twelve children – might live in such a room as that. Perhaps you are too proud. Perhaps you spurn such poor people . . .'

'No, I do not. But Mrs Gunner's room is noisy. The servants shout and laugh and there's the clatter of the kitchen things.'

'There will be no noise. If I give the order: "no noise", there will be no noise. You will move, please, on Sunday.'

She tried to speak but Gurgur held up his hand. She need say no more. She went, near tears, to her room, thinking: 'The cleverness of the vulture.' He would not challenge the government by unhousing them. He was merely taking back the room to which, in any case, they had no right, and offering an alternative. This way, they had no cause for complaint.

'What did he want?' Hugh asked, when he returned to luncheon.

'He wants us to move into Mrs Gunner's room.'

Hugh ingested this fact in silence while Kristy sat with her head hanging, brought down by a sense of failure. She felt, had she been her old self, she could have dealt with Gurgur and somehow kept their room. But she was a fettered personality now, weakened as though by sickness. And what, in fact, could she have said or done? The quarrel over the moth had pre-defeated her. Hugh thought she had been a fool and perhaps Hugh was right. The clever ones, the ambitious ones, the ones who planned to get everything they could get, never quarrelled with anyone. They did not quarrel with the most debased. Not even with Gurgur, for who might not, by devious means, find his way to power?

Her eyes glinting wet, she murmured: 'I'm sorry.'

Looking at her, Hugh said: 'We're not going to move.' His face had taken on an expression that Kristy, during their married life, had seen only two or three times. He became pale, his mouth grew taut and his cheeks seemed to swell as though the muscles had thickened. It was an obstinate and yet vulnerable expression. She wanted to say: 'No, don't do anything. You're not strong enough,' yet he was doing what she wanted him to do. He was taking on Gurgur for her sake. He was summoning forces within himself. He had decided to fight.

'I shall telephone Ambrose from the office.' He spoke firmly but with the caution of one who moves in a bureaucracy. He would not use the Daisy telephone. No one must overhear his call. Gurgur must not be forewarned. He went back early to his office so he could put the call through from an empty room. The Praslin telephone girl took so long to find Ambrose that Hugh imagined him to be in some other world, a world so remote from the Fosters' adversity, it seemed tactless to mention it. When at last Ambrose came on the line, his charming insouciance caused Hugh to apologize: 'I do hate to trouble you but we hope you can help us. Gurgur's forcing us out of our room.'

Ambrose, who did not seem to grasp what Hugh was telling him, invited the Fosters to Sunday luncheon: 'The buffet is famous throughout the southern seas. Yachtsmen call in here simply to have lunch on Sunday. You can tell me all about it then.'

Kristy was relieved by the invitation, imagining that their absence on Sunday would confound Gurgur and delay the move. They felt it safer to slip away unseen so walked down to the harbour to find a taxi.

Ambrose, who met them among the fountains and orange-trees of the Praslin's main room, was wearing another new suit. When they expressed admiration, he said: 'I had three made by the Indian tailor down on the Harbour. Not quite Maddox Street, but a good imitation. I feel I've earned them. No need to tell you: my life at the Daisy was not spacious. Mrs G. even nagged me not to waste the bath-water. *I ask you!* Things are very different here, I can tell you. Now, what are we drinking?'

The dark amber of the window glass muted the outdoor dazzle and gave the interior the glow of gold. The half-light flattered Ambrose who looked that morning not much older than Hugh. As though suffused by his new life with new energy and impulses, he was attentive to Kristy in a flirtatious way. After seating her in one of the long cane chairs, he collected cushions to place at her back, treating her like an invalid, but a productive invalid whose condition called for approbation and respect. Hugh was irritated by her indolent acceptance of these attentions. They had come here to appeal to Ambrose. It seemed to him that Kristy, taken by Ambrose's improved appearance, was diverting him from their cause. Hugh was the more irritated because he had come to rely on her forthright habit of speech. He felt it too bad that now, when it might have been of some use, she blandly said nothing and left Hugh to break the barrier of Ambrose's urbanity. He could see he would be forced to do what he most disliked doing: make a complaint.

The hotel was quiet. Most of the guests were at the pool and the safragis were preparing the buffet on the terrace. They could be seen passing and re-passing, carrying dishes to the buffet and placing them among mosses and leaves. A screen of transparent cords – silk or nylon, Hugh thought – hung round the awning, enclosing the terrace and splintering the light into rays of red and blue.

The buffet would soon be ready and Hugh wondered whether he should speak now or wait till after luncheon. He caught the creamy smell of a cigar and, looking round, found Lomax standing behind him, waiting for an invitation to join the party. The last person Hugh wanted here was Gurgur's friend, Lomax. He thought: 'For God's sake, go away' but Ambrose, with off-handed liberality, said: 'Sit down, do. What are you going to drink?'

Lomax sat next to Hugh and they both watched Ambrose

fooling with Kristy, talking nonsense that served as conversation until the head safragi pushed open the doors to the terrace and announced that the buffet awaited them.

Ambrose caught Kristy's hands and pulled her up: 'Are you hungry?'

'I'm always hungry.'

'Then let's serve ourselves before the wolves come up from the water-hole.'

Out on the terrace, Hugh saw that the fringe round the awning was not silk or nylon: it was water. Water flowing over the awning and falling like rain to the ground, made the terrace as cool as the rest of the hotel. The guests, coming up from the pool, splashed in through the water curtain and shook themselves with a lot of laughter. They were probably not the people that Hugh and Kristy had seen on their first visit, but they looked the same: big, blonde, busty women withered by the sun and self-satisfied men flaunting their virile good looks. The safragis, though they should have become immune by now, were still goggling at the naked bosoms. As the guests crowded in, shouting to each other, piling their plates with the sea-creatures that had died to feed them, the air that had been cool and vinegary became steamy with the heat of so much flesh.

Ambrose, a guest himself, made his way good-humouredly through the press of bodies as he led his party back to the room: 'Pleasanter to eat in here, I think.' They sat down where they had sat before.

Lomax spoke quietly to Hugh: 'Something is worrying you, Mr Foster.'

'I'm afraid so.' Hugh looked at Ambrose but Ambrose was taking Kristy back to the terrace so she could refill her plate. For want of anyone else to whom he could tell his troubles, Hugh told them to Lomax: 'I know Gurgur is a friend of yours. It was unfortunate that Kristy was rude to him. Now he's turning us out of our room at the Daisy. He wants to put us into Mrs Gunner's old room which is scarcely big enough for one person, let alone two. Kristy – I don't need to tell you – is having a baby and it's unfair to move her now. I came here to have a word with Ambrose. I'm hoping he'll speak to Gurgur.'

'Will that do any good?'

'The Daisy belongs to him. Surely the final word will be with him?'

A smile afflicted Lomax's face and he turned his head as though to hide it. It was a smile of embarrassment and discomfort. The gold table in front of them had an inlay of coromandel wood. As though unwilling to say what he had to say, he traced one of the rose-purple markings with his finger, murmuring, 'I don't know ... I don't think ...' He finally said: 'The Daisy doesn't belong to Ambrose. Technically, at the moment, it belongs to no one: but Gurgur is the virtual owner. He has paid a large sum into Ambrose's account and as soon as the will is proved, the pension will be made over to him.'

Hugh, unable to speak, let his breath out with a sigh.

'It is a pity Mrs Foster was impolite to Gurgur. He is a strange man. He has a great fondness for ladies and is kind to the girls he employs. Had your wife not been impetuous. ... Had she, for instance, reproved him lightly, he would have taken it differently. You would have had no trouble.'

'She does fly off the handle at times.'

Hugh watched Kristy and Ambrose coming back from the terrace hand in hand, coquetting absurdly with each other, and he realized she had been courting Ambrose to ensure his protection against Gurgur. Hugh felt sorry for her.

With some idea of warning her and putting a stop to her nonsense, he said rather too sharply: 'We must go, Kristy.'

His tone bewildered her. Ambrose put his arm round her: 'Of course you mustn't go. You can't take Kristy away. I want her to have some millionaire's salad. Do you know why it's called that? Because it is made of palm heart. To get one dish of salad, they have to sacrifice a whole tree.'

'I wouldn't like that,' Kristy said.

'Neither would I.' Hugh stood up. He had intended to go without explanation but his disappointment had been too painful and he spoke in spite of himself: 'How could you sell the Daisy to Gurgur? To Gurgur, of all people?'

Startled, Ambrose said: 'Who told you that?'

It was evident that his dealings with Gurgur, probably illegal, were to be kept secret. He glanced at Lomax, recognized the culprit then looked back at Hugh, trying to justify himself: 'What could I do? Gurgur wanted the Daisy and I wanted the money. I may say,' he became confiding as though what he had to say made all good, 'the Daisy's days are numbered. Gurgur's only interested in the site. He wants to pull the house down and build an hotel.'

'He won't get planning permission.'

'He will, sooner or later. He knows his way around.'

'I hope he bloody well gets his fingers burned.'

Ambrose, who had not known that Hugh was capable of anger, stared unhappily at him: 'Be reasonable, Hugh. Don't spoil the party.'

Hugh signalled to Kristy who was no more ready to stay than he was. Lomax came with them to the hall, offering them a lift back in his car. Ambrose followed with a lame look, his great face settled again into the rubbery mounds and runnels of late middle age.

When they were in the car, Lomax spoke through the window: 'I could telephone Gurgur and try to talk him round. He might change his decision.'

'We'd be grateful if you would.'

Nursing this slight hope, they were driven back to the uncertainties of the Daisy.

7

When Monday came, the Fosters were still in the balcony room.

'And I've every intention of staying there,' Hugh said. He would not tell Kristy what he had decided to do but, inspired by the fact she now seemed the weaker of the two, he sent in a request for an audience with Sir George Easterbrook

The request had to be made through Pedley who treated it with suspicion: 'What d'you want to see him about?'

Hugh, grown cunning, said: 'Kristy's having a baby. I've decided to put in for a permanent appointment.'

'Ho, ho!' Pedley could not hide his delight that Hugh, who had flaunted his independence, was now seeking a way into the machine: 'I don't think they'll wear that. You scraped into a temporary post because of special skills but I can tell you this, for one thing: pukka officials are not allowed to owe money to the Inland Revenue.'

'I'm paying it off. I'll be out of debt in a year or so.'

'Yes, well, perhaps. Sir George's a busy man. Don't expect he'll see you.'

At the end of the morning, Hugh was summoned to Sir George's office. This time the summons did not disturb him. He went to his appointment with the cool resolution of a friendless man who has nothing to lose. He was equally unmoved by Sir George, who welcomed him as an old and trusted colleague whom he was glad to see: 'Hope you're settling down all right, Foster?'

The only thing that disconcerted Hugh was the fact he did not have Sir George to himself. Two Arab engineers were in the room, squatting down by the skirting board which they had pulled out from the wall so they could get at the wiring behind. Fearful of being overheard and reported back to Gurgur, Hugh edged his chair closer to the desk and spoke in a quiet voice: 'I need your help, sir. We live at the Daisy Pension. Six months ago, when we arrived here, we were put by mistake into a room reserved for Mr and Mrs Ogden. The Ogdens very kindly allowed us to keep it.'

'I heard something about that.' Sir George spoke sympathetically but, to remind Hugh that time was precious, he pulled up his cuff and exposed his wrist-watch.

Hugh spoke more quickly: 'The problem is this, sir. The pension has been taken over by a Mr Gurgur who has ordered us to move into a small, airless, noisy room beside the kitchen. My wife is very upset.'

'Um.' Sir George shook his head slowly: 'I foresaw this sort of thing. Ten years ago I indented for a residential club to house the lower-paid officials but the F.O. said: "No go." To them the Daisy was as good as government property and Mrs Gunner immortal. They've been proved wrong. I'm old in the service. I've seen the empire go down. Once we were as gods: now we're beholden to the whims of a levantine brothel-keeper.' Sir George drew in his breath and slowly let it out: 'But what can I do?'

'You could requisition our present room and keep us in it.'

'Only in an emergency.'

'This is an emergency. I was given this temporary job because no one in the service could do . . . I mean, wanted it. I've no perks or pension rights but, having come all this way, I think we've a right to reasonable accommodation. My wife is going to have a baby. No one should have to keep an infant in the room Gurgur has offered us. If we're forced into it . . .' Hugh had meant to say he would take his wife back to England but in the face of Sir George's kindness, he said: 'our position will be intolerable.'

He could see that his anguish, his obvious need, impressed Sir George as threats would not have done. Sir George picked up his pen: 'We'll have a go. I'll slap an order on him and if he ignores it . . . well, we'll think again.'

The order was written. Putting it in an envelope and handing it to Hugh, he said: 'Get Pedley to send that.' He rose and held out his hand. Hugh, amazed that he had accomplished so much, expressed his lightness of heart by asking about the engineers:

'What are they doing?'

'Don't ask me. They've been going round all the upper floors. The contractors balled-up the wiring and these fellows are putting things right. Good-bye, Foster, and good luck.'

Hugh went away, glowing with the comradeship that he felt to be between them.

That same morning, returning from her walk, Kristy found three strange women in her room. They were unpacking suitcases. Akbar, in the background, making no move to help, was watching them with a protective benevolence.

The women were surprised when Kristy entered. She said: 'This is my room.'

They looked at one another and spoke in French among themselves. Kristy saw that two of them were teenage girls, the other a woman of forty; a mother and daughters, dark, plump, short, pretty, all much alike. The girls, puzzled and timid, put down the clothes they were holding and moved behind their mother. She eyed Kristy, noting her pregnancy and her appearance of emotional weakness, and was about to approach her when Akbar took over the situation. Assuming his most domineering manner, he pointed to the door and ordered Kristy out.

'Yo' go now, *sayyida*. Yo' room now Mis' Gunner room. Akbar take all yo' things Mis' Gunner room. No more here. All gone. Yo' go Mis' Gunner room.'

Kristy stood at a loss, afraid if she opened her mouth she would burst into tears. The woman, unimpressed by Akbar, said: 'So this is your room, yes? I might have known there was a trick being played. This fellow,' she indicated Akbar, 'let me think he was the Praslin courier. He had a taxi waiting and brought us here. I asked: "Can this be the Praslin?" He said it was better than the Praslin and cheaper and there was a very nice room. We looked and, yes, the room is nice. I said we would take it, but . . .' she swung round on Akbar, nodding in a threatening way: 'I should have known. I should have known.'

Akbar, furious that his trick was turning against him, caught the woman by the shoulder and pushed her towards the balcony:

'Yo' stay there, *sayyida*. This not yo' business. This Akbar business. Yo' not speak her.'

The woman struck off his hand. Beside herself that he had dared to touch her, she seemed to spark with rage. Breaking into Arabic, she set about him with virulent contempt. Akbar, used to the liberal, inhibited manners of the English, had forgotten that there were others less forbearing in their dealings with servants. Kristy did not know what the woman was saying, but she saw its effects on Akbar. He was deeply shocked. His eyes rolled in horror and his dark, bloomy skin took on a greyish tinge. He made a croaking noise but could find no words and, abjectly silenced, he looked to Kristy as though she should defend him.

Kristy, troubled by the whole scene, said: 'It's probably not his fault. The owner here has been trying to get us out of this room.'

'No matter.' The woman turned to Kristy: 'I have told him to get me a taxi. I will not stay here to be touched by a dog, a jackal, a descendant of slaves.'

Akbar, his great, globular eyes almost falling from their sockets, spread both his monstrous hands on his chest and cried: 'Akbar no slave man. Akbar very big fellow in Soudanese country.'

The woman, shouting '*Halan, halan*', waved him away then patted Kristy's arm: 'You English do not know how to treat such people. Now, we pack again and go to the Praslin. You ask me, why did we think at all of this pension?' She laughed: 'I do not know. Sometimes it seems good to save a little money, but how foolish! I hope all is well with you, *ma chère*.'

When the taxi arrived, Hassan and Negumi were sent up for the luggage. Akbar kept out of sight. The taxi drove off with the three women and Kristy went in search of her clothes and Hugh's clothes. They had been thrown down roughly in Mrs Gunner's room, some on the bed and some on the floor. The wardrobe stood open and Kristy saw that Mrs Gunner's garments were still hanging inside. They were bright garments, mostly red or gold, sequinned dresses and jackets, child-size trouser suits, little shoes, all bearing the imprint of her body and redolent of gin and cigarette-smoke.

Kristy carried the Fosters' possessions back to the balcony

room, transporting them in five trips, then she fell on the bed and slept, exhausted.

Since the incident with Akbar, the Ogdens had kept themselves in mental seclusion. There were no affable exchanges with Simpson, no friendly talk with the Axelrods, no word at all from them until the day Kristy found the women in her room. That evening, coming in to dinner, Ogden quietly announced that he and his wife were leaving the Daisy. Mrs Hampton, hearing how Ogden's dignity had been affronted, had invited them to share her villa for the few months that remained before his retirement. There were murmurs of regret at their going and envy of their new dwelling-place, but the remarks were fraught with uncertainty and shame. For the sake of peace and comfort, their friends had failed them and Ogden, though he reproached no one, looked sadly from face to face. When he reached the Fosters, he looked not only sad but worried as though he felt they had failed him most. He had given up the balcony room to a young couple in love, an ideal young couple wrapped up in bed together 'like puppies in a basket', a vision that may have reminded him of his own youth. And how mistaken he had been!

When the day of their departure arrived, Mrs Axelrod tried to break into the Ogdens' restraint, saying: 'I won't say "good-bye" because you'll be coming back to see us very often.'

Ogden agreed: 'Oh, yes, indeed!' but no one believed him.

A few days before this, the office porter had delivered Sir George's letter of requisition. Kristy, sitting in the salon, saw Akbar and the porter talking in low voices with exaggerated gestures of dismay and horror. The porter, who gossiped with the typist, knew what was in the letter and though the matter had nothing to do with him, courtesy required him to condole with Akbar and condemn the British and all their works. Akbar, carrying the letter through the salon, was stopped in his tracks by the sight of Kristy and opening his eyes very wide, he gave a long hiss of indignation.

She foresaw some dramatic reaction to the letter, expecting Gurgur to rush out on her or other strangers to appear in her room. Nothing happened at all. That evening she and Hugh drank to Sir George and Kristy, pressing Hugh's hand, said: 'You've been very clever.' Hugh laughed, feeling that when he cared to take action, he could do as well as the next man.

He was surprised to find at the office, next day, that he had roused Pedley's rancour.

'A nice bit of business, I must say,' said Pedley, 'that letter you got Easterbrook to send. The others won't like it, you know.'

Hugh could not understand why anyone should dislike it. No one had a good word for Gurgur. It was not known whether he lived at the pension but the sense of him pervaded the house as though a corpse had been walled up in its fabric.

'Why should they mind?' Hugh asked.

'It's your attitude they don't like. You think, because you're the bright swinging chicks, you should get the best room in the pension. If you don't, you rush upstairs and blackmail Sir George.'

'I told him my wife's having a baby.'

'And why can't your wife go back home like every other wife who has a baby? Because, whatever happens, you're a special case. You don't even mix with your own group in the service. I'm told you're seen around with a pretty dodgy crowd. In this place, it doesn't pay to mix with outsiders.'

'What is Gopal? – insider or outsider?'

Pedley stared at Hugh, the yellow growths standing out from the liverish white of his eyes, and spoke distinctly: 'Gopal is a source of information, though he doesn't know it. He thinks he's the clever one. He thinks he's the fixer. Fact is, he talks too much. He gives himself away. All these speculators who see money in Bustan – they all go to work through Gopal. When he comes asking for favours, I know just who's on the make now. At the moment he's working on behalf of your friend Lomax and it'll do Lomax no good at all.'

Pedley, having proved himself the clever one, turned on his heel and left Hugh to reflect on what he had learnt. Hugh said to himself: 'At least we've beaten that bastard, Gurgur.' With this consoling thought, he returned to the Daisy at midday and found Kristy sitting bleakly on the edge of the bed. All her papers had been thrown on the floor. The writing-desk had been taken while she was out for her walk.

'In future,' Hugh said, 'we'll keep the door locked.'

'What good would that do? The room has to be cleaned and Akbar has a pass key.'

Had it not been for Pedley's strictures, he would have gone back to Sir George for help but now he was inhibited, realizing he seemed to the others a spoilt, demanding junior. If he could not go to Sir George, who else was there? Not Ambrose. And Simon Hobhouse had taken himself off again. Only one name occurred to him: Lomax. Lomax had offered to speak to Gurgur. Lomax was in a position to make peace between them. When he returned to the office, Hugh telephoned the Praslin. As soon as he heard Lomax's voice, he knew that whatever plea had been made for them, had failed.

Sounding remote and embarrassed, Lomax said: 'I tried to reason with him, but it's gone too far. He refused to discuss it. I am afraid I can do nothing.'

Who else was there? There was no one else.

The pension linen was changed every other day. The Fosters' towels and bed-linen were not changed. The cloth on their table was replaced by one that was not only not clean: it was very dirty. A cup of coffee had been spilt across it and the large, salient stain seemed to mark them as friendless and victimized.

Hugh could go to his office but for Kristy there was no escape. She was sitting on the balcony when Akbar entered without knocking and surveyed the room as though deciding what to take next. He had brought three safragis with him and they, seeing Kristy, began to retreat but Akbar recalled them sternly.

Kristy entered the room to ask: 'What have you done with my writing-desk?'

'That desk too big. That desk belong Mas' Gurgur: he need it.' Akbar looked out at the balcony table and chairs: 'Mas' Gurgur say he need these one, two things.'

'He has no right to them. The furniture has been requisitioned.'

'No, only room rekwishoned. Furniture Mas' Gurgur furniture.'

Kristy returned to her chair on the balcony and put her feet up on the opposite chair and the safragis were confounded. They dared not move Kristy and Kristy refused to move.

Akbar said grimly: 'We come back *bukra*' and next day, while the Fosters were at breakfast, not only the balcony furniture but the arm-chair and sofa were moved out.

If the other guests knew what was happening, they said and did nothing. They had not supported the Ogdens, so why should they support the Fosters? Besides, they had other cause for complaint. If they brought their own wine up from Aly's, Gurgur charged them corkage. If someone wanted a meal in his room, Gurgur put an extra ten rupees on the bill. Mrs Gunner had kept the Daisy as an English preserve. Gurgur was willing to take all comers. The room left vacant by the Ogdens was let to an Egyptian couple. Mrs Gunner had served meals to residents only. Gurgur pushed the tables closer together, added more tables and advertised that his restaurant was open to everyone.

Mrs Axelrod was angered most by the Egyptians, a fat elderly man with a young wife. The man, who wore his fez at the table, roused in her so much consternation that her husband could not keep her quiet.

'What have we got sitting with us?' she asked aloud. 'A bloody safragi?'

The Egyptian, on his first appearance in the dining-room, called Akbar and explained that his wife was slimming. She did not eat luncheon so he required a rebate on her food. Both men were Arabic-speaking but, to Mrs Axelrod's joy, neither could understand the other's Arabic and they were obliged to speak in English. Akbar went to consult with Gurgur and returned to say that a rebate could not be allowed. During the long argument that followed, Mrs Axelrod broke in every few moments with appreciative hoots of 'Hah!'

It was decided in the end that the Egyptian would eat his wife's luncheon as well as his own. After his first meal, he would stroll round the garden to prepare himself for the second. This solution so transported Mrs Axelrod that she spent every luncheon watching the Egyptian throughout his meals and commenting on his progress.

The Fosters, lost in their own troubles, gained little from these diversions. They could only wonder what Gurgur would do next.

One evening, Kristy, coming out on the balcony to view the

sunset, looked into the Lettuce Room and saw it was filled with Gurgur's girls. The girls must have noticed her for they at once began to pull down the blinds. While this was going on, Kristy saw a male figure leave a car and make a cautious detour in order to reach the Lettuce Room unseen from the windows of the Daisy. She recognized Culbertson, the Chief of Police. He went in through the new rear door and she heard him greeted by female cries of delight. Culbertson was not the only member of the force to visit the Lettuce Room but he was the only Englishman and his patronage of Gurgur gave her a bitter sense of betrayal by her own kind. Then it occurred to her that Gurgur had wanted to dispossess them because of this vantage point. They would see too much and know too much and in her nervous state, she began to imagine Gurgur murdering them – poison in the food, an attack in the dark – simply to get rid of them.

Hugh, returning each evening as harassed as she was, would ask: 'Has anything happened?' Within a week, the room had been denuded of everything except the bed and a bedside table that had to accommodate the reading-lamp and all Kristy's make-up pots. Thinking about it, she began, at the dinner-table, to laugh hysterically.

Hugh, on edge, said: 'For God's sake, stop that.'

She pointed to the stain on the table-cloth: 'Look, it's like a giraffe. And the room: it's like that place the Tibetans believe in. A sort of half-way house in the next world. What's it called? Braham?'

'I've never heard of it.'

'When you get there, you make your own surroundings. You can think up exactly what you want but you have to keep a sharp look-out because it's a thought structure and parts are liable to disappear. The room's like that. We keep losing bits of it.'

Hugh frowned, not liking this sort of talk.

'But not just the room. Everything, everything.' Kristy gulped, making an effort to control herself: 'It's the same with the world. I hate the destructiveness. One wants to save it, to cling to what's left but every day . . . I feel I'm holding on to one corner and then another corner, and they're all slipping away.'

She seemed on the verge of hysteria and Hugh checked her sharply: 'Shut up. Don't let them see you crying.'

She kept her head down for several minutes then whispered: 'Do something.'

'What can I do?'

'Go and see Easterbrook again.'

'I can't. He'd only think I'm a nuisance. We get what we pay for: bed and board. We're on our own. We have to fight this ourselves.'

Kristy brooded a while, staring at the stain on the cloth, then, gathering her strength, she said: 'O.K., we fight.'

Hugh watched anxiously as she lifted her end of the cloth and put the dishes and cutlery on the bare wood of the table. When the cloth was clear, she threw it on to the floor. Negumi, quite bewildered, picked it up and took it to Akbar who appeared to be scandalized. Frowning darkly, he took the cloth to the Fosters and asked: 'Why yo' do dat?'

'The cloth is dirty,' Kristy said.

'No surprise. Yo' very dirty people.'

'You're quite right. So we're better without a table-cloth.'

'Bad people. Bad, bad people,' said Akbar as he returned to his post.

No one appeared to disapprove Kristy's action. On the contrary, Mrs Axelrod looked appreciative and Simpson smiled at her like an old friend. For the first time since their arrival, Hugh felt rather proud of his wife.

Another cloth was put on the table; not a clean cloth but one that was tolerably half-clean. The bed-linen, however, was not changed and being constantly sweat-soaked, it soon had a putrid smell that became the smell of the room. Conditioned to it, Kristy was the more surprised when she returned one day to find the air heavy with her Balmain scent. The bedside table had gone and everything on it had been tipped on to the bed. She was careless with bottle tops and the scent had soaked through the bedclothes. The combination of odours made her feel sick. When Hugh came home, she said:

'The boat arrives tomorrow. Let's pack and go.'

'Nothing would please Gurgur more.'

'How much longer can we bear these filthy sheets?'

Even the servants, it seemed, felt that the sheets disgraced the pension. Hassan approached Kristy in a nervous, secretive way and whispered: 'Why you not ask Akbar to help you?'

'*Akbar?*'

'Give Akbar little money, you have new sheets, new towels.'

'I can't believe it.'

'Yes, yes, *sayyida*. Akbar say ten rupee and all towels new. Come now, *sayyida*, it better for you.'

Kristy handed over the ten rupees and the bargain was kept. Not only did they get clean sheets and towels but Akbar began to take a paternal interest in their table. Two days later they were given a clean table-cloth. The Fosters, amazed, realized that Akbar, the magnificent, had needed only to be bought.

But the furniture was not returned. Now that she was heavy and dull-footed, Kristy found the size of the room a burden. She was always crossing empty space to reach the cupboards or bed or balcony. There was nowhere to sit except the bed. She began to feel that any room, even Mrs Gunner's room, would be preferable if in it she could feel secure and free from persecution. She said to Hugh, desperately: 'Let's do what he wants. Let's move.'

For a moment Hugh looked as though he, too, would be thankful to move, then an obstinate expression came over his face: 'A nice couple of fools we'd look, moving now when he's taken all he can take. There's nothing left but the bed and if that goes, we've real cause for complaint. He's done his worst. Now he'll have to leave us alone.'

But Hugh had overlooked the vulture's skill at picking the last shred of sinew from a denuded bone. Or so Kristy thought. In fact, he had not overlooked it, he simply turned his back on it. His work, he felt, was tedium enough without the strain of returning to the pension in fear of some new reprisal. When Kristy came down to dinner with the air of one still in the fight, he wanted to say: 'Don't tell me.'

Her appearance disturbed him. She looked breathlessly elated, yet strange. Her face seemed to have shrunk and her cheeks had lost their colour but she was more vivacious than she had been for many a month. She said: 'He's taken out the light bulbs.'

'So we're without light?'

'No. I borrowed a chair from Simpson's room and got the bulbs from the corridor. I put them into our room.'

'Then you'd better take them out again.'

'Like hell I will.'

Her gaiety seemed unnatural to Hugh: 'Are you all right?'

'I feel marvellous,' she said but there had been an aberrant instant when, reaching up to the chandelier in the room, her consciousness shifted. When she thought of it, it still seemed that in that instant she had lost her balance and fallen into a void. But she had not fallen. She found herself where she had been: on Simpson's chair, putting the bulbs into the chandelier in the dark room.

It was to be a memorable evening. While they were sitting over their coffee in the salon, Ambrose entered the pension with the assurance of a proprietor. He paused, expecting a welcome, but the only welcome came from the Fosters.

Though they had quarrelled with him, they were, in their forlorn situation, thankful to see him. He joined them rapturously and called on Negumi to bring him coffee. Hassan, abandoning the bar, ran to his old employer. Ambrose, struggling to his feet, embraced Hassan who was so overcome that a tear rolled down his worn, yellow face. Returning to the bar, he sent Negumi over with three glasses of brandy and only after argument would he accept payment for them.

The small jocular party of Ambrose, Hugh and Kristy was islanded in a sea of disapproval. Unfriendly eyes viewed Ambrose's new elegance and air of well-being. How had he achieved them? By selling the Daisy up the river.

The Fosters, unable to forget their wretched plight, were a little hysterical in their merriment. This went unnoticed by Ambrose who was eager to pass on an amusing piece of news.

He said: 'Believe it or not, Lomax is in love.'

Kristy had been laughing too much. Now she attracted attention by shouting wildly: 'You're joking!'

'I assure you, I'm not. He met the lady while he was in Beirut and she's followed him here. And, I may say, he's not done badly. She's a pretty widow with a house in the Lebanon and orchards and vineyards. What more could anyone want?'

'How about two pretty daughters?'

Ambrose's eyes opened as he gazed on Kristy: 'But she *has* two pretty daughters. It's most unjust, a cold fish like Lomax getting not one woman but three.'

'You wicked old thing! You want her yourself.'

'Well, I will say she finds me quite entertaining. But he saw her first. I'm afraid they're already engaged.'

When they had talked right through Lomax, the Fosters could not keep from mentioning Gurgur and what he had done to them. They joked about the disappearing furniture hoping, in spite of their laughter, that Ambrose could set things right. Ambrose was quick to promise help: 'I've come to pick up Mrs G.'s clothes. He rang me to remind me they were here. I said I'd look into the Lettuce Room before I go. Don't worry, I'll have a word with him.'

'Lomax tried . . .' Hugh said.

'Oh, Lomax! He doesn't know how to tackle Gurgur. I'll see the old thing: I'll get round him.'

The Fosters, in spite of everything, were elated by Ambrose's self-assurance. Why should he not succeed where Lomax failed? He had a charm that Lomax lacked. Seeing them delivered from misery, Kristy, still wideawake at eleven o'clock, was as vivacious as she had ever been.

Hugh told Ambrose: 'It must be your company. She's usually dead on her feet by ten.'

Ambrose, taking her vitality as a compliment to himself, flirted with her and held her hand in his, but at last he had to go. Lomax's car awaited him and the chauffeur was brought in to carry the little bright garments outside.

'What will you do with them?' Kristy asked.

'He'll distribute them among the girls at the Dobo. Very much their *goût*.'

Ambrose went, as promised, to the Lettuce Room and was gone so long that only the Fosters remained when he put his head into the salon. He called 'Be seeing you' and sped away.

221

Kristy cried: 'Go after him. Ask him what Gurgur said,' and Hugh, running out into the darkness, caught the car as it was about to move off. He looked into the window and Ambrose seemed to shrink from him.

'It was no good. He wouldn't listen to me.'

'Thank you for trying.'

As he returned to Kristy, Hugh thought he had touched the nadir of dejection yet the next day's events were so much worse, they reduced Gurgur's vengeance to insignificance.

Hugh had gone first down to breakfast, expecting Kristy to follow him. She did not follow and when he had eaten, he went back to the room, fearing fresh persecution. He found her still in her dressing-gown, standing on the wide, empty floor, crying helplessly. All he could feel was an exasperated inertia.

'What's happened now?'

She shook her head, unable to speak. He went to her and put an arm round her: 'Kristy, what's happened?' She was soaked with tears but he was troubled less by her tears than the limp despair of her whole body. He shook her: 'Tell me what's happened.'

'It's dead.'

'What's dead?'

'The baby. The baby's dead.'

'Of course it isn't dead. Don't be silly.' He led her over to the bed and sat her down. She had been wringing a towel between her hands. He took it from her and wiped her face with it: 'Where did you get this idea?'

She said that while lying in the bath, she had noticed a crease across her belly. The distended flesh had shrunk, only slightly but she was frightened because it was a reversal of the natural process. She tried to remember when she had last felt the child move. Not during the night, not the previous evening. She got out of the bath, dried herself and placed her hands over her stomach. She *sensed* a lack of life.

'Last night I was wide-awake at eleven o'clock. Now I know why.'

Hugh did not believe any of it. He tried to reason with her but she only dropped down on the bed and wept afresh. It had occurred to him that the pregnancy might end itself, and what a relief that would be! But now, disturbed for Kristy's sake, he went to telephone Mueller and the expected relief came only when Mueller laughed at Kristy's alarm.

'I will see her today,' he said. 'But, Mr Foster, you need not be alarmed. Ladies have these ideas at such a time.'

That confirmed Hugh's own opinion but when he returned at lunch-time, he found Kristy lying as he had left her, in a half-waking stupor, the parturient bloom all gone from her face.

They walked up to see Mueller in the mid-afternoon. The trade wind, hot and dusty, was blowing fiercely against them. Hugh supporting her, held her hand with the tenderness of their earliest days together but Kristy offered no response. In her spiritless silence, she looked a figure of such desolation that even Dr Mueller stopped laughing when he saw her. He regained himself quickly and taking her from Hugh, said in a comforting tone: 'It'll be all right, you will see.'

When she returned, Hugh, confident she would come out reassured, looked into her face and knew that her fear had been confirmed.

Blundering downhill, head hanging as though nothing could ever rouse her again, Kristy would not let him take her hand. He felt guilty, having wished the child away. He blamed himself as though, by wishing, he had killed it; and, at the same time, he shared the shock of loss. He had, he felt, rejected the one thing that would have brought purpose into their lives and his punishment was the sight of Kristy, desolate. But too late was too late. And now he must comfort her as best he could. He felt an acute pity for her, an acute sense of his responsibility. He caught her hand and held to it against her inclination and gradually her fingers relaxed in his hold. When he saw she was weeping again, he put his arm round her shoulders and drew her close to him.

8

It would be a week or two before Kristy could go into hospital. Dr Mueller had to send to Durban for the drug that would induce delivery. He warned her that as she was nearly seven months' pregnant, the induction would take a little time.

'But only a little time,' he said, still trying to put a smiling face on things. 'You must not be afraid. There is nothing in this to harm you.'

'I am not afraid for myself.' Kristy was very dull these days, letting herself be examined and organized as though she had lost the incentive to live.

Mueller, whose concern was with life, was at a loss with her. He tried to revive her spirits by telling her: 'This is something that does not happen often. It is, indeed, rare. Next time, it will not happen, I promise you. So do not worry. You feel well, don't you?'

'I feel like a walking cemetery.'

The simile shocked him yet she realized that other people were inclined to the same idea. From the furtive glances of the women in the dining-room she knew the matron had put the news around: the child, though still inside her, was dead. She was a curiosity. Even Hugh could not reassure her about this. In Mrs Gunner's day they could have taken their meals in their room but now they could neither ask for privileges nor hope they might be granted.

Kristy no longer went for morning walks but sometimes, in the afternoons, Hugh would persuade her to go down to the harbour or up to the plantations. He began to be oppressed by these two walks, all that the island could offer, and said: 'When this is over, let's go away somewhere.'

'Where could we go?' Kristy spoke as though the island had so narrowed in on her, there was no escape from it. Still she trudged uphill or downhill, making no complaints. Hugh would have preferred a stream of self-pity which he could try to combat, but she said nothing. When he talked, he wondered if she were listening, if she were there at all. It was as though, unable to live with the dead, she had moved out of herself.

For moments her depression weighed on him so he became exasperated and said: 'Don't take it so badly. After all, you have a life of your own.'

They had reached the plantations. She said: 'I'd like to walk to the mango tree.'

'I really haven't time.'

'Don't worry. I can go alone.'

She hurried across to the lane, moving, for once, as though she had some reason for moving. Contrite, he followed her and caught her up when she stopped in front of the tree. She was staring up into the branches.

'What have you found?'

She shook her head: 'Nothing. The bird has gone.'

On the way back they met three young Arabs; three Arabs like the three who had met Lomax under the bread-fruit tree. Not only that, but two of them were the men he had seen working in Sir George's room. He was surprised that they recognized Kristy and stopped to speak to her.

One of them, who wore Arab dress, said with a half-humorous irony: 'Have you been looking for our friend Gopal? He is not here, you know. He has been sent on an important mission to the coast. He has taken the ministers to observe parliament sitting in Nairobi.'

Kristy introduced the men to Hugh. Musa looked him over with a smile of sardonic interest then said: 'Will you come with your wife to visit me? Please come. I would like you to come on Thursday at six o'clock.'

Kristy explained that she would be in hospital at that time. Musa, swinging round on Hugh, said: 'Then you will come alone, Mr Foster. I should be honoured by your visit.'

'It would be impossible. I have to be in my office at six o'clock.'

'I am sorry to hear that.'

Throughout this fervent invitation, Musa smiled his sardonic smile and was still smiling when he lifted his hand to Kristy and walked away. Hugh felt that Musa was laughing at him but the other two men, when he looked at them, were regarding him with reflective seriousness. He said: 'I saw you working in Sir George Easterbrook's office.'

One of them replied: 'I am an engineer', and they hurried after Musa.

Hugh, bewildered by the invitation, made so precisely for a certain day and hour, said: 'Is he usually as strange as that?'

'Was he strange?' Kristy asked, her mind on other things.

Required to spend the day fasting, she went early to the hospital on Wednesday. Hugh, alone at the breakfast-table, feeling conspicuous and futile, was thankful when Ambrose came in looking for him.

Ambrose had a solemn expression, conveying the fact that whatever had got him up and dressed and to the Daisy at that hour, was weighty business. He sat opposite Hugh and bending across the table, said in his smallest voice: 'I'm leaving on the boat. I've a taxi waiting. I just looked in to say my adieux. How's Kristy?'

Hugh described the calamity that had come down on them, not out of a clear sky, but a sky so occluded with vexations and tensions, he had not, at first, been able to comprehend Kristy's sense of loss.

'But I feel it now, more than I would have thought possible.'

'I'm sorry. Deeply sorry.' For a moment Ambrose hung his head in sorrow but there was the pressing matter of his imminent departure: 'I'm afraid I can't stay. I must . . .'

'But where are you going? When are you coming back?'

'I can't tell you at this juncture, but I'll write. I'll explain everything.' Ambrose squeezed Hugh's hand.

'You're not in trouble, I hope?'

'No. *Au contraire*.'

'What about the treasure? You're not dropping that?'

Ambrose laughed: 'What a piece of nonsense that was! I

226

must fly. We'll meet again one day. I've always been fond of you.'

'And I of you. Let me come down to the harbour and see you off.'

'Dear friend, no.' As Hugh made to rise, Ambrose pushed him back into his chair: 'I'm not alone. A lady. Three ladies, in fact. Three delicious girls. When we meet, I shall have not only a wife but two daughters. But, meanwhile, good-bye and love to Kristy.'

Hugh was not much surprised when Lomax rang him at the office and asked him to luncheon. He was about to refuse when Lomax said: 'I beg you to come. I must talk to someone.'

With a desolating sense of being forced to add to his own unhappiness, Hugh accepted and was picked up by the chauffeur at one o'clock.

Lomax sat alone in the brown gloom of the Praslin's main room. He was drinking a martini. Hugh, served with the same, found it was practically neat gin.

Lomax looked unusually flushed: 'Do you know that Ambrose has left the island? My friend, Mrs Namier – we were on the point of becoming engaged – is with him. Her daughters, too. They all went without a word. I came down to find them gone. Mrs Namier left a letter which was handed to me. I wish you to read it.'

The letter, on three sheets of hotel writing-paper, was in Ambrose's small hand. Taking it reluctantly, Hugh asked: 'Must I read all this?'

'If you would be so kind.'

The letter, which had been written to Mrs Namier, was a declaration of love. 'A blinding attraction,' Ambrose called it. 'Truly love at first sight.' His passion, he said, had developed rapidly until he was possessed by only one wish in life: to make her his wife. He was not the most handsome of men, or the youngest, or the richest, but he could offer her his experience and a devotion in the highest traditions of an English gentleman. He was a squire and his understanding of estate management would be of considerable use to her. Till recently, he had kept up the family home of the Gunners . . .'

'I can't read any more.'

'Please read the last page.'

The last page began: '. . . but you will say "What of Lomax?" I feel bound to tell you that Lomax is an abnormal man. His desire to marry you is a last desperate throw. He is a depressive and a homosexual who, having failed to attract me and the male sex in general, now wants to try his luck with the female. . . .'

Hugh put the letter down and took up his drink: 'Why do you show me this?'

'Ambrose was my friend. He was also yours. I thought you should know his true character. There is no truth in what he says about me. It is slander. I have no abnormal tendencies.'

Acutely embarrassed, Hugh said: 'He may have misunderstood you. You *did* tell me that you loved him.'

'Is it abnormal to love a friend? In Shakespeare a man will say he loves another man.'

'Yes, but nowadays we do not use the word so widely.'

Lomax called the safragi to bring more martinis. He drank, staring reflectively before him and after long consideration of his case, said sadly: 'So I was misunderstood. I am afraid that must happen very often. I am very much alone. I know how to make money but I do not know how to spend it. I do not know how to make friends. It is not that I do not want people: I feel they do not want me. When Ambrose approached me, I was pleased. . . . Yes, I was pleased.'

Hugh saw that Lomax knew too much about himself. Had he been less sensitive, he might have blundered through as well as another. He went on talking, explaining that when he was young, he thought he had only to make money and everything else would be added to him. He had been surprised to realize that it was the poor who attracted friends, not the rich. Hugh, hearing his voice coming as from the other side of a chasm, thought: 'That is tragedy: to be aware of one's shortcomings yet unable to surmount them.' He soon grew bored with Lomax's tragedy and his thoughts went to Kristy. What was happening to her at that moment? He remembered her grief when she knew the child was dead. He had been moved at the time but now she was in Mueller's hands, he could ask why so much love had been wasted on a creature she had never seen? A burden that had brought her

228

creativity to a stop? Certainly she had wasted no love on him. He was like Lomax, a loser where relationships were concerned.

Lomax, smiling his agonized smile, said: 'I suppose I suffer from the disease of the rich. If anyone approaches me, I think "He does not want me: he wants my money."'

'Does it matter so much what someone wants? Is it better to be wanted for your looks? Looks are the result of a genetic accident: they don't last. Money, if you take care of it, is yours for life.'

Lomax, merely puzzled by this attempt to reassure him, sighed, perhaps feeling he had called across the chasm and found nothing there. Hugh wondered if Lomax had hoped he might replace Ambrose. He thought: 'poor devil' and liked the man no better than before.

Lomax took out a packet of Gauloises and was about to light a cigarette when the luncheon bell rang. He put the cigarette carefully back into the pack and lit, instead, Ambrose's letter to Mrs Namier. They left it burning in the ash-tray.

Luncheon was a strained and depressing meal. Lomax, laughing suddenly, said: 'There will be no treasure hunt!'

'You did not give Ambrose the money?'

Lomax made a movement of the head that did not say yes or no. Hugh, realizing the man could not bear to say more, let the matter drop.

When they had eaten, Lomax strolled out on to the terrace and walked on over the grass, under a sky so brilliant the eye avoided a direct glance. He seemed not to know what he was doing and Hugh followed, concerned for him. At the pool, the bathers had retreated under awnings but Lomax walked on beneath the white-hot sky and came to a stop beside the mangosteens. He stood in the wind blowing hot off the blaze of the shore. The sea had the blue-blackness of ink. Occasionally the long roller bent the surface, moving slowly and frothing in whiter than the sand.

Finding the light acutely uncomfortable, Hugh said: 'I have to go to the hospital to see my wife.'

'Ah! Your baby is coming?'

'No. We have lost him.'

Lomax contracted his shoulders regretfully: 'I will send for my chauffeur and he can drive you.' When they parted, he held out his hand: 'You were kind to listen to me. I appreciate your kindness.'

Hugh was not allowed to see Kristy. The matron told him she was too drowsy to recognize him and her condition was unchanged.

9

The Indian nurse told Kristy that the room she was given had been Mrs Gunner's room.

'You mean, she died here?'

'This very old hospital. In every room people die.'

The small cream-washed room with its brown hospital furniture looked towards the cemetery. The nurse thought this an advantage as the front rooms, exposed like bird-cages on the island's façade, could be unpleasantly hot. The back room, though in shadow, seemed suffocating to Kristy as she lay sweating in the unfamiliar, narrow bed, the pitocin drip passing into her outstretched arm. The only effect of the drug was to deaden her consciousness. The day wore on: the spasms started and stopped, started and stopped, and the matron, annoyed by the perversity of Kristy's pelvic floor, increased the drip and tried to speed the birth for Dr Mueller's sake. Even so, it was midnight before he need be summoned and dawn was breaking when he at last managed to drag the unaiding foetus out of the birth canal.

Kristy, feeling she had reached the limit of human endurance, whimpered: 'Put me to sleep. Why don't you put me to sleep?' but no one listened to her. Dr Mueller, his shirt-sleeves rolled above the elbow, sweated in the heavy night-time air. The matron stood by, exhausted but determined to see what there was to be seen.

To Kristy it seemed she had become for them no more than an awkward portmanteau that had to be unpacked. Feeling a raw and crunching sensation as the flesh was pulled from her flesh, she ceased to control herself and screamed aloud.

The matron had no ears for her but Dr Mueller looked surprised as though he had forgotten he was handling a sentient being. As the matron stared keenly at the product of so much pain, Kristy turned her face from it and said: 'I don't want to see it.'

The matron said: 'It's a girl,' adding reflectively but reluctantly: 'It's perfectly formed.'

'Let me sleep. Only let me sleep,' Kristy said. 'Why didn't you give me an anaesthetic?'

'Oh, come, come, Mrs Foster!' Now that he had earned his fee, Mueller was his old jolly self: 'It was so quick.'

'It took all day.'

Kristy slept till the early afternoon when she was awakened in the mysterious half-light of her small room by the opening of the door. Dr Dixon looked in and, satisfied she was awake, nodded to her and said: 'I have examined the foetus. The cord was around the neck so the child was strangled. I thought you should know it was not your fault.'

Kristy tried to find strength to ask: 'Who said it was my fault?' but she did not need to ask. Behind the old doctor as he moved away, she saw the matron's simpering, sheepish face.

The Indian nurse came to tell Kristy that, as a government wife, she might lie on the balcony. She accepted the privilege but it did not mean much to her. She scarcely bothered to glance down on the Residency garden and the idyllic shore where the Chief Secretary and his friends went water-skiing.

Hugh, coming to see her before going to the office, saw she was once again the thin, pallid young woman he had married, but her vitality had not returned. Dr Mueller was sitting beside her. Patting her hand, he cheerfully said: 'You must be pregnant again straight away. Now, at once, immediately. Do not wait. And next time, I promise, all will be well.'

'How can you be so sure?'

'I am sure. You can believe me.'

Kristy did not believe him. She gave him a stare of dislike and took her hand away. She wanted no more of Dr Mueller with his self-confidence and the physical intimacies of pre-natal examinations. She was disgusted by all of it.

Disconcerted by her coldness, he rose, saying: 'For a little while, good-bye. Soon I shall see you again.'

When he was out of hearing, Kristy said: 'I want to go back to England, it doesn't matter how. I'll go steerage from the Cape, if that's the best we can manage. You've only got another five months here. I'll find us a flat. I'll see you have a job to come home to. I'll rally the friends. Something is sure to turn up.'

Greatly relieved that she was again her managing, independent self, he said: 'Yes, it'll take your mind off things.' He knew he would return to find the world organized for him.

The matron, excusing herself, came out and shook up Kristy's pillows, then said with an insinuating sweetness: 'So Mr Gunner has left us? I'm told he went with a lady and those who saw them said they seemed very close.'

Hugh said: 'The lady and Mr Gunner are about to be married.'

'You don't say! Who'd've thought it?'

She took herself off and Hugh and Kristy sat in silence. They could go, they could start again, but here they had been defeated. Hugh felt the inertia of low spirits, thinking of the dull evening ahead and the lonely supper-table. Realizing that that would be his whole life after she had gone, he was dejected, feeling that without her, he would be in limbo.

She put out her hand to him and asked: 'What has happened to your friend Hobhouse?'

'I think he's camping on the other side of the island.'

'What does he do there?'

'I don't know.'

Hugh remained with Kristy till the sun touched the horizon then he had to set out for the office. As he walked down the road, the first flame streaks of the sunset reached out overhead. He was late but refused to hurry. The evening show of scarlet and aurum filled the sky then in an instant, like a conjuring trick, the colours were gathered into the black of night. He quickened his steps. The stars, appearing almost at once, looked to Hugh unusually clear and brilliant. He saw the reason for this when he reached the square. The upper road was unlit. The Government Offices were in darkness. He could see the flash of torches as men moved about inside, probably trying to trace the fault. He found the porter standing in the doorway and decided to wait there with him till the lights came on.

'In one, two minutes, all good,' the porter said. The lights had failed to come on after sunset but, luckily, the engineers had been on the spot and were putting things right.

Standing in the darkness, Hugh could hear the rustle of the land-crabs as they made their nightly journey down to the stream. He breathed in the scents of the lemon vine, the white cleodendrum, the fabled cereus, the gardenia trees and felt their luxury was overpowering. This world was not for Kristy and him. Could he, he wondered, break his contract and return home with her?

A van drew up in the square and two men jumped out of it. As they approached, Hugh saw they were carrying a large laundry-basket. One of them shouted: '*Manashef nadtheefa*' and the porter, cheerfully standing aside for them, said jokingly: 'You work late tonight.'

Laughing good-humouredly, the men went into the dark building and the porter, full of a sense of his important position, told Hugh a long story about rivalry among the suppliants who were still sitting on the white seat, not caring whether the lights were on or off.

The story was in mid-flow when a group of men, six or eight of them, came pelting across the hall and flung themselves out of the door with a vigour that was like panic. Each was holding an electric torch and as a light lit on Hugh's face, one of the men caught his arm.

'I am Mohammed. Musa's man. Run. Run quickly.'

'But why?'

Mohammed made no reply but gripping Hugh fiercely by the wrist, he propelled him across the square and up the road past the church. Looking back and seeing no one was following, Hugh could make nothing of this treatment. If there was cause for urgency, the fact was known only to those who ran with him. He shouted: 'Haven't you warned the others?' but as he spoke, it was too late for warning. The explosion came in a chain of noise, one detonation rising from the other, and as the blast rushed between Hugh and his captor, Mohammed let go his hold and Hugh was blown against the Residency wall. The adobe surface gave as he struck it and he was no more than half-stunned

as he went to the ground. Mohammed, bending over him, said:
'I go now. I go.'

Hugh dropped his head, unwilling to move, and feeling the
earth sinking beneath him, he clung to it and let it carry him
down.

PART THREE

The Rain Forest

1

Kristy, still on the balcony, was shaken out of her indifference by the explosion. She roused herself and watched in amazement as blocks of white coral, rising into the distant darkness, were caught in the yellow glimmer from the hospital windows. They rose in an unhurried way, like bubbles rising in water, then, turning as in some elaborate juggling act, they fell back and others took their place. Landing somewhere, they made a slapping noise as though they were striking water.

There had been an earlier alarm when the lights failed. The Indian nurse had been on her way to Kristy but turned, calling: 'I come back' and went to see what the trouble was. There had been darkness filled with the cries and chatter of the patients, then the hospital dynamo was started up. Emergency lights came on and the patients laughed though the lights were so weak that some were red and some yellowish-brown. The Indian nurse had just returned to the balcony when the uproar started below.

'What is it, you think?' she leant over the balcony rail then, as though time were running swiftly backwards, she was swept into the corridor and flung against the table.

Kristy, alone on her precarious eyrie, heard the explosions gathering force, swelling and breaking into reverberations and counter-reverberations, striking the cliff behind the hospital and making the whole building rattle. The windows broke, glass crashed to the ground outside and the patients wailed in terror.

The noise died out at last and Kristy found herself unhurt.

Simon Hobhouse, driving down from the Medina, picked out a body by the light of his headlamps. It was a male body in European dress and as people passed, excitedly running down to the square, they tripped over it or jumped over it. Simon stopped because it looked familiar. When he bent over it, he found it was Hugh Foster, the man he had been going to visit.

'What on earth are you doing here? I nearly ran you down.' Getting no reply, he dragged Hugh into the back seat of the Land-Rover, shone a torch on his face and finding he was alive, threw a blanket over him.

By this time the road was packed with people, all eagerly making their way to the scene of the detonation. Driving slowly through them, Simon reached the church and decided to go no farther. He could just discern by the light from the stars the vast pyramid of coral that had once formed the Government Offices. Crowded round its perimeter were Arabs, Indians and Negroes, all in a state of admiration, gazing, shouting but doing nothing else. Simon was no more inclined than they to start rescue work. Backing the Land Rover in beside the church, he turned and drove uphill against the flow of pedestrians and cyclists. All the way up to the plantations, they came rollicking down on either side, slapping the Land-Rover on the bonnet and bawling excitedly across it.

Some distance along the plantation road, Simon met the cavalcade coming down from the police barracks. As the vehicles manoeuvred to pass him on the narrow track, Culbertson leant out from his armoured car and gazed into the Land-Rover: 'Who's that? Hobhouse? Where d'you think you're going? Don't you know the Offices have collapsed? Our chaps are under the rubble? Aren't you going to give a hand?'

Simon stared at Culbertson, considered the proposition, and said: 'No.'

'God damn it, Hobhouse, you're a doctor. We'll need all the help we can get.'

'You'll find plenty down there, if you can organize it. And you'd better hurry. They're buried and pretty soon they'll be smothered.' Simon threw back his head and laughed, then, mounting the earth at the side of the road, accelerated and passed the procession while Culbertson bawled after him. He drove round the Medina wall and stopped in the car park. He looked for the owner of the petrol pump and finding the café empty, he took the pump key from the ledge where it was kept and filled his petrol tank. He did not stop again until he was through the orchards and had reached the Moslem cemetery on the edge of the grasslands. He shook Hugh and asked: 'Are you all right?'

Hugh mumbled and put an arm over his face.

Simon went on, his headlights touching the gravestones that were all much alike: a narrow pillar capped with a stone turban for the males, a wave of hair for the women. Chameleons, disturbed, swivelled their eyes and scuffled out of sight. As the Land-Rover rocked over the grassland, Hugh sat up and wondered where they were going.

'How do you feel?' Simon asked him.

'All right. My head hurts.'

'We'll clean that up when we get to the camp.'

Hugh dropped down again, knowing, in his lower consciousness, that if he tried to discover his reason for being there, something would force him to return to whatever he had left behind. With Simon, he felt the contentment of a child in the hands of his father. They were going somewhere. He did not know where but the journey roused in him a creative expectation. Something remained to be discovered.

He lay with his eyes open, watching the darkness pass. Near the top of the grassland they came into a region of standing objects, large phallic shapes that could have been menhirs, showing more darkly than the dark. The headlight, touching them, revealed a broken surface. If they were stones, they were patterned stones. Their spaced presence seemed ominous to Hugh but Simon stopped among them and said they would stay there till daybreak.

'The col's no place for night driving. You keep the blanket. I've got a sleeping-bag.' Simon went off with his sleeping-bag to lie down among the menhirs. Hugh, wrapping himself in the blanket, fell into a deep sleep and did not wake till the mountainside was lit by the dawn. He sat up and saw that the menhirs were not stones but plants. He asked Simon what they were.

'Lobelia and tree daisy.'

Hugh laughed and let it pass. Through the back window of the Land-Rover, he could see the barracks, the island's northern outpost, a long way below them. He had not realized that the grassland, usually hidden by mist, was so extensive. Now, in the cool, clear light, he saw it rolling down to the Medina, a pasturage for sheep, goats and camels. He had not even known that there were camels on the island. An Arab shepherd was riding among his flocks. Other horsemen were coming through the north gate of the city, cantering and cavorting their horses as though in pleasure of the morning. Looking down from this height, he was surprised to see patches of green among the pink and cream roofs of the city. There were gardens, vegetable plots, small pieces of tillage inside the Medina. The whole of its north-west corner was a park surrounding a residence of considerable size. The whole brilliant and soundless scene looked to him like a mirage of the world the Arabs had left centuries before: a world in little, that belonged elsewhere, incongruously transported to the southern seas.

As they drove on, the Medina slipped down out of sight. Hugh, with no distractions, had to face his own doubts. He said: 'There was an explosion last night. I've just remembered it.'

'It knocked you out. I found you lying beside the road. Something blew up.'

'But shouldn't we be down there? We might be needed.'

'It was nothing much. The police were there in force. They can manage without us. But I hope Easterbrook's all right. I'm composing another riposte for him and I don't want it wasted.'

Simon's face was gleeful and Hugh thought of that other man – was it Samuel Butler – who spent his intellectual fortune on squibs to put under the statues of the great. He said: 'You may be above social restriction but you're not above social combat. You enjoy quarrelling with people.'

Simon laughed: 'I know I've made enemies. One day I'll show you my more maleficent letters. I think you'll be entertained.'

'But what exactly happened down at the offices?'

'A wall blew out. It'll disrupt the routine, I imagine, and that gives you an excuse for taking a week-end trip.'

'Is that what we're doing? – taking a week-end trip?'

'We'll be back on Sunday.'

Hugh felt both disappointed and reassured by the briefness of the excursion. It had seemed to him, on waking, that he had deserted someone or something but while lying half-stunned on the back seat he had had, in the darkness, a dreamlike belief that he was being carried away from the limitations of the known world.

They were going steadily uphill. The grass was becoming coarse and sparse. The fingers of rock that stretched down into it, gradually broadened until there was no grass, only rock. There was no life of any kind and no track. The Land-Rover glanced off the uneven rock and skidded in small moraines of shale and swayed like a ship in a heavy sea, but it kept going. Conditioned to the steamy heat of the lower areas, Hugh felt the mountain cold and wrapped the blanket about him. Simon had an anorak on the seat beside him, but he did not stop to put it on.

The peaks, already misted over, became visible as they approached and for all their impressive immensity, were revealed as merely stone. The col between them was the valley of a little stream that gently, through the millennia, had cut the mountain in half. The floor of the col, just wide enough to take the Land-Rover, was strewn with rock pieces and dank with the water that trickled between them. The mountainsides permitted no sunlight but a luminosity, reflected down from the top, lit the crevice with a ghastly twilight. On previous trips, Simon had cleared a way through the rocks but there had been fresh falls and it was Hugh's job to get down and move obstructions as they met them.

Hugh wanted to know when had Simon come first through the pass?

'Two years ago. I came with an expedition that was financed partly by government funds and partly by a firm prospecting for metals. The agents for the firm found nothing and the rest of us didn't find much. For some time there'd been an idea that the north of the island might lend itself for industrial development, but it's what used to be called an 'inhospitable shore'. There's no natural harbour, no ground suitable for an air-strip and the cost of clearing the forest would be prohibitive. Also, as you'll see for yourself, the place has a discouraging atmosphere. It's no tourists' trap, I can assure you. The team, what was left of it, soon felt they'd had enough. I was the only one with any ambition to return.'

'What brought you back?'

'Curiosity. Something interesting occurred on the survey. Unusually interesting. There were seven of us: five mineralogists and an engineer. I went as medico and general factotum. Three of the mineralogists fell ill. They had temperatures between 103° and 105° and were too sick to crawl out of the tent. I gave them camoquin but it had no effect. That evening, when I went in to look at them, I found them dead.'

'Of what?'

'What indeed? I have no idea. There had always been a rumour among the Arabs that the slaves who escaped here, did not last long. It was put down to propaganda. No one was much interested. The north of the island has always been seen as a wasteland not worth the cost of clearing. But now the world has grown small and people are hungry for land. I suppose, sooner or later, even this bit of forest will be destroyed.'

'So that's why the forest is out of bounds? – because the men died?'

'Yes.' Simon slid his eyes round to look at Hugh and asked with an amused irony: 'You aren't nervous, are you?'

'No, but I'm not suicidal, either.' Hugh spoke rather sharply, but, remembering the story of Ambrose and the smallpox patient said nothing more.

Simon stopped the Land-Rover and pointed to a rivulet that came out of the rock: 'There is the begetter of the twin peaks. Without that little fountain there would have been no pass and the slaves would have had no escape route. Look, you see that point of rock! It divides the stream so that one half goes south and the other north. There are, in effect, two streams. The one flowing north will provide us with our drinking water.'

Driving on, Simon talked, taking it for granted that Hugh's desire for knowledge was as dispassionate as his own. He said: 'I am particularly interested in the possibility of a new virus; or, rather an undiscovered virus. Some scientists believe we are due for another viral assault. When one species has over-bred itself, as we have, nature strikes back with a decimating force.

We keep parrying the blows but one day a blow will come from an unexpected quarter. It *could* come from this little area of forest.'

Hugh moved uneasily: 'You might have warned me that coming here, I'd be at risk.'

'One's at risk everywhere. You could go down any day with a dose of flu.'

'Flu,' Hugh said with contempt.

'Flu killed fifteen million people after the first war. That was a viral assault all right.'

'Where did it come from?'

'Who knows!'

The col ended. Bumping down a flight of stone, the Land-Rover came to rest on a flat rock and Simon paused to let Hugh survey the forbidden territory.

It was, as Simon had said, discouraging and the most discouraging factor was the light. It was mid-morning, the time when on the southern side the light was like honey, containing within its gold a spangle that was more gold. Here the light was sickly, thrown from a sky that was white with the exhalations from the forest. The grassland, spacious on the other side, here dropped abruptly for not more than half a mile. So Hugh had the impression that the forest was only just below them. The front ranks of trees stretched from shore to shore and behind them the forest was a neat map of darkness. There was no break of any kind. Nowhere, it seemed to him, where an entry could be made.

'Yet you've managed to get into it?'

'But not through here. I did try to cut my way in but even a band of machetes could not get you far. The vegetation grows behind you. It encloses you. You feel it stifling you.'

Hugh's uneasiness became acute: 'Don't you think we've come far enough?'

'Good heavens, no. I didn't bring you here to show you the view. I've discovered something. I want you to see it.'

They bumped slowly down the grassland towards the two tents that Simon had set up. The tents, that offered refuge of a sort, were to Hugh the only congenial objects in the whole distasteful scene. The vapour veils were thickening over the forest and forming into clouds that drifted and dispersed and gave way to new formations that dispersed in their turn. As the mist grew heavy, the white disc of the sun, appearing and disappearing through the vapour, gave out a glare that fretted the nerves. Hugh felt himself abducted indeed, and he was no longer complacent and suddenly he remembered Kristy. This was the day he was supposed to pick her up and take her back to the Daisy.

As they drew near the forest line, it broke into detail and he saw that the trees were joined by a matting of creeper. Some of the tree daisies stood like monuments about Simon's tents and pointing to the sunbirds that fluttered about them, he said: 'There are my companions. I feed them and two or three are so tame now, they come into my tent. Here, you see, I have not only a house but a garden. I sleep in the small tent and work in the larger one. This is my living-room.'

Simon folded back the flaps of a large, square tent and Hugh saw it was furnished with a table, canvas chairs and a military chest. Sparse, orderly and self-contained, it could have been the headquarters of a general in the field. A microscope stood on the table beside a drawing-board, paper, pens and a bottle of Indian ink. A primus lamp hung from the roof.

'What do you live on?' Hugh asked. 'Is there game of any sort?'

'Nothing edible and I'm not keen on killing. I live as the blacks did: on cassava and plantains. I suppose you can manage on that for a couple of days?' Simon handed Hugh a canvas bucket: 'If you fetch the water, I'll get a fire going. We can have coffee. I don't eat till evening.'

Hugh found the stream running with a white sediment that had stained the grass for several yards on either bank. He was doubtful of the water but Simon laughed at him.

'I've been drinking it for weeks without harm. The sediment is only a fibrous mineral from a volcanic bed near the ridge. The blacks used it to decorate their dwellings. When we've had our coffee, I must get down to work.'

It was arranged that Hugh should have the camp-bed in the small tent and Simon sleep in the living-room. Hugh, still sick from the bruise on his head, lay down on the camp-bed, intending to sleep for an hour but did not wake till late afternoon. When he opened his eyes, he was oppressed by the heat and an elusive sense of nightmare. Through the tent opening, he could see the edge of the forest and the tree trunks compacted by the binding of creeper. It looked what it was; impenetrable: and it brought down on him the claustrophobic terror of his dream. Imagining the weight of vegetation holding him down like a coffin lid, he leapt up and hurried into the open air.

Hearing him outside, Simon shouted to him to get another pail of water. As he returned to the stream, the sun dropped behind the peaks that in shadow looked more immediate than they had been at midday. Hugh was startled by the sight of them. There was something shocking about their nearness and immensity, the naked stone rising from the grass like teeth from gum. This simile was peculiarly troubling because the peaks had an inward curve. Putting his tongue against the back of his lower front teeth, Hugh could follow an identical curve and it seemed to him that on this side of the island he was within a brain: a blurred, disordered and minatory brain.

Everything about the place repelled him, even the stream trickling like milk through the chalky grass. As he returned with the water, the shadow of the peaks stretched out rapidly over the grassland. On this side of the island the mountains hid the glory of the setting sun and the lambency of reflected colour increased the hostility of the place.

Under shadow, the black pelt of the forest was still, then the night wind sprang up. There were squawks from the nocturnal birds and the fruit bats set out, a long stream of them, rising one after the other, the fur of their bodies and the webbing of their wings sharply visible against the ochre sky.

Simon was pumping up the lamp. He motioned Hugh to close the tent flaps before he produced a light. For a couple of minutes the two of them, invisible to each other, were in stifling, humid darkness, then the gas flared and lit the small interior with a livid brilliance. Simon had cleared his work from the table and set two places for supper. They sat on the canvas chairs, enclosed in the compact tent as in a well-ordered cupboard. The supper comprised two plantains each and bread. The bread was so dry that Hugh had to wash it down with coffee. He asked: 'What is it?'

'Cassava or, as the blacks call it, manioc. It's the stuff we were given at school. We knew it as tapioca. I found an old plantation left by the escaped slaves. Excellent food if you know how to prepare it. You peel the tubers, slice them and soak them in the stream, then you boil them until the starch forms into grains. The grains can be ground into flour.'

'Do you have to do all that?'

'You certainly do. Raw manioc is full of hydrocyanic acid. It's a killer. The Africans must have learnt to deal with it by trial and error.'

'Need you eat this stuff? Couldn't you bring bread and tinned foods over with you?'

'I could, but I choose to be self-supporting. Don't you like it?'

'I'm not mad about it.'

Simon laughed and reaching across to the military chest, he opened a drawer and took out a sheet of cartridge paper. He threw it over to Hugh: 'What do you think of that fellow?'

'Good God, is there such a thing?'

The creature, drawn in ink, solidly black, filling the imperial page, looked like a spider but was the size of a large tortoise.

'There is such a thing. I found him among the dead fronds at the base of the cyathea. I'm inclined to think he may be what I'm looking for.'

'And what is that?'

'A carrier. If there's a virus lying fallow here, it would be most likely transmitted by some insect or other. Take a look at this one.'

Pushing aside the food plates, Simon put his microscope on the table and adjusted it so Hugh, when he looked in, could see a black speck between two slides. It was the spider. He laughed: 'That's too small to harm anyone.'

'It's the size of a flea. Think what the flea did when it carried the plague from China to Western Europe!' Simon spoke as though delighted by the flea's depredations and his pale face flushed with enthusiasm. Bending again over his spider, he said: 'Structurally, this chap resembles that deadly little monster

Lathrodectus Katipo, but he's smaller and there are certain differences. I've never seen his like before. He's an original that's been cut off here since the mountain range sank beneath the Indian Ocean. He can't get away because he can't swim and the air of the ridge is too cold for him. So here he is, a potential destroyer of the human race, cooped up, poor chap, in this little bit of primordial forest.'

'Which is just as well.'

'Oh, I don't know. Suppose we put a few dozen of his relatives into a Thermos flask and transported them to the other side and released them – where? How about the Residency garden? Sooner or later, of course, some scientific busybody would track him down but before that happened, he could depopulate the island. Al-Bustan would return to the pristine innocence of those days when the birds were so secure, they did not need wings.'

'Would you do that, if you could?'

'I don't know. I might. Consider the mayhem done by the human race on this one small area of earth. First the pirates: they felled the best of the timber and wiped out the wingless birds: then came the Arab slavers, growing rich and working their slaves to death: then the British – self-important donkeys for the most part but better than the others. At least they stand out against haphazard development. But after them, total destruction. What will we have here? The Las Vegas of the southern seas. Another Hawaii. The only thing that can save this place is fear. Fear would ward off the invasion. People are damned careful of their bloody skins.'

'And what about you? Aren't you afraid? How will you prove your theory about the spider? Would you let it bite you?'

'It has bitten me.'

'With what result?'

Simon gave a shout of laughter: 'None. No result at all.'

'So it was all a joke?'

'Yes, a joke.'

Hugh gazed with new understanding at Simon: 'And when you took Ambrose in to see the smallpox patient, was that a joke?'

'You must admit that was very funny.'

'And picking me up and bringing me here? – another joke?'

'Not entirely. I felt I could do with a bit of company for a couple of days.'

Simon laughed and Hugh was disturbed, aware suddenly of the absurdity of his illusions about this man. Whatever there was in the cold colour of Simon's eyes, there was nothing paternal.

'You didn't give a thought to my wife? She does not know where I am, and she's in hospital. You didn't know, of course, we've lost the baby.'

'Oh!' Simon glanced away: 'I won't pretend to grieve. In our overcrowded world, the loss of an infant is not a tragedy.'

'It is for her. You know: the fox's child, the fox's very own child.'

'That is the egoism that's done for us all.'

Hugh appealed to him without much hope: 'Simon, I must go back. Please drive me back tomorrow morning.'

Simon, making one of his feline movements, sprang to his feet, laughing: 'My dear fellow, don't be ridiculous. What does one day matter? We'll make our trip into the interior and you'll be back with your wife on Sunday. Meanwhile, you'll see what you will see.'

He left the tent and coming back with his sleeping-bag, spread it on the floor: 'We'll doss down now. We have to make an early start tomorrow. I'll wake you at first light.'

Hugh shut the flap of his tent but could not exclude the shrieks, whistles and chatter of the forest. It was too early for sleep and, lying in the dark, he wondered if Kristy had taken herself back to their denuded room in the Daisy. Without Ambrose, she had no friend on the island. He remembered her as she had stood in the room, weeping, and saying: 'It is dead.' Now, without him, she was alone. And, it occurred to him, that he, without her, was alone. The thought of her, as she probably was that afternoon, dressed and waiting for him to come with a taxi, made him realize the distance that now lay between them. He considered the extensive grasslands on the other side, the drive through the col, the run down on this side, and guessed they had come some thirty miles. How long would it take him to walk back? Too long. He might as well see it through with Simon.

For there was no hope of a reprieve. Simon had decided they would go and Hugh was too weak to stand up to him. He was a determined man, a practical and self-reliant man who made independent decisions and stuck to them. But was he more than that? It occurred to Hugh that he might learn much from Simon, but would he discover anything? He thought, if Simon had more imagination, he would be more easily moved. His jokes, too, would be less frightful. But then he would be dependent on others, and no better man than Hugh himself was.

2

When the explosion finally died out, silence – a momentous silence – came down. Kristy left the day bed and went down the corridor to the Indian nurse. She said: 'Are you hurt?' The girl did not reply. The table had fallen sideways, striking her across the waist. Kristy pushed at it but, ineffectual as a child, she could not deal with its weight. Giving up, she knelt down and put her arm under the girl's head. The head lolled lifelessly and placing it back on the floor, she sat beside it, not knowing what to do next. She noticed, with detached surprise, that her own body was shaking violently. In the end, too weak to give any more thought to what had been happening, she stretched out on the floor and went to sleep.

The African nurse wakened her, saying crossly: 'What you do there, lady? You come to bed this minute.' The nurse, a big, stout girl, lifted her easily and took her to her room. She did not wake again till the safragi brought in her breakfast.

'What happened last night?' she asked.

'Nothing happen.'

'How is the Indian nurse?'

'Not very well.'

'Is she dead?'

The safragi shook his head and said in a low voice: 'Yes, poor girl dead.'

No one else came to speak to Kristy. After breakfast, she got herself out of bed, dressed and put her things together. She was still weak but she was determined to go when Hugh came for her at midday. She sat for some time on the bed then, becoming bored, she went out to the balcony and leant over the rail, trying to see something of last night's eventuality. Foliage obstructed her view but she could hear a thudding, as though the bricks she had seen rising in the air were still falling to the ground.

There was no sign of life in the Residency garden. Lady Urquhart, it was said, had followed her daughter to England and Urquhart was alone in the great palace.

The day bed and chair had been removed from the balcony and Kristy, soon tired of standing, was about to go indoors when she heard footsteps below. A file of Arab labourers came round the corner of the hospital, each with a spade on his shoulder. She realized they were making for the cemetery and, going back to her room, she was in time to see them unlocking the cemetery gate.

The African nurse found her at the window and sternly said: 'Now, lady, you go back to bed.'

'Why don't you tell me what's happening?'

The nurse, looking as though too much were being asked of her, became more stern: 'Why you want to know what happening? How I know what happening? I know nothing. You go back into bed this minute.'

'But my husband is coming for me. I'm leaving today.'

'No, you not. Not today. You stay in hospital and no go on balcony. No one go on balcony today.'

'Why?'

'How I know? Matron say no one go on balcony today.'

As soon as she was alone again, Kristy went out to the corridor and found the doors to the balcony shut and locked. She lay on her bed, waiting for Hugh, trying to read but impeded by boredom and the deadening heat. When midday passed and Hugh did not arrive, she wished that anyone, even the matron, would come to answer her questions. She could hear in the distance the steady thudding she had heard from the balcony. During the afternoon, it became desultory and died out At the back of her mind, at first unadmitted then emerging and growing stronger, was suspense. Hugh's non-appearance, the nurse's refusal to communicate, the sense of a catastrophe of which she could discover nothing, all oppressed her until she could no longer bear her ignorance and isolation. She decided to discharge herself.

Downstairs, she found the whole hospital staff gathered like a reception committee at the front door. Shocked by the sight of her, the matron said: 'You can't go out. Back to bed with you.' Though the words were commanding, the tone was uncertain and Kristy knew that, not ill enough to be controlled, she was an embarrassment in the hospital.

She said: 'I've been expecting my husband. Have you heard anything from him?' For answer, the matron turned and hurried away.

Looking around at nurses, porters and safragis, Kristy met pitying half-smiles or heads turned from her. No one spoke. Moving rapidly, she dodged through them, determined to get away. No one tried to detain her. She realized they preferred her to go and make her discoveries for herself.

It was a day of full sunlight. Half-way down the path, under the trembling, sparkling eucalyptus trees, she saw Aly's driver coming towards her in his delivery van. He had to slow down to pass her and she put her hands on the open window edge and begged him to stop. She said: 'What was the explosion last night? Tell me what's happened.'

The driver, his thin dark face drawn with concern, shook his head slowly: 'Memsahib. You are not well, memsahib. Everyone knows the Government Offices fell down and all are dead. Even the Governor is dead.'

'And my husband? Do you know anything about my husband?'

'I know nothing. If he was in the offices, he must be dead.'

Kristy ran on. When she came to the main road, quickened in an ecstasy of panic, she did not follow the road bends but scrambled through the vegetation, dropping from one level to another until she could look down on the square. She saw the ruin of the government building. The site was only partly cleared. An atmosphere of weary discouragement hung about the men who were climbing over the coral bricks, occasionally lifting one and tumbling it off the others. Dust hung heavily in the air, so the scene looked faded and remote like a photograph taken long ago.

She tried to run again but stumbled and fell. When she made to rise, it seemed her mind did not extend as far as her feet. She crawled back to the road and there, managing to pick herself up, she proceeded slowly on level ground. She looked in through the

Residency gate and saw the police guard at his post and the flag flying at the mast-head. There was no one left to order things differently. The church, however, was a background for calamity. Its doors had been propped open and the hospital ambulance stood outside them. The rear doors of the ambulance were also open and Kristy saw that the bunks were folded away to accommodate a cargo of coffins. When she asked the driver if he knew anything of her husband, the man directed her in to Mr Pierce and Dr Dixon who had charge of the dead. For the first time since her arrival on Al-Bustan, she entered the church.

It was a small church, full of sunlight that yellowed the wood and the lozenge-shaped panes of the windows. Bodies, each wrapped in a sheet, lay on the pews and between the pews, and already the air was heavy with a low, warm smell of decay.

The two men stood together near the altar, their faces benumbed yet uplifted by the fact of their survival The minister, in his vestments, holding a prayer-book, appeared to be in control. There was smugness about him for he had work to do while Dr Dixon had none. The sight of Kristy disturbed them both.

She said: 'I'm looking for my husband.'

Fussed and at a loss, Dixon said: 'You should be in bed,' but he had a list of the officials who had been identified and, consulting it, he said: 'Not here. They haven't found him.'

'Then where is he? There are only five police and an Arab officer down there. Most of the work is being done by Indians. Where's Culbertson? Why isn't he . . .' Kristy's voice broke and Dr Dixon, putting a hand on her shoulder, led her out of the fetid air.

'The police were working all night. When he realized that they'd find no one alive, Culbertson took most of the men back to the barracks for a few hours' rest. He sent the wives home because they were worn out and doing no good, standing there watching. He's given orders that all women are to stay away from the square. I'm afraid, my dear, there's no need for haste because . . . there's no hope.'

Kristy stared at him, feeling nothing.

Dr Dixon patted her shoulder and went on talking, telling her all he knew of the night's work. The explosion that had occurred, they thought, in one of the wash-rooms, had been caused by a device of considerable size. There was some delay after the building collapsed because the porter had been stunned and there was no other responsible person to give the alarm. When he picked himself up, he had to go to the Residency to telephone the barracks. By the time the police arrived, anyone not killed outright was likely to have been suffocated. Then the work of moving the blocks was hampered by lack of light and Culbertson had to send men to the Medina for flares. In order to enhance the appearance of the offices, the blocks had been cut unusually large and helpers found them difficult to lift. Instead of carrying them clear of the ruin, they were throwing them to one side so while uncovering one victim, they were possibly piling weight on another. Meanwhile, people were crowding about the site and some of the Arabs, regarding the explosion as an Arab achievement, were gleefully climbing about over the bricks in order to hamper the rescue work. There was also the likelihood of loot. The building had been too big to be properly guarded, the island's resources being limited, and now its remains were too big to surround and patrol.

Eventually a searchlight was brought up from the harbour and when it was erected, Culbertson turned it on the faces of a group of stupefied women who had come up from the Daisy. He shouted at them: 'Get back. You're only a nuisance here', but the women were hemmed in by the crowd and had to remain where they were.

The only outside help came from the Indian shopkeepers who cleared the south-west corner of the site and found Pedley and two women secretaries. All three were dead. The Indians worked near the women from the Daisy. They worked in silence but between them and the women there was an understanding created by years of business contact. People came up from the Dobo and offered to work for money. The more likely ones were employed. The Dobo men brought the news that the Praslin had also suffered. The detonation had brought down a cliffside which had buried the hotel.

'I don't know what's being done there,' Dixon said: 'There aren't enough police to deal with two sites and, of course, the offices are of first importance. I'm told that some of the Dobo people are scrambling about the Praslin – no doubt looking for pickings. Well, Mrs Foster, I advise you to go no farther. The ambulance can take you back to the hospital and you'd be wise to have another day in bed.'

Kristy shook her head and said: 'I'll stay here till they find him.'

She went on towards the ruin of the offices. As she reached the edge of the block heap, one of the Indians gave a cry and the others hurried over to see what he had found. From their excitement, she knew they had discovered someone alive and, running to them, she shouted: 'Who is it? Who is it?' They were too intent to answer her and she climbed over the blocks till she could see for herself.

The men were uncovering an oblong steel case with a grille on its upper side: the office lift. Within, someone lay on his back, quite still, his arms down at his side, as though in an over-size coffin. The figure was so covered with dust, it looked like one of the human shells found in the ruins of Pompeii. It did not move but one of the Indians assured her: 'He is alive. He opened his eyes and looked at me. He looked directly into my eyes and he knew I was the one who had found him. Yes, he is alive and I found him. With these hands, I lifted the blocks and uncovered him. He should be grateful.'

They all stood round and looked down on the man in the lift. Those who had not come to help but merely to see what was to be seen, were particularly gratified by the spectacle of the trapped, dust-covered body that looked more dead than alive. The police officer pushed through the crowd and took over the discovery. He tugged at the lift gate but it was jammed and could not be opened. As the grille was shaken, the man inside opened his eyes and Kristy recognized him. She called: 'Mr Simpson, are you all right?' Simpson looked at the faces above him with an expression of bleary inquiry, then he closed his eyes and did not open them again.

The officer shouted for the police to move the lift but the cable was buried in debris so even if they could raise it, the lift could not be moved. While the matter was being discussed, Kristy saw Simpson's mouth fall open and she knew he had quietly died.

She said: 'Don't waste time. There may be others alive. My husband is here somewhere. We must go on looking.' She started pulling at broken pieces of rubble and one of the police, a large Negro, burst out laughing. 'No, lady,' he said, 'you no damn good. You go away, away. We find your husband.'

Taking herself to the perimeter of the square, Kristy sank down on the ground and set herself to watch. Though Simpson had been found alive, the men still worked half-heartedly. Simpson had been protected by the lift. The other officials had had no protection. Not a sound came from under the debris. And – a worse omen – a stench of death was filling the air.

As the bodies were found, they were placed at the back of the square and later carried on stretchers to the church. Kristy went to view each of them. They looked much alike, shrouded in the white dust, but she was sure that none of them was Hugh.

Mechanics were brought up from the harbour to release Mr Simpson and behind them came a procession of women from the Daisy. They were a bedraggled company, led by Mrs Axelrod with her hair hanging about her face, her skin glazed by weariness. She had probably not slept the previous night but she advanced with an exaggerated air of purpose, as though even now she would lead the others and defeat their despair. She glanced at Kristy then looked back as though trying to decide who she might be.

Kristy, scratched by thorn apples, dress torn, face and hair grey with dust, said: 'I'm Kristy Foster. They haven't found my husband.'

'They haven't found mine.' Mrs Axelrod spoke angrily, pushing back her damp red hair with fierce, trembling hands: 'Culbertson said they're all dead but now they've found Simpson alive. So they're not all dead. If the police won't put their backs into the job, we'll do it for them. No good you sitting there, moping. Get up and give a hand.' As Kristy got herself up, Mrs Axelrod took another look at her: 'No. I forgot. You look all in. You stay there and we'll let you know when we come on him.'

She formed the women into two groups of four. Each group was instructed to tackle a block between them. As soon as they started work, the men came to a stop and stared at the extraordinary spectacle of English women exerting themselves. Mrs

Axelrod shouted at the men, trying to shame them into greater efforts, but they only gawped and grinned until Culbertson arrived with a convoy of cars.

'I thought I told you to stay away,' Culbertson said and Mrs Axelrod, on the point of breakdown, screamed at him, accusing him of incompetence and heartless indifference. He turned from her and went to supervise the release of Mr Simpson. The lift gate was opened and Simpson lifted out. Culbertson returned and said to Mrs Axelrod: 'Simpson is dead. We don't intend to work with women. Now, either you clear off and leave us to finish the job or I take my men back to the barracks.'

Mrs Prince said wearily: 'Come on, Dulcie. Leave the men to it. I know I'm no use and I'm going, anyway.' She walked off, leader in the hour of defeat, and the other women followed. Mrs Axelrod went after them but first made a furious show of contempt for Culbertson. Kristy, forgotten, was left alone.

She moved to a corner where Culbertson would not notice her. His presence speeded the work so that by five o'clock the black and white hall floor had been uncovered. The last of the dead were the supplicants, the only non-British victims for, with Gopal and the ministers away, the ministerial floor had been empty when the explosion occurred.

During the afternoon there had been visitors to the square. Mrs Hampton had driven down in her Mini-Minor, bringing with her a weeping Mrs Ogden. Akbar and the cook from the Daisy had stood for a while, gazing blankly at the ruin. Other English-women, some of whom Kristy had never seen before, came to the edge of the site then went to the church. Kristy herself went to the church and confirmed that Hugh's body had not been found. She saw other women in tears but she could not cry because she had nothing to cry for. Even after Culbertson and his men had driven away and the Indians were returning to their shops, she went on sitting in the square, expecting Hugh to reappear and explain himself.

Just before sunset, Musa with his court of friends came down the road and paused on a piece of high ground near the church. They kept close together, with a sort of cautious insolence, and surveyed the fractured, dusty chequer-board that had been the hallway of the Government Offices. The young men – Kristy recognized several of them – were in Arab dress and Musa wore the gold algol of rank. When no one accused them, or even spoke to them, they came slowly down into the square. Seeing Kristy still sitting in her corner, Musa sent one of the men to speak to her. The man was Mohammed. He said: 'I am your good friend, *sayyida*. I saw your husband at the office and said to him: "Run, run." I ran with him. I put my hand here,' he slapped his hand down on his own shoulder, 'and I made him come with me. He is alive, sayyida.'

'But where is he?'

'I cannot tell. He fell up there by the wall, but he was alive. I could not stay and cannot tell where he went.'

Mohammed returned to the group and Musa raised his hand to Kristy in a gesture of farewell. Then, twitching their robes about them, the young men turned together and went, like conquerors, up the hill.

As the sun dropped and the sky became coloured over with sunset, Mrs Axelrod returned and spoke firmly to Kristy: 'You can't spend the night here, young woman. Get up.' She caught Kristy by the hand and pulled her to her feet.

Kristy said: 'My husband is missing.'

'My husband is dead.'

Mrs Axelrod's face crumpled and dropping her chin to her chest, she broke into hoarse and violent sobs. Appalled by this grief, Kristy realized how great was her own good fortune. Hugh was not dead: and she knew, with sudden, inspired certainty, that wherever he was, he would return to her. Caught up in a fervour of compassion, she put her arms about Mrs Axelrod and led her gently back to the Daisy.

3

Simon wakened Hugh by flinging a pair of wellington boots into his tent, ordering him: 'Put these on. If they're too big, stuff something into the toes.'

It was still dark but before Hugh was dressed, the eastern horizon had split like a ripe pomegranate and the sky had flared up. A crimson light coloured everything with its own colour. The grass was crimson. The great peaks and the rocks of the ridge, all sheened like glass, glowed under the crimson sky.

Hugh, who seldom saw the dawn, said: 'It's like the last day of the world.'

'Or the first. Come on.'

As they drove eastwards, keeping parallel to the forest edge, Simon said: 'I'll show you something you've never seen before: a shore without a footprint.'

'I don't share your enthusiasm for an empty world. Those peaks, for instance. They're too close for comfort. They threaten me.'

'What? Those!' Simon looked at the peaks with quizzical scorn: 'They're about as threatening as a couple of ice-cream cones.'

The forest clamour had ceased as though its creatures were hiding from the daylight. Driving beside the solid baulk of trees, Hugh heard no sound from it except the occasional squawk of a parrot. Simon went slowly, choosing his route over the uneven ground, so nearly an hour passed before the sea came in sight. When they stopped beside Simon's cassava plantation, the sun was high enough to hold a spark of the day's heat. A few yards away was the shore, a white crescent of sand touched by nothing but the delicate feet of sea-birds. Looking to the left, Hugh saw the landfall he had once tried to surmount. This pretty strand, on which the sea threw laces of foam, looked to Hugh the only natural thing on this side of the island. But they were not going that way. They were going in the other direction. There, where the forest met the sea, the shore was rough with pebbles and fallen trees.

Simon had brought a small rucksack that contained medicaments and coffee. They had had no breakfast and would not eat until their return in the evening but at least they would get coffee.

'Come on. No time to waste.' Simon jumped down to the littoral and strode away between the forest and the sea. Palms and thorns hung out over the sand, often forcing the men to wade in water. The edge of the forest was a low cliff of earth so clotted with roots that they groped out, seeking sustenance among the stones. Some had stretched so far, they were blanched by sea-water. The trees that had fallen across the shore, thrust out by the swelling life of the forest or washed by storms from their beds, now lay with roots exposed and heads drowned. Their lacings of creeper had come with them and bushes, torn up by the upheaval of the roots, had rolled down to the water and were washing about in the waves. There was something disquieting about all this, a menacing wildness so Hugh knew what Simon had meant when he spoke of an inhospitable shore.

Simon took the hazards with an athlete's ease, vaulting over the smaller trees, ducking under the larger ones and climbing over those that were so large, their weight had carried them to the ground. Hugh, struggling behind, ignorant of the dangers of the place, tripped again and again and putting his weight on rotting wood, fell on his face when it caved in beneath him. The wood had become riddled with ants that swarmed over his hands and bit his flesh with white-hot venom. Spiked by thorns, a-tingle with ant bites, suffering the continual attacks of wasps and forest bees, Hugh gave up his first attempt to keep Simon in sight. Plodding after, he was thankful that, if nothing else, he had the wellingtons to protect his feet.

As the heat grew with brutish force, the forest moisture turned to steam and clouded out from the trees, rank with rotting vegetation.

259

Rounding a turn in the shore line, Hugh saw Simon a long way ahead, waving to him to hurry. When he was near enough to hear, Simon shouted: 'If we don't move fast, we won't get back before dark.'

Hugh kept moving with an obstinate perseverance that Simon seemed to enjoy. He waited till Hugh caught him up, then laughed at him:

'Want any help?'

'No.'

'The ants have been at you. I've got some Ultradil in the pack. I'll get it out when we have coffee.'

It had occurred to Hugh that, forced on this jaunt, he could employ the strategy of the weak and bring to it such impatience, unsympathy and unexpressed anxiety that Simon would be glad to cut it short. But it was not a thing he could do. Though he felt disillusioned about Simon, the man's attraction remained. His independence, his energy, his eager pursuit of knowledge, inspirited Hugh so he had to follow. Simon, though limited in his humanity, seemed to him, in spite of everything, an exceptional human being.

Simon clambered on to a bank of sand and stood there until Hugh came up beside him. They had reached the mouth of a small river. Hugh, gazing into the channel that the water maintained between the trees, saw that here was the way into the forest. They were to walk through shallow water which had a bottom of brown sand. He began to tug off his boots, thinking he could move faster without them, but Simon told him to keep them on: 'The leeches would make a meal of you.'

The shaded river seemed to offer relief from the sun but beneath the trees, the air was clogged with heat and full of the steamy effluvia of decay. Added to the wasps and bees, there were now mosquitoes. Though the transparent, quietly moving stream made for easy going, there were obstructions here, too. Trees, brought down by lightning, lay across the water, their thick ligatures of creeper stretching like nets about them. In places the undergrowth reached out of its overcrowded environment to meet the undergrowth on the other side.

A grey-green twilight hung on the air with here and there a spot of sunlight lying like a coin on the water. They came into a region of romantic beauty where dragonflies skimmed the river and the hanging creepers were in flower. The trees were grown over with ferns, orchids, moss and lichens. Some of the orchids were blue and some of the red and gold kind that Simon called Vallambrosa. As the stream narrowed and they made their way into a tunnel of gloom, the flowers were left behind. Here the fallen trees were white with age and bearded over with lichens.

Closed in by trees, the men were assailed by a whining, galactic army of wasps, bees, mosquitoes and tiny flies. The forest came so close that Hugh could peer between the interwoven branches and creepers but he saw only the inner darkness. He felt a nervous dread of the forest coming too close to him. For stretches of this monotonous walk in oppressive heat, reality left him and he felt himself back in the suffocating mystery of his dream. He was lost, with no more knowledge of his surroundings than a grub hatched in a carpet. They were supposed to be moving towards an objective, but how could he be sure of that? For all he knew, the forest darkness was an eternity, like space, without habitat or goal.

He stopped for a moment, trying to throw off his surroundings that were like a sack over his head, smelling of vegetable death, and asked: 'Is it all like this?'

'No. The trees naturally crowd towards what light there is but farther on, the stream opens out and becomes a swamp. Just beyond it is . . .' Simon paused and did not go on.

'What is beyond?'

Simon was silent and Hugh wondered if he, too, were affected by their stifling passage along the stream. After a moment, Simon regained himself and answered the question: 'The place where they made their last stand.'

'The slaves made a stand? But against what?'

Hugh again had to repeat his question before Simon, laughing, gave an answer: 'Forgive me. Yes. Against what? I don't know and there's no one left to tell us.'

The stream was petering out and the water, that scarcely covered their boots now, trickled over a wide area of ground, forming a swamp. Patches of scrub and saplings had grown up among the several small tributaries of water. Where the water formed pools there were the large, raft-like leaves of water-lilies. Some of these pools were covered with emerald weed and Hugh, walking on what looked to him firm ground, sank into slime that threw up a sickening stench. At the edge of the swamp, trees lay lifeless and brittle. Those that survived were covered with fungoid growths that extended from them, pink, like deformed hands. The forest stood as firm-set as ever on either side of this diseased area and closed in beyond it. But they were reaching something which showed through the tree tops, flashing white against the solid blue of the sky. A few yards ahead, they came out of the forest and Hugh saw a cone-shaped structure set inside a wall. It was the first of some thirty or forty buildings, all alike, that faced each other across a passageway choked with weeds. There was no sign of human life and no noise except the forest noises.

Hugh came to a stop, feeling the buildings held him under surveillance, and Simon said: 'What do you make of this?'

Hugh did not know what to make of it. He said: 'I suppose they're huts? Standing like this, they look like a monstrous halma set.'

'Yes, they are huts. Fortified huts. People once lived in them – or, rather, they existed. Look at those walls. This one's about fifteen feet high. Some of them go up to twenty feet, with no doors or entrances. The place is difficult to explore because of the undergrowth. I cleared a path here last week and the weeds are already springing up again.'

The cleared path, running between maidenhair, thorns and young trees, led to a ladder propped against the wall of the first hut. Simon went to it and gripped the sides, saying: 'No ants in this wood. It's been treated with lime or potash, a trick learnt from the Arabs. Do you know why this ladder was left here?' As Simon turned, Hugh noticed that his cheeks were flushed and his eyes were unusually brilliant: 'I think the very last of the colony shinned up and left it here because he was too weak to pull it in after him. He'd come home to die.'

'Why do you think that?'

Simon took out a handkerchief and pushed it over his face, making an impatient movement of the body as though to shoulder back a physical annoyance: 'He collapsed on the other side. He's still lying there, what's left of him. His first need would be to make the place impregnable. Only weakness – a dire weakness – could cause him to leave the ladder here. They were terrified. They really lived in a state of siege. It's possible they feared one another. I've heard that some African tribes make arrow poison so strong that their own people are frightened by it. Or they may have feared the gods.'

'You think they had gods?'

'Naturally. Having escaped one set of tyrants, they would at once fit themselves out with another.' Simon took off the rucksack and found the tube of antibiotic cream: 'Put some of that on your scratches, then we'll take a look inside. Be careful not to touch the wall. The plaster's riddled with insect life. Ants everywhere. Look down there.'

Ants, yellow in colour, were marching out of the weeds, crossing the cleared ground and entering the weeds on the other side. They were in close formation, twenty abreast, a steadily moving band of bodies, broad and glistening as a python.

Simon propped himself against the ladder for a while then, pulling himself together, leapt up it and gained the top of the wall. There he paused and put a hand to his head.

'Are you all right?' Hugh asked.

'Fine. Perhaps a touch of fever. I hope it's not malaria.'

Hugh watched him anxiously as he again mopped his face: 'Let's go back now. I've seen all I want to see.'

Simon laughed and without answering, swung his legs over the wall and went down on the other side. He had, it seemed, regained his energy but his movements had lost their cat-like grace. Hugh followed him up the ladder and found wooden footholds and a handrail on the other side. As Simon had told him, the householder lay where he had fallen on the other side: a stretched-out pattern of crumbling bones. Jumping to avoid them, Simon did what he had told Hugh not to do: he touched the wall of the hut. The plaster cracked like paper and ants poured out. He stood and watched them as they assembled about his feet, saying: 'We can be thankful they're not scorpions. Still, they're unpleasant enough. People think that ants don't eat the living but they're wrong. I heard of a fellow who went back drunk to his bungalow and passed out. The bungalow was in the path of an ant army and next morning our drunken friend was no more than this skeleton here.'

Though there were no windows in the round, tapering hut, there was an opening about five feet high and Simon, stooping, went in. Hugh refused to follow but, looking in, saw a small, circular room where the ashes of a long dead fire were heaped under a vent in the pointed roof. Beside the door were more bones, a huddle of bones large and small that fell apart as Simon touched them with the toe of his boot.

He said: 'The family. Probably waited here for the one who dared to venture out.' He paced the diameter of the room: 'About five feet. A self-made prison.'

Cooking pots and animal bones were heaped between the walls and Hugh, going to look at them, stepped quickly away from them. The heap had become a habitat for large white spiders that sat quivering amid a complex of webs. He turned his back in disgust and when Simon emerged, said: 'Why did you bring me in here?'

'Don't you find it fascinating?' Simon glowed with his own interest in his discovery but his colour looked unnaturally high: 'Think what an existence these people led! The women and children cooped up here in terror of the outside world, never going out, never seeing anything, never admitting a stranger to the little compound. And the one who went out to hunt or take part in some ceremony – the gods always demand ceremonies – getting back in as fast as his legs would carry him. I've climbed into three of these huts and there were skeletons in all of them. And drums. I found several drums. They must have communicated by drum beat. They were savages who had escaped slavery and here tried to reconstitute the life they had known in Africa. And this is how they ended up. Why? Because of fear. Doesn't that fascinate you?'

'I hate the place.'

'Yes, but think what it proves! Fear can confine you to a space so small, you might as well be in a grave.'

Simon smiled quizzically at Hugh and Hugh, feeling baited,

said angrily: 'I didn't want to come here and I don't want to be here. I'm getting out of this compound.'

The climb back to the lane gave him an illusion of deliverance: but, of course, he was not delivered. He was still inside the abominable village and the village was surrounded by forest. The place imposed on him such an anguish of repulsion, he felt sick.

Waiting, with no company but the steady, glistening flow of the ant army near his feet, he listened to every movement that Simon made inside the wall. There was no other noise. It was midday and the forest was silent under the heat. Damp, drawn up from the ground, was forming a haze over the sky. The sun was fading back and humidity hung in the air.

When Simon at last appeared at the top of the wall, Hugh said fervently: 'Let's go back.'

Coming down the ladder, Simon missed a step and slipped to the ground. He remained seated, his head hanging and Hugh said: 'Drink the coffee.'

Hugh took the flask from the rucksack and filled the cup. When he had swallowed down most of the coffee, Simon said: 'Look in the pack. See what you can find.'

Hugh brought out a phial of yellow tablets: 'Paludrine?'

'Might work. Not the usual symptoms, though. No initial drop in temperature, no rigors.' Simon swallowed two tablets with the last of the coffee and said: 'Bitter. The wrong sort of bitterness. Wish there was more coffee.'

Sweat beaded on every pore of his face and neck. Hugh, seeing he was in danger of falling into the path of the marching ants, went to the wall on the other side of the lane and began clearing the ground. He tugged up the heavy fern-roots with a fury that helped to keep his anxiety at bay. He did not consider the insects that, at any other time, would have unnerved him. Unlike the ants, that moved in such numbers they could devour a living man, the spiders and centipedes fled as he uncovered them. When there was space enough, he took Simon under the arm-pits and dragged him across the lane and put him down in the new clearing with the rucksack for a pillow. He opened his eyes and smiled: 'You're still there?'

'Did you think I would run away?'

'I expect you're hungry. You'll have to forage.'

'Forage? Is there anything to forage for?'

Simon tried to rise on his elbow and failing, waved a hand towards the far end of the village: 'Down there. Old plantain grove. Better go before the rain starts.'

Looking down the lane between the fluting of the walls, Hugh saw how the day had changed. The moisture in the sky was now so heavy that it hid the sun. The end of the lane was fogged by a thunderous shadow. Hugh took a step then paused, nervous of the clogging weeds: 'Are there land-crabs here?'

'No.' Simon closed his eyes and smiled with his old irony: 'Nothing to fear.'

'All right. I'll see what I can find.'

Like a non-swimmer forced into water, Hugh struck into the weeds with a blundering deliberation, swallowing back his aversion from the place. Half-way down the lane, he glanced back and was amazed to see how far he had come without mishap. Simon was right. There was nothing to fear.

At the end of the lane, he felt the suck of water under his boots. Here he was among reeds that rose above his head and became so thick, he had to force a way through them. The reeds gave suddenly and he fell out on to a platform of stone.

When he got to his feet, he understood Simon's talk of gods and ceremonies. Here were the gods, staring at him with monstrous eyes. There were two of them, set up side by side on the natural stone. They had probably been carved from tree trunks but like the huts, they were plastered over and whitened. Their whiteness flashed against the purple bruising of the sky. The black of their eyes and red of their lips and cheeks caricatured human features, but they did not look human. They had the teeth of wolves.

He thought he could see in the pair a reference to the peaks. These, too, were guardians, built to frighten off whatever was feared. But there had been more to it than that. The feet of the figures were soaked with blood and the stone was stained with it. Piled around the figures were the skulls of the slain. Hugh felt an aroma of terror here but it was not his own terror. It was the terror of those who had waited to die.

The surrounding forest, as though affected by the squalor it enclosed, was hung with grey moss. Hugh looked among the trees and saw, on the other side of the stone, a few old plantain palms.

To get to them, he had to walk under the idols, among the skulls.

Now he knew why Simon had smiled. Another joke!

Hugh crossed the platform, kicking the skulls as he went, and reached the palms. Inside the light green, silken leaves, he found a single bunch of fruit, greener than the leaves. The fruits were the size of small runner beans. He picked one, peeled it, tasted it and spat it out. He felt disgust at Simon's arrogance and a profound sense of betrayal. Picking up a skull, he flung it and hit the nearer figure. Then, determined to overthrow the pair of them, he picked up skull after skull, throwing them wildly so the whole platform became covered with shattered bone. Grinning like Aunt Sallies, the figures shuddered and rocked, but they did not fall.

In the midst of this exercise, Hugh was startled by a tearing, hissing sound. Rain was rushing across the open ground. It struck him harshly and, remembering Simon lying helpless beneath the storm, he took to his heels, leaving the figures still upright behind him.

Holding up his arms to shield his face from the cataract of water, he blundered through the reeds into the lane. Lightning was darting about in the upper air. A rivet of red struck down into the forest and the following thunder peal renewed the rain.

Hugh found Simon prone, eyes half closed, rain beating on to his face. His skin had taken on an earthy colour and he looked, in the grey light, as gaunt and contracted as an old man. Uncertain whether he was alive or dead, Hugh knelt beside him and felt his hand. Raising his eyelids a little, Simon whispered: 'Very cold.'

'It's the rain.'

'Five days since the spider bit me. Remember that; five days. Could be significant. Not sure. Interesting. Wish I knew.' Taking his hand from Hugh's hold, he opened it and displayed the key to the Land-Rover: 'You'll have to find your own way back.'

'I won't leave you.'

Hugh sat down against the wall, putting the rucksack behind his own head and pulling Simon's head onto his lap. He settled himself to wait.

The forest was no distance from them and through the howl and clatter of wind, he could hear the trees groaning together, their branches cracking and breaking, and, when the rain slackened, he could see the leaf crowns turning like mops in the whirl of wind. Sometimes a tree fell, bringing down with a rush of sound everything about it. The earth shook. To Hugh it seemed that roots were moving in the ground beneath him.

A glow touched the air and he knew that above the storm, the sun was setting. The glow was soon gone. Darkness came down and there was nothing to be seen but the lightning that for an instant would reveal the forest by its lurid light.

Putting the rucksack on to his shoulder, he dropped his head on to it and tried to sleep. As the hours passed, the noise of the storm blurred and took itself into the distance. He woke to a tranquil world, pink with daybreak, silent except for the tentative whistles of the storm-shocked birds.

Warmth had returned to the air but Simon's hand was cold. He had died while Hugh slept.

Hugh thrust out his legs to ease the cramp in them, then rolling from under the weight of Simon's head and shoulders, he rose unsteadily. Looking at the dead man, he wondered what he could do for him. He could not bear to leave the body exposed there but had not the means to bury it. He went to the forest edge where branches in full leaf had been torn down during the night. He gathered an armful then, turning to go back, he saw the huts reflecting the dawn glow. In the delicate pink of the light, they looked mild and placating, an enemy overcome.

When he reached the clearing, he saw that the ant army had broken in half and the rear echelon had changed direction. It was marching across the lane, straight towards the dead body. Hugh realized that for the dead, whether in the ground or on it, the result would be the same. Taking the key out of the stiff hand, he began to put the branches in place. Simon's face had regained its normal pallor and look of youth. The remarkable blue of the eyes glinted between the half-closed eyelids. Already the ants were moving through the black beard and into the delicate nostrils and over the fine pale lips. Hugh dropped the last branch to hide the spectacle of this spoliation. Then, putting the key into his pocket, he set out to find his own way back.

FOR THE BEST IN PAPERBACKS, LOOK FOR THE

In every corner of the world, on every subject under the sun, Penguin represents quality and variety – the very best in publishing today.

For complete information about books available from Penguin – including Pelicans, Puffins, Peregrines and Penguin Classics – and how to order them, write to us at the appropriate address below. Please note that for copyright reasons the selection of books varies from country to country.

In the United Kingdom: For a complete list of books available from Penguin in the U.K., please write to *Dept E.P., Penguin Books Ltd, Harmondsworth, Middlesex, UB7 0DA*

In the United States: For a complete list of books available from Penguin in the U.S., please write to *Dept BA, Penguin, 299 Murray Hill Parkway, East Rutherford, New Jersey 07073*

In Canada: For a complete list of books available from Penguin in Canada, please write to *Penguin Books Canada Ltd, 2801 John Street, Markham, Ontario L3R 1B4*

In Australia: For a complete list of books available from Penguin in Australia, please write to the *Marketing Department, Penguin Books Australia Ltd, P.O. Box 257, Ringwood, Victoria 3134*

In New Zealand: For a complete list of books available from Penguin in New Zealand, please write to the *Marketing Department, Penguin Books (NZ) Ltd, Private Bag, Takapuna, Auckland 9*

In India: For a complete list of books available from Penguin, please write to *Penguin Overseas Ltd, 706 Eros Apartments, 56 Nehru Place, New Delhi, 110019*

In Holland: For a complete list of books available from Penguin in Holland, please write to *Penguin Books Nederland B.V., Postbus 195, NL–1380AD Weesp, Netherlands*

In Germany: For a complete list of books available from Penguin, please write to *Penguin Books Ltd, Friedrichstrasse 10 – 12, D–6000 Frankfurt Main 1, Federal Republic of Germany*

In Spain: For a complete list of books available from Penguin in Spain, please write to *Longman Penguin España, Calle San Nicolas 15, E–28013 Madrid, Spain*

OLIVIA MANNING

Olivia Manning's *Balkan Trilogy* and *Levant Trilogy* form a single narrative entitled *Fortunes of War*, which Anthony Burgess described in the *Sunday Times* as 'the finest fictional record of the war produced by a British writer. Her gallery of personages is huge, her scene painting superb, her pathos controlled, her humour quiet and civilized. Guy Pringle is certainly one of the major characters in modern fiction.'

THE BALKAN TRILOGY

THE GREAT FORTUNE

Set in a Bucharest throbbing with the tensions of war, *The Great Fortune* introduces Harriet and Guy Pringle who have just embarked on married life. As they discover more about each other, the story of an expatriate Russian émigré unfolds, observed in minute detail.

and

THE SPOILT CITY
FRIENDS AND HEROES

THE LEVANT TRILOGY

THE DANGER TREE

Cairo in 1942, just before the battle of Alamein, is rapidly becoming the clearing-house for Allied soldiers and civilians marooned by the fall of Rumania and Greece. With the flotsam and jetsam are washed up Guy and Harriet Pringle – strangers in a strange and unfriendly land.

and

THE BATTLE LOST AND WON
THE SUM OF THINGS